BETTER BUSINESS BETTER FUTURE

BETTER
BUSINESS

BETTER
FUTURE

ELISABET LAGERSTEDT

FUTURE NAVIGATORS

Better Business Better Future
© Elisabet Lagerstedt 2021
www.elisabetlagerstedt.com

Cover design, layout and illustrations
Cecilia Pettersson, Pica Pica
www.picapicadesign.se

Images
Unsplash, www.unsplash.com

Published by
Future Navigators, Sweden
www.future-navigators.com

Printed by
BoD – Books on Demand, Norderstedt, Germany

First edition

ISBN 978-91-527-0795-1

To my loving parents, my patient and supportive husband,
and my wonderfully amazing children Axel and Saga.

To the brave business leaders of the world
who are now stepping up to make a meaningful
difference for generations to come.

In love of life and for the future of humanity
and our planet.

CONTENTS

PREFACE

"The future is unwritten. It will be shaped by who we choose to be now."

CHRISTIANA FIGUERES AND TOM RIVETT-CARNAC[1]

As I write the final words of this preface, we have reached the very end of 2021. A year that together with 2020 will go to history due to the Covid-19 pandemic. We have however also experienced extreme weather across the globe—from alarming floods in central Europe and China to severe heat and fires in North America, Siberia and Southern Europe; from serious drought in Iran to monstrous monsoons in India. Scientists say that global warming is likeliest the culprit and that its consequences will not show up in a distant future. The consequences of climate change are already here and is having an impact on the world as we know it. [2] After a few stumbling steps in the right direction during the UN Climate Change Conference in Glasgow in November (COP26), it is clear that some of the greatest challenges of humanity still remain, and that it will take an extraordinary effort to change from business as usual.

Events and insights like these do not reduce my inherent optimism for humanity or the planet. Rather, they call to my business strategist and inner change maker for answers and action. They also inspire me to continue to expand my perspectives, because we will not solve our problems with the same thinking we used when we created them. This means that surfing will not only be of interest to companies like Patagonia going forward. Instead, we, as business leaders, will need to learn how to surf the monumental waves of the sustainability revolution to stay relevant and attractive in business. It will simply be a key to surviving and thriving, because we are all parts of the larger life-sustaining system that we call Earth. Patagonia has already realized that. Have you?

This endeavour will take courage to unlearn and relearn, go beyond business as usual, and inspire humanity to step up and move forward. We could certainly all use some of the expanded perspective and rebellious spirit of Steve Jobs and Apple from the early days of the digital revolution. Remember their iconic commercial from 1998, where they celebrated those who dare see things differently because those are the ones that can change the world? Their one-minute ad featured images of 17 inspirational personalities, such as Albert Einstein, Thomas Edison, Amelia Earhart, Richard Buckminster Fuller, Martin Luther King and Mahatma Gandhi—all indeed great change makers. It went like this: "Here's to the crazy ones. The misfits. The rebels. The troublemakers. The round pegs in the square holes. The ones who see things differently. They're not fond of rules. And they have no respect for the status quo. You can quote them, disagree with them, glorify or vilify them. About the only thing you can't do is ignore them. Because they change things. They push the human race forward. And while some may see them as the crazy ones, we see genius. Because the people who are crazy enough to think they can change the world, are the ones who do."

This time, however, it is the sustainability revolution that needs our full attention to mindfully design the future that we want rather than let the opportunity slip through our fingers. It will be our collective responsibility to move things forward, inspired by activist business leaders like Yves Chouinard (Patagonia), Anita Roddick (BodyShop), Paul Poleman (Unilever) and Emmanuel Faber (Danone)–who have all dared to think different.

Why is this so important? Well, let us consider that the business case for sustainability has long been proven. Then reflect on the tremendous business risks in letting wicked problems like climate change and biodiversity loss accelerate even further. Large investors are already demanding that corporate leaders act to protect their assets long-term. And venture capitalists have long placed bets on the tremendous business opportunities that lie in this transformation, which is now only accelerating. Not to mention the implications that business as usual would have on the planet and humanity.

My mission with this book is to inspire you, as a corporate business leader, to get in touch with your inner change maker, elevate your perspective and move beyond business as usual to co-create Better Business and healthier futures. The time has come to step up, to re-envision the future of corporate business, transform your organization, and capture the vast business opportunity that the sustainability revolution presents.

/ Good business is simply good for business and seriously needed in solving the world's wicked problems /

This requires us using a strategic and holistic, yet practical approach that includes not only our businesses but also our business ecosystem, as well as the larger world beyond it. It also requires for us as corporate business leaders to step into our full human potential. Why is this so vital? Because good business is simply good for business and seriously needed in solving the world's wicked problems. And as a corporate business leader, you are crucial in this transformation. In understanding the challenges and providing purpose, direction, and resources, you can contribute to meaning, transformation and growth and help enhance the wellbeing of both people and our planet—all while futureproofing your corporate business to ensure that it stays relevant and attractive and can thrive going forward.

What feels truly promising is the growth of impact startups and impact investors who aim to solve some of the world's most urgent challenges and wicked problems. Among corporate businesses, there also seem to be a sense that the traditional measures of corporate social responsibility are no longer enough and that sustainability is not only crucial going forward, but a key business risk and opportunity that cannot afford to be overlooked. The Vision 2050 initiative driven by the World Business Council of Sustainable Development (WBCSD), for instance, shows promising proof of insight in their ambition to create a world where more than nine billion people are living well within planetary boundaries by mid-century.[3] Still, studies show that while this is an area that big businesses today speak ambitiously about, their activities so far have been far more superficial than transforming. Losing the initiative, however, is not an option.

It will be far from enough to acknowledge the need for Better Business or to put a selected set of aspirational initiatives into action, such as the increasingly popular—and important—NetZero target for carbon emissions. First and foremost, we need to think and act holistically and strategically to capture the opportunity of Better Business and integrate sustainability into the core of our businesses—that is, into purpose, mission, vision, values, strategy and offering, as well as into business models and operating models. We also need to embrace our business ecosystem to proactively support its evolution and aspire to change the world for the better.

In the late 1990s I was part of the pioneers in this transformation as I led one of Sweden's first sustainability brands. A journey that has always been with me although I spent the majority of my later career in what I now simply call business as usual. So, when I was asked a few years back to help Oatly facilitate the co-creation of their strategies for sustainability and innovation to help them change the world, I knew I had to step up to the challenge. Their transformational journey had already started in 2012, and by the time I got engaged, they were already well on their way and growing exponentially. This, of course, became truly interesting client projects, with additional time spent on their digital strategy and exploring exponential, agile, dynamic, adaptive, and teal organizations as platforms for human growth. And, as always, there were no easy answers. Instead, it became a search into building something new. This left me with the feeling that we were on to something important. So important that I continued to explore the area even more in depth after the projects closed to understand what companies and business leaders can do to integrate sustainability more systematically into their core and strategically transform their businesses into a force for good. I also explored what types of business leaders we need to become and what types of organizations we need to build to handle the increasing challenges and complexities of the world and co-create the future that we want for the generations to come. I looked high and low, wide and deep and slowly unfolded the riddle, one step at a time. This was also a natural extension of the work for my last book, *Navigera in Framtiden* (*Navigate into the Future*, published in 2018), where I explored and identified some of the key business and leadership principles of coping with a VUCA world of accelerating change.

Now, this book has finally come to life through the contributions of an amazing network of business leaders and sustainability experts on the frontlines of Better Business. I have indeed learned a lot on the way.

As I share this, I would like to express thanks to my many teachers, some of which are considered the finest management thinkers in the world, such as Clayton Christensen, Rebecca Henderson, Linda Hill, Michael Tushman, Alexander Osterwalder and Yves Pigneur. I would also like to extend my deepest respect and gratitude to all who, over the past few years, have contributed to the book being brought to life in different ways. If someone is missing in the list of acknowledgment, my memory is the only one to blame. My deepest gratitude especially to Dr. Joyce Miller and Dr. Antoinette Braks, who have helped me expand my perspectives beyond what I ever could imagine on my own journey of adult development.

A big thank you also to you, who now aspire to read this book and are inspired to make a meaningful difference. I believe you will find the book worthwhile and helpful. What took us here is not what will take us there—into the future that we want. It is simply time for us to step up to the challenge.

More resources and downloads can be found on
www.elisabetlagerstedt.com and www.future-navigators.com.

Warmly,

Elisabet Lagerstedt
Höllviken, Sweden
December 31, 2021

ACKNOWLEDGEMENTS

Torbjörn Lööf, former Chief Executive Officer at Inter IKEA Group

Lena Pripp-Kovak, Chief Sustainability Officer at Inter IKEA Group

Karen Hamilton, Global Vice President of Sustainable Business at Unilever

Richard Aldwinckle, Sustainability and Purpose Consultant, formerly at Unilever

Nigel Stansfield, President Europe, Africa, Asia, Australia at Interface

Vincent Stanley, Director of Philosophy at Patagonia

Anders Eldrup, former Chief Executive Officer at Dong Energy (today Ørsted)

Thomas Ollendorf, former Director of Sales and Country Manager Sweden at Dong Energy (today Ørsted)

Toni Petersson, Chief Executive Officer at Oatly

Christel Kinning, Chief Transformation & People Officer at Oatly

Carina Tollmar, Sustainability Manager at EON, formerly Sustainability Director at Oatly

Ashley Allen, Chief Sustainability Officer at Oatly

Hanna Meinl, Nordic Market Development Manager at Oatly

Erik Osmundsen, Partner at Verdane, formerly CEO at Norsk Gjenvinning

Rolf Ladau, Chief Executive Officer at Paulig Group

Anita Laxén, former Director of Communications & Brand at Paulig Group

Najla Vallander, former Business Developer at TooGoodToGo, currently at Worldfavour

Kaj Török, Chief Sustainability Officer at Max Burgers

Sandya Lang, Sustainability Manager at Nudie Jeans

Björn Magnusson, Investment Director at H&M Group

Jonas André, Corporate Responsibility Director at Volvo Group

Johan Lannering, Head of Sustainability at SKF

Kerstin Lindell, President and Chair of Board, Bona Group

Pontus Cornelius, Chief Executive Officer at Bona Group

Anders Hülse, Chief Executive Officer at Fristads Kansas

Jörgen Hermansson, President at Södra Building Systems

Tina Andersson, Chief Consumer Officer at Fiskars Group

Tomas Granlund, Vice President New Business Development at Fiskars Group

Cynthia Figge, Chief Executive Officer and Co-Founder of CSRHub and Co-Founder of EKOS International

Soulla Kyriacou, Chief Operating Officer at Blueprint for Better Business Foundation

Maria Smith, Secretary General at Axfoundation

Lyn White, Director of Strategy at Animals Australia

Dorota Laughlin, Director of Operations at Animals Australia

Nille Skalts, Corporate Activist and Movement Maker, founder of the B-Corp Nordics community

Tomas Bjoersdorff, Planet & Profit Management Consultant, Certified B-Corp Leader

Claudia Juech, former Chief Executive Officer at Cloudera Foundation

Jennifer Campbell, Systemic Leadership Expert and Founder of the Systemic Leadership Summit

Heléne Clark, Ph.D., Director at ActKnowledge, and President at Centre for Theory of Change

Mark Workman, Director at Foresight Transitions, and Co-founder of the Carbon Removal Centre

Jan Agri, Sustainability Consultant, Founder and Circularity Expert at Tricircular

Karin Lundqvist, founder of Energibyrån, formerly at Öresundskraft and Vattenfall

Emma Järund, independent Sustainability Consultant

Thomas Kalling, Professor of Strategy and Innovation Lund University School of Economics and Management

Ronald Wintzeus, Executive Search & Board Advisory Consultant, Mercuri Urval

Sofia and **Conor Fürstenberg Stott**, Founders and Partners at Fürstenberg Maritime

Joakim Hökegård, Business Developer and Communications Strategist at HiQ

Bas Roelofs, Business Designer and Circular Innovation Strategist

Carl-Henrik Sundström, former Agile Project Manager at Future Navigators, currently at Netlight

Sofie Piilmann, co-founder of Sirqularity and former project leader at Future Navigators, currently at Accenture

Camilla van den Boom, PhD, Founder and Strategy Director at Sturrm

Cecilia Pettersson, Designer and Owner at Pica Pica design

A special thank you also to the Board of Directors and the Executive Management team of Duni Group–who is now accelerating the company's transformation towards Better Business and beyond–in particular Thomas Gustafsson, Chair of the Board; Robert Dackeskog, Chief Executive Officer; Marielle Noble, Executive Vice President Strategy, IT and Communications; Malin Cullin, Executive Vice President Sustainability, People & Culture; Linus Lemark, Executive Vice President BA Duni; Magnus Carlsson, EVP and Chief Financial Officer; and Pauline Lindwall, Board Director & Senior Advisor. Also, a special thank you to Erik Lindroth, Sustainability Director; Elisabeth Gierow, former Sustainability Director; and Johan Mårtensson, Innovation Manager at Duni Group.

INTRODUCTION

"The sustainability revolution has the magnitude of the agricultural and industrial revolutions but the speed of the digital revolution."

AL GORE[4]

In *The Future We Choose*, authors Christiana Figueres and Tom Rivett-Carnac—who led the United Nations' (UN) negotiations during the Paris Agreement of 2015—outline two futures for humanity in 2050. One describes a dark and gloomy world in which we fail to meet the Paris Agreement's climate targets. The other paints a more positive picture of a regenerative world with net-zero emissions. They also show that the latter is possible if governments, corporations and each and every one of us work to fend off disaster and grow on the way. [5]

In the face of this massive adversity, it is, of course, easy to feel too small to make a difference. But instead of seeing our potential contribution as limited, we need to realise that our zone of influence as corporate business leaders can be much larger than we tend to think. This is because the world of corporate business is particularly well equipped to help solve the problems of the world through the ingenuity, creativity, collaboration and resources that it can so often call forth more effectively and efficiently than other human organizations. And we, as corporate business leaders, can go far beyond demonstrating in the streets. We can actually move capital, minds and action, and cooperate to nudge consumers into making choices that co-create the healthy future that we want and need for our business, humanity and the generations to come—our own children and grandchildren included.

Because the digital revolution is now being followed by a sustainable one, the message from the World Economic Forum is clear: "Like the digital revolution before it, the sustainability revolution promises to change everything. Yet, just as with digital, many companies are moving too slowly, taking an incremental approach to a challenge that demands a radical rethink."[6] The pandemic only seems to have accelerated the trend. In the wake of this development, some real and important change is happening, but we are also seeing a flood of seemingly empty promises and greenwashing from businesses across the globe.

What has been especially striking to me in the deep dive into relevant research and reports for this book is that the emergency that we are now experiencing in the field of climate change and biodiversity loss is far from new. The first conclusions from the ambitious undertakings of The Club of Rome, published in their 1972 report *The Limits of Growth*, Medows and collegues[7], clearly outlined the challenges and predicaments of modern society. The same year, the world's first global conference on the human environment was held in Stockholm, the capital of Sweden.[8] There, the participants adopted principles for "sound management of the environment" based on the scientific findings and insights of their time. Already there was an understanding of the link between economic growth and the pollution of the air, water and oceans and the well-being of people across the globe. These insights, however, seem to have taken far too long to trickle down to other members of society, including policymakers, entrepreneurs and corporate business leaders across the globe. And since the 1970s, growth has increased exponentially, lifting billions out of poverty, but at the same time accelerating the environmental damage to all life systems. Hence, we have not been able to decouple growth from its negative environmental impact.

I need only look at my own business career and personal development to see this being mirrored in the work that I have done over the past 25 years. Even though I came early on to study economic history, sociology and management, and built a well-rounded understanding of the evolution of the world and society as we know it, it took me a very long time to truly realise and internalise this major challenge for humanity. And even though in the late 1990s I became responsible for one of the first environmentally friendly and commercially successful brands in Sweden targeting environmentally conscious consumers–and especially the parents of future generations–I at the time still lacked the insights needed to truly make a difference from a broader perspective. Interestingly, what I came to know as environmental best practices in business back then—more than 20 years ago—is still far from common practice. In this VUCA (Volatile, Uncertain, Complex and Ambiguous) world of accelerating change, global warming and biodiversity loss, a transformation beyond business as usual is, however, both urgent and important. Sustainability is no longer something for conscious consumers and brands in some of the most developed countries in the world but something that concerns us *all*. Across the world. Across industries. It should have been since the beginning of the industrial revolution. As corporate business leaders (and consumers), we have seriously contributed to the dire situation that our planet is currently in. We have far too long left it to others to solve the problems that we have created. But what got us here will not get us into the future. We must realise that the challenges ahead are bigger than what we could have ever imagined and rethink how we do business so we can hand over a thriving planet and society to the coming generations.

We also need to realise that this is not only about climate change (as if that was not enough). Consumers are already taking social and environmental issues more seriously and rewarding businesses and brands that do good, even though they still have major challenges in adjusting their own behaviours and consumption, and need our help in doing so. This will increasingly be embraced by purpose-driven companies and brands that aim to 'build back better' in the post-pandemic era. The companies that aim to rebuild a more equitable and greener world will not only unlock new business opportunities but also gain competitive advantages and be rewarded with renewed trust and a social licence to operate.

Today, even investors have come to understand that the values they have built up over the past century may be at risk if corporate leaders fail to act and ESG (Environment, Social and Governance) investment is gaining ground. BlackRock, one of the world's leading investment firms with a focus on sustainability, can testify that the investor community is waking up: "[They are] driven by an increased understanding of how sustainability-related factors can affect economic growth, asset values, and financial markets as a whole".[9] BlackRock have also stated that they will proactively challenge companies that are not pursuing this agenda. Already today, there are no contradictions between sustainable returns and sustainable investments. On the contrary. As the CEO of Credit Suisse told CNBC, "In many cases, sustainable investments are actually higher returning than non-sustainable investments." He added, "I think companies that are behind the curve in terms of sustainability, they are already forced to pay higher cost of capital."[10]

Many companies are facing not only increasingly demanding investors but now also nimbler and more adaptive startups and new competitors that are less wasteful and damaging to the environment – and not afraid to say so to challenge the establishment. Others have their own customers asking for more sustainable solutions, or employees and future talent requiring transparency and action. Many have realised that sustainability will need to be an integrated part of their core business as they strive to stay relevant and fit for the future. Some have completely transformed and changed their business models already. A few even aim to become fully regenerative and planet positive. Most companies have at least found that applying some of these principles to their own businesses has helped them reduce risk, become more effective and efficient, and at the same time attract both customers and talent. Also, many have realised that the sustainability revolution is opening vast new business opportunities. Amazingly though, far too few are really on the ball. Several studies have shown that we are still seeing more talk than action.

Interestingly, no single industry seems to have risen above the masses and taken the lead in this transformation - at least if you study aggregated ESG measures going back a decade, which have not improved substantially over time and are surprisingly even across industries.[11] It is, however, clear that some industries now experience stronger transformational forces than others, with the energy industry being in the middle of this vortex. In the research for this book, I have also seen indications that the energy industry is closely followed by the automotive and transportation sectors; fashion; agriculture, food and beverages; mining and heavy manufacturing; and construction. This is illustrated in Figure 1 as a schematic Sustainability Vortex, where the industries currently experiencing the strongest disruptive and transformational forces are found in the very centre of the vortex.[12]

Leading companies from industries close to the centre of this vortex have indeed been a key inspiration for this book. What has become increasingly clear to me, however, is that sustainability is not "only" a matter of transformation. It is rather a multi-dimensional journey that changes as our world changes and evolves over time. The transition to a low-carbon economy will take decades, but the future starts

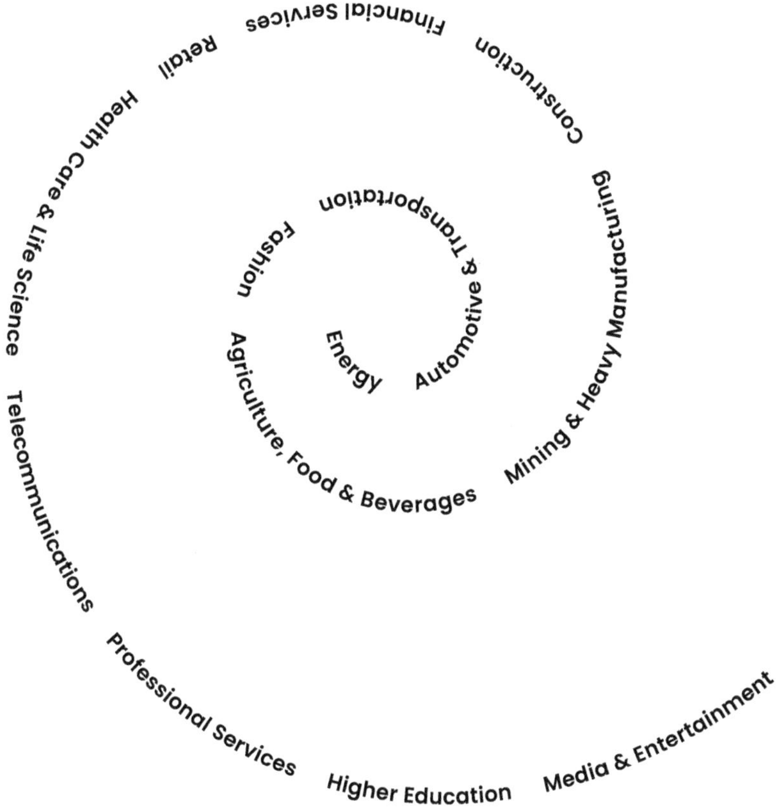

FIGURE 1

The Sustainability Vortex illustrates industries experiencing a high level of disruption and transformational forces in the middle of the sustainability revolution.

now. Only if we dare to listen to our hearts and visualize the future that we want, play our cards right, change our consumption patterns and utilize the progress in technology and innovation for good, will we be able to co-create a better world and companies fit for the future. This will, however, not happen by itself. As business leaders, we will simply need to embrace this unique situation with all its opportunities and threats, roll up our sleeves, and step up to the challenge on both strategic and operational levels going forward.

As a first step, we will need to build Better Business.

WHAT IS BETTER BUSINESS?

What are then the characteristics of Better Business? To define this, we first need to understand 'business as usual'.

In 1970, economist Milton Friedman wrote a New York Times article titled *"The Social Responsibility of Business Is to Increase Its Profits."* [13] In the article, Friedman argued that business leaders have no other responsibility than to increase the profits of the firm, and that anything other than a pure focus on profits is to be considered theft from shareholders, and socialism. This 51-year-old article has been attributed to the origin of the short-sighted shareholder capitalism that we have seen far too much of during past decades and is a key characteristic of 'business as usual' today. Consequently, short-term value extraction over time became the norm rather than a focus on the total value that the business creates or gives back to society. Calls for more ethical, stakeholder-oriented, sustainable and even regenerative business practices have, however, been brought forward by many, even from business leaders themselves, and from The Business Roundtable—a non-profit association whose members are chief executive officers of major US companies. [14] Some are now wisely suggesting that the role of business is to advance human prosperity within the boundaries set by nature. Better Business will, however, not get us there. Regenerative Business will.

But what does regeneration mean? SustainableBrands.com suggests that it means: (1) "restoring, renewing and/or healing systems we all depend on, while also (2) improving the ability of said systems to restore, renew and/or heal themselves more effectively."[15] A carbon-capture machine can, for instance, help us restore climate stability by withdrawing carbon out of the Earth's atmosphere. A carbon capture machine is, however, not regenerative, as it does not directly improve the Earth's own ability to restore climate stability. Compare this with a tree. A tree accomplishes both withdrawing carbon and restoring climate stability—and is hence regenerative.

A *Regenerative Business* has regenerative practices, cultures and leadership and truly goes beyond what we today see as 'business as usual'. It has already been described by visionaries such as Carol Sanford (2017), Daniel Wahl (2016), Ethan Roland et al. (2013) and others. As a simplified concept, it is similar to Net Positive Business, as described by Forum of the Future, and Paul Polman.[16]

So, what is it?

Plainly said a Regenerative Business is a for-profit organization that return more to society, the environment and the global economy than it extracts or takes out. It is focused on all stakeholders for the good of society and our planet. It respects the rights of all other living beings; has robust circular flows; is innovative, adaptive and responsive; contributes to the health and well-being of the whole; works collaboratively across ecosystems; and balances collaboration and competition. It values all 'rightsholders', including natural, social and living capital, as well as financial capital. As explained by Harvard professor

Greg Norris, it is inspired by nature and "boldly seeks to increase its socio-ecological *handprint*". As such, it aims to restore the health of individuals and communities as well as the planet, and not only to reduce its footprint, but to give back more than it takes from both the planet and society.[17]

/ Regenerative Business models are open to exploration not only for startups but also for all of us who have grown up in the corporate world of business as usual /

Even though interest in Regenerative Business is currently on the rise, it is still in its inception, and there seem to be no peer-reviewed academic studies from which to learn. SustainableBrands.com has put together a report with a few short cases that can give you a hint of what this could mean in practice.[18] One of those cases is about Guayakí, an organic energy beverage company founded in 1996, based in California, US, with 600 employees and a current revenue estimated at $210 million USD.[19] Guayakí drinks are based on yerba mate, a plant known for its energizing properties (it contains caffeine) that was first cultivated and used by indigenous communities in South America. Around their beverage offering, the company has created what they call a *market-driven regeneration business model.* In that, they explicitly seek to regenerate life on land. They do that by sourcing from and promoting regenerative agriculture while they support, empower and partner with smallholder farmers in parts of South America. Even though Guayakí aspires to be regenerative, their reporting reveals that after 25 years in business, they still have a negative footprint and are not fully regenerative yet. They are however a Certified BCorp and seek to achieve net-zero by 2030, and as such, apply the highest standards of sustainability today.

An interesting sidenote is that Guayakí's new CEO, Stefan Kozak, was recently recruited from a position as CEO for Red Bull North America, with earlier experience as managing director of Coca-Cola bottling operations in Brazil.[20] On his LinkedIn profile, he describes himself as any other successful business leader would do: "20 plus years of leadership roles with proven ability to create visions, develop strategies, and build organizations and systems/processes that deliver top and bottom-line growth."[21] So why did he take on this position? In a press release sent out by Guayakí, Stefan Kozak said, "I am thrilled to be joining Guayakí Yerba Mate, a product I love and a company that aligns with my experience, skills and most importantly, values. Given the state of the planet and Guayakí's longstanding commitment to sustainability and social good, I can't imagine a better and more meaningful place to work. I look forward to building on the great work the founders and their teams have established over the past 25 years, and lead Guayakí Yerba Mate – its business, ideas, and ideals - into the future. 'Come to Life' is not only Guayakí's mantra, but perfectly describes my feelings while embarking on this new journey."[22]

To me, this means that Regenerative Business models are open to exploration not only for startups but also for all of us who have grown up in the corporate world of business as usual. My own 25 plus years of business experience, however, tells me that Regenerative Business models probably feel rather unfamiliar—and far away—for most business leaders, having led their whole professional lives and careers in 'business as usual' and having been successful in that arena. Changing the game always feels risky, but in the long run, regenerative business models will be the only way forward.

Could there potentially be a first stop on the way that does not feel as radical, but that could help us get started on this important journey—and even act as a bridge between today and tomorrow? There is. I simply call it 'Better Business'. See Figure 2.

Some of the distinctive characteristics of 'business as usual', Better Business and Regenerative Business are highlighted in Table 1. As you can see, these organizations are all for-profit. Other than that, much differs, especially on the parameters of time, value creation, operation logic, choice of arena, business integration and the interpretation of corporate responsibility.

/ Better Business can be described as a company that has a long-term perspective and is guided and inspired by a higher purpose /

In this context, a Better Business can be described as a company that has a long-term perspective and is guided and inspired by a higher purpose that helps the organization create, deliver and capture value to stakeholders, while minimizing ecological and social costs, engaging its business ecosystem and reducing its footprint. It could be a Certified B Corporation or a Benefit Corporation, but it does not have to be. Better Business also opens a whole new field of opportunities that are more sustainable and circular—from new value propositions to new business models and new customer segments.

/ Regenerative Business will ultimately need to evolve into the new normal /

Even though Better Business still may sound rather far away for some, I believe that it is only a stage of development—or a bridge to what is emerging—rather than a new state or status quo. It is definitely better for people and the environment than business as usual, but it is still not fully regenerative. Regenerative Business will ultimately need to evolve into the new normal in order for humanity to thrive within the natural boundaries of this planet over generations to come. We are already seeing more and more companies developing into Better Businesses, and like Interface—one of the world's leading and most recognized companies in this field—some companies have already raised the bar and aim to become fully regenerative.

Interestingly, Better Business is a conceptual area that was pioneered in the mid-1970s (even though the term Better Business was not used) and is already inhabited not only by its pioneers but also by early adaptors and an early majority. It is now going mainstream as more and more companies strive to use business as a force for good. Hence, there are several companies to learn from, and even 'only' Better Business can be considered far beyond business as usual for anyone with a more traditional business mindset and skillset.

But how do you transform your corporate business from business as usual into Better Business? And what can we learn from those already in the frontlines of Better Business? Those are the key questions that will be addressed in this book.

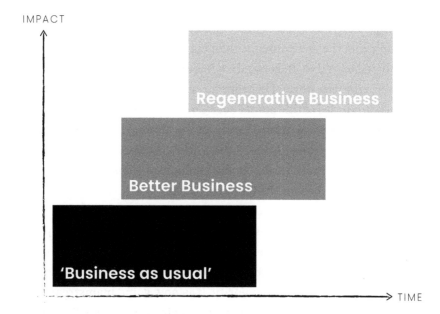

IMPACT

Regenerative Business

Better Business

'Business as usual'

TIME

FIGURE 2

The development of 'business as usual', Better Business and
Regenerative Business over time.

	'Business as usual'	Better Business [23]	Regenerative Business [24]
Form	For-profit	Purpose-driven for-profit, potentially a Benefit Corporation or Certified B Corporation	Purpose-driven for-profit, potentially a Benefit Corporation and Certified B Corporation or beyond
Time Perspective	Short-and mid-term focus	Long-term focus	Generational focus
Value Creation	Maximise value for shareholders	Creates shared value for stakeholders	Creates value for all 'rightsholders', including natural, social and living capital, as well as financial capital
Operating Logic	Take-make-dispose	Increasingly sustainable and circular	Fully circular and regenerative
Arena	Direct transactional business environment	Business ecosystem	Planet and society
Corporate Responsibility	Traditional CSR initiatives applied to reduce risk and protect and enhance reputation	Purpose driven, aiming to minimize social cost and ecological footprint	Purpose driven, aiming for a higher good with zero footprint and a positive "handprint"
Business Integration	Sustainability is not a systematically and deeply integrated part of purpose, strategy, offering, business model, or operating model. Opportunistic approach if a sustainable business opportunity arises	Sustainability becoming integrated into purpose and strategy. Systematic efforts taken to make current offer more sustainable and circular; also, in opening opportunities in new value propositions, business models and operating models	Sustainability, circularity and regeneration are completely integrated and natural parts of purpose, strategy, offering, business model, and operating model

TABLE 1

Characteristics of 'business as usual', Better Business and Regenerative Business.

THIS BOOK

This book is written for business leaders with a genuine interest in exploring and co-creating a true strategic transformation towards a more sustainable and regenerative business and future. It is based on a rigorous search for a holistic, yet strategically and practically applicable perspective, and intended to inspire you to step up to the challenge of our lifetime, integrate sustainability into the core of your business, capture what may be the biggest business opportunity in our history, and co-create a better future for your children and the generations to come. What is considered 'business as usual' today will not be accepted as 'business as usual' in the future. And those who still believe greenwashing is the answer will be caught with their pants down going forward in this world of increasing transparency.

The aim of this book is to help you understand the big picture that is unfolding and decode the good and evolving practices of those in the frontline of Better Business in order to strategically choose where to play and how to integrate sustainability into the core of your corporation. Ultimately to transform into a Better Business.

I simply suggest that you read the book from start to finish, because the later chapters of the book build on an understanding of the big picture that is presented in the first chapters of the book.

 Throughout the book, please take the opportunity to mindfully write down your thoughts and reflections on your discoveries and insights. Simply regard it as a note to self.

The first two chapters of this book will help you understand the big picture—the sustainability revolution and why Better Business is key for the future success of your business, the planet and for the generations to come. You will also be invited to explore the business opportunity and to reimagine a better future.

In the third chapter of this book, you will learn from six companies who have already travelled far on this journey and integrated sustainability into their very core—Patagonia, Interface, Ørsted, Unilever, IKEA and Oatly.

In the fourth chapter of this book you will be introduced to the StepUp framework and the Fit for Purpose Model, and several good practice examples that will help you shape your own integrated Better Business strategy going forward.

As we close the book with our fifth chapter, we will summarize our learnings, and then take a closer look at the important role of you as a business leader in this transformation in the epilogue.

After having read the book, you will be invited to apply what you have learned in a brief self-assessment of your corporate business.

The self-assessment as well as other resources can be found at www.elisabetlagerstedt.com and www.future-navigators.com.

DEFINITIONS

"The limits of my language mean the limits of my world."
LUDWIG WITTGENSTEIN

Language defines our world and shapes our reality. The language we know, speak and understand defines—but also limits—how we think, act and behave.

As with any other area, the field of sustainability is filled with jargon and acronyms, where you, as a reader, will need to understand at least the most frequently used terms. So, before we move on, I recommend that you read through the definitions section on the next pages. This is especially important if you are not already well versed in the field, as it will help you better understand the terminology and the many different types of companies that you can read about in media. What used to be just business is evolving into a jungle of different types of organizations, often with slightly unclear definitions.

SUSTAINABILITY or **SUSTAINABLE DEVELOPMENT** is often defined as the ability to meet current needs without compromising the future generation's ability to meet their needs.[25]

The **SUSTAINABLE DEVELOPMENT GOALS (SDGs)** were set in 2015 by the UN General Assembly and are intended to be achieved by 2030. The SDGs are included in the 2030 Agenda (also called Agenda 2030), which is a UN resolution. A UN resolution is a decision voted on by all member states of the UN in the General Assembly, the main deliberative, policy-making and representative organ of the UN. In more practical terms, the SDGs are a collection of 17 interlinked goals and 169 designed targets that can be seen as "a blueprint to achieve a better and more sustainable future for all". They address the wicked

FIGURE 3

The 17 Sustainable Development Goals. More information is available on the UN website. [27]

problems that humanity is currently facing, including poverty, inequality, climate change, environmental degradation, peace and justice. [26] See Figure 3.

UN GLOBAL COMPACT, started in July 2000, is a voluntary initiative based on CEO commitments to corporate responsibility and sustainability, and acknowledged by the UN. 9 000 plus companies have already joined the community. They aim to drive change across all areas of corporate sustainability, including the SDGs, and to catalyse action, partnerships and collaboration, provide frameworks, best practices, resources and networking events. You can read more about their *ten principles* on their website. [28]

For decades, **CORPORATE SOCIAL RESPONSIBILITY (CSR)** or **CORPORATE RESPONSIBILITY (CR)** has been about how a company can become a "good corporate citizen". It includes elements such as corporate philanthropy, social responsibility and environmental sustainability. Companies can, in this sense, become socially responsible by following the law and mitigating some of the ethical, social and environmental concerns that their business might bring, for instance, by donating to charitable causes that they see as beneficial connections. [29] Today, CSR is normally referred to as having three pillars (from the *triple bottom line* concept): environmental, social and economic. **ENVIRONMENTAL SUSTAINABILITY** implies that the Earth's ecological systems should be maintained. **ECONOMIC SUSTAINABILITY** should ensure that reliable sources of livelihood and economic activity are available to all. **SOCIAL SUSTAINABILITY** means that basic human rights and necessities should be available in order to maintain healthy communities. This all sounds good, but in reality, CSR practices are most often not integrated into business strategy, but rather are an add-on to mitigate some of the negative effects of running 'business as usual' in order to reduce reputational and legal risks and to live up to minimum standards of investor requirements.

A **STAKEHOLDER** can be described as a person with an interest in or concern in something. In a business context, the term stakeholder is generally considered to be the different interest groups in a company's internal and external environment. Employees, managers, and owners are generally considered internal stakeholders, while customers, suppliers, shareholders, governments, creditors and society can be considered external shareholders. Since the 1970s, the shareholder has been given increasing supremacy and has morphed into being considered the most important stakeholder—not seldom at the expense of the others. This is something that is now changing.

ENVIRONMENTAL, SOCIAL AND GOVERNANCE (ESG) ratings specifically help investors and other stakeholders understand the material risks, ethical impact and sustainability of a company. It is increasingly used by financial analysts and investors to guide investment recommendations and decisions. It is becoming mandatory for stock-listed companies to disclose a selection of ESG relevant metrics and practices. It is also increasingly both expected and demanded by investors. An ESG and sustainability consultancy highlights that "…recent research shows that that 65% of institutional investors look at ESG ratings at least once a week, and companies with high ESG ratings receive 15% more investment and 10% reduction in costs of capital."[30] ESG ratings are provided by several actors – mainly as a service to investors. Major ESG rating providers are for instance MSCI and Sustainalytics, which can both be easily found online.

A **'B CORP'**, or a **CERTIFIED B CORPORATION,** is a for-profit company that has reached a set of predefined levels of standards in the field of sustainability and received a private certification for that. It is issued by B Lab, a non-profit organization that started in the US in 2006. B Lab aims to create viable alternatives to the current economic system and build a global movement of people using business as a force for good. Their vision is an inclusive, equitable and regenerative system for all people and the planet. The B Corporation certification is, in short, offered to companies that score more than 80 points (out of 200) on their B Impact Assessment. On their website it is described like this: "Certified B Corporations are businesses that meet the highest standards of verified social and environmental performance, public transparency, and legal accountability to balance profit and purpose. B Corps are accelerating a global culture shift to redefine success in business and build a more inclusive and sustainable economy."[31] Ben & Jerry's and Patagonia are examples of Certified B Corporations.

An important observation is that high *ESG* ratings and high *B Corporation* assessment scores generally seem to point in the same direction. Hence, if a company has a high rating in the B Impact Assessment, they are very likely to be a strong ESG performer. The B Impact Assessment can be accessed and used for free online by anyone aiming to assess their own practices. Standards and methods for ESG ratings are instead mainly developed for investors, can vary between different rating providers and are provided from 'the outside' based on a myriad of sources that are scrambled from across the internet (e.g., yearly reports, websites, articles, press releases, memberships etc). One source says, "ESG ratings and analyses provided by independent research firms can help investors to better understand ESG risks related to their securities and their portfolios. However, these metrics have several shortfalls that make them difficult to use. They are not always objective and the data they are based on may be unreliable... Note that ESG ratings can vary depending on the provider due to the different methodologies, metrics, data and weightings they use."[32] This indicates that any ESG rating is less transparent and difficult to understand than the open and straightforward B Impact Assessment, which any company can do for themselves – and hence also be in control of their strengths and weaknesses – and systematically work to improve their rating as well as their own narrative.

A **FOR-PROFIT ORGANIZATION**, in general terms also called a **BUSINESS** or a **COMPANY**, is traditionally defined as an organization with the overall goal of making a profit and maximizing shareholder value.

A **CORPORATE BUSINESS** or **CORPORATION** is a legal entity that is separate and distinct from its owners. A **BENEFIT CORPORATION** is a legal entity and a type of for-profit company (and, as far as I know, it is still only available in 35 US states and a few countries outside of the US). A benefit corporation is legally allowed to strive for something more than just profit and maximising shareholder value. As its defined goals by law, a benefit corporation includes—in addition to profit—a higher purpose and a positive impact on society, its workers, their community and the environment.[33]

As to Wikipedia, a **NON-PROFIT ORGANIZATION** can be considered "a legal entity organized and operated for a collective, public or social benefit, in contrast with an entity that operates as a business aiming to generate a profit for its owners."[34] Examples are organizations like public schools, business associations, political associations and many more. A **NON-GOVERNMENTAL ORGANIZATION (NGO)** can be described as a group of people from different countries acting together for a cause. The organization is, however, not connected to a government. Again, as to Wikipedia: "Usually, non-governmental organizations are non-profit—that is, they are trying to do something other than make money for the people who run them." An iNGO is an international non-governmental organization, such as Oxfam and Red Cross.[35]

A **FOUNDATION**, or a charitable foundation, is typically a category of non-profit organization that provides funding and support for other charitable organizations through grants. They may also be directly involved in a selected social or environmental cause through a wide set of activities. In connection to the business world, we often find private foundations that are commonly endowed by or for an individual or family to support a given cause. An example of a contemporary and hands-on foundation (or 'think and do tank', as they call themselves) is Axfoundation, a non-profit organization working practically and concretely towards building a sustainable society.[36]

A **SOCIAL BUSINESS** could be described as a business aimed at addressing specific social causes, with a vision of contributing to social welfare rather than profits. These often exist in the areas of healthcare, housing, education and financial services to the poor. In this scheme, there may be a small profit; investors may get their money back after a certain time or not at all. Success is, however, not defined by profit, but rather as the amount of impact and positive change that the company is able to generate.[37] An example of a social business is Kiva, which is "a platform for individuals and organizations to lend money directly to entrepreneurs who would otherwise not get funding, such as those in the developing world." [38] They charge a small fee to cover the operational costs but are not driven by profits.[39]

IMPACT STARTUP is a term often used for a fairly newly-started for-profit company on a mission to solve a big social or environmental problem—often supported by a unique business model, offering and/or new technology, and aiming at scaling fast.

IMPACT INVESTING generally refers to an investment strategy that not only generates financial returns, but also creates a positive social or environmental impact. Impact investors may or may not expect lower-than-average returns on their investments.

CONSCIOUS BUSINESS is a terminology often used to describe businesses run by conscious business leaders who choose to pursue a business purpose and strategy that promote an intelligent pursuit of wellbeing to all its stakeholders and the planet, while creating both short-term and long-term profit. A conscious business is characterized by four principles: a higher purpose, stakeholder orientation, conscious leadership and a conscious culture—all mutually reinforcing. Whole Foods Market is often presented as an example of conscious business.[40]

A **CIRCULAR BUSINESS** is based on a circular business model and is a key element of the **CIRCULAR ECONOMY**. In a circular economy, economic activity builds and rebuilds overall system health based on designing out waste and pollution, keeping products and materials in use and regenerating natural systems. A circular business model describes the logic of how an organization creates, offers and delivers value to its broader range of stakeholders while minimizing ecological and social costs. Circular businesses are particularly involved in the product usage phase. As to Ellen McArthur Foundation: "They generate revenues through provisioning services instead of selling physical products; they rethink the conventional producer-consumer-relationships, value creation activities and the structure of value chains; ecological and social factors complement the overall business culture and philosophy." [41] Many companies are currently aspiring to develop circular solutions, or even to become circular. EU also aspires to become a circular market.

Finally, a few words to define biodiversity, ecosystems, global warming, climate change and the associated terminology that we currently run into more and more often in the business world.

In layman terms, **BIODIVERSITY** can simply be considered the rich variety of life on Earth. As to World Wildlife Fund (WWF), "Biodiversity is all the different kinds of life you'll find in one area—the variety of animals, plants, fungi, and even microorganisms like bacteria that make up our natural world. Each of these species and organisms work together in *ecosystems*, like an intricate web, to maintain balance and support life. Biodiversity supports everything in nature that we need to survive: food, clean water, medicine, and shelter."[42] Due to human activities, such as resource extraction, the Earth is today rapidly losing biodiversity: "WWF's 2018 Living Planet Report found an average 60% decline in global populations of mammals, fish, birds, reptiles, and amphibians since 1970. The 2019 landmark *Global Assessment Report* by the Intergovernmental Platform on Biodiversity and Ecosystem Services (ipbes) reported one million animal and plant species are now threatened with extinction – the highest number in human history."[43] Biodiversity is also effected by global warming.

NASA defines **GLOBAL WARMING** as "the long-term heating of Earth's climate system observed since the pre-industrial period (between 1850 and 1900) due to human activities, primarily fossil fuel burning, which increases heat-trapping greenhouse gas levels in Earth's atmosphere. The term is frequently used interchangeably with the term **CLIMATE CHANGE**, though the latter refers to both human- and naturally produced warming and the effects it has on our planet. It is most commonly measured as the average increase in Earth's global surface temperature."[44]

NASA defines **CLIMATE CHANGE** as "a long-term change in the average weather patterns that have come to define Earth's local, regional and global climates. These changes have a broad range of observed effects that are synonymous with the term. Changes observed in Earth's climate since the early 20th century are primarily driven by human activities, particularly fossil fuel burning, which increases heat-trapping greenhouse gas levels in Earth's atmosphere, raising Earth's average surface temperature. These human-produced temperature increases are commonly referred to as global warming. Natural processes can also contribute to climate change, including internal variability (e.g., cyclical ocean patterns like El Niño, La Niña and the Pacific Decadal Oscillation) and external forcings (e.g., volcanic activity, changes in the Sun's energy output, variations in Earth's orbit)."[45]

Created in 1988, **THE IPCC (*THE INTERGOVERNMENTAL PANEL ON CLIMATE CHANGE*)** is a UN body assessing science related to climate change.[46] They also publish reports with assessments of the state of climate change to support policy makers. As stated in their factsheet: "The IPCC is committed to preparing reports that aim for the highest standards of scientific excellence, balance, and clarity. Multiple stages of review are an essential part of the IPCC process to ensure a comprehensive, objective and transparent assessment of the current state of knowledge of the science related to climate change." [47]

THE PARIS AGREEMENT, adopted in 2015, is a legally binding international treaty on climate change. Its goal is to limit global warming, preferably to 1.5 degree Celsius (at least well below 2 degrees) as compared to pre-industrial levels.[48]

Many companies currently aspire to become *carbon neutral, net-zero or even carbon positive* to live up to the targets set by the Paris Climate Agreement. In fact, only 29 years remain to reach net-zero emissions globally. What does this mean? Apart from being critical to the survival of humanity, the definitions are best summarized by topic experts (here PlanA Academy):[49]

- **"CARBON NEUTRAL** means that any CO_2 released into the atmosphere from a company's activities is balanced by an equivalent amount being removed."

- **"CLIMATE POSITIVE** means that activity goes beyond achieving net-zero carbon emissions to create an environmental benefit by removing additional carbon dioxide from the atmosphere."

- "**CARBON NEGATIVE** means the same thing as 'climate positive.'"

- "**CARBON POSITIVE** is how organizations describe climate positive and carbon negative. It's mainly a marketing term, and understandably confusing— we generally avoid it."

- "**CLIMATE NEUTRAL** refers to reducing all GHG (greenhouse gas) to the point of zero while eliminating all other negative environmental impacts that an organization may cause."

- "**NET-ZERO CARBON EMISSIONS** mean that an activity releases net-zero carbon emissions into the atmosphere."

- "**NET-ZERO EMISSIONS** balance the whole amount of GHG released and the amount removed from the atmosphere."

THE GHG PROTOCOL sets the global standards on how to measure and manage greenhouse gas emissions (GHG).[50] Greenhouse gas emissions are categorized into three groups or 'Scopes'. As to the CarbonTrust these are defined as follows: "**SCOPE 1** covers direct emissions from owned or controlled sources. **SCOPE 2** covers indirect emissions from the generation of purchased electricity, steam, heating and cooling consumed by the reporting company. **SCOPE 3** includes all other indirect emissions that occur in a company's value chain." [51]

THE SCIENCE-BASED TARGETS INITIATIVE (SBTi) "mobilizes companies to set science-based targets and boost their competitive advantage in the transition to the low-carbon economy. It is a collaboration between CDP, the United Nations Global Compact, World Resources Institute (WRI) and the World Wide Fund for Nature (WWF) and one of the We Mean Business Coalition commitments. The initiative defines and promotes best practice in science-based target setting, offers resources and guidance to reduce barriers to adoption, and independently assesses and approves companies' targets." The SBTi has furthermore launched the first science-based global standard for corporate net-zero targets to ensure that companies' targets translate into action that is consistent with achieving a net-zero world by no later than 2050.[52] So far approximately 1000 companies have approved **SCIENCE BASED TARGETS (SBT)** and many more have committed to.

 **NOTE TO SELF**

CHAPTER 1

THE SUSTAINABILITY REVOLUTION

"We've watched the COVID-19 situation unfold at incredible speed… The climate crisis is playing out on a much slower timeframe. We know roughly what to expect and when to expect it, and we should be preparing with the same level of urgency."
DR. DE MENOCAL [53]

We are literally going to start this chapter on a burning platform. But probably not one you would expect.

One July night in 1988, Daryl Connor, a consultant and writer, was watching the news on TV when he heard about a horrific explosion on the Piper Alpha oil rig in the North Sea just outside of Scotland. The explosion and subsequent fires destroyed the platform and claimed 167 lives. What captured his interest was the story of one of the survivors, Andy Mochan.[54]

The explosion had abruptly woken Andy up in his quarters and injured him badly. He still somehow managed to escape to the platform edge. Daryl Connor writes: "Beneath him, oil had surfaced and ignited. Twisted steel and other debris littered the surface of the water. Because of the water's temperature, he knew that he could live a maximum of only 20 minutes if not rescued. Despite all that, Andy jumped fifteen stories from the platform to the water. When asked why he took that potentially fatal leap, he did not hesitate. He said, "It was either jump or fry." He chose possible death over certain death. Andy jumped because he felt he had no choice—the price of staying on the platform was too high."

/ It helps us realise that we often don't move until we have to—or until we have a real crisis on our hands /

Daryl Connor used the story in one of his 1990s management books as a metaphor for describing the determined commitment needed to create a significant change. Today, the metaphor is most often used to convey the message that remaining with the status quo, or staying put, is not an option and that something needs to be done even if it may be both risky and uncertain. The story may, however, create slightly different associations than it did 25 years ago when the oil and gas industry was booming. Today, it is an industry in transformation due to another burning platform (climate change) and an increasing focus on renewable energy. As a metaphor, however, it is still highly relevant because it shows the difficulty and importance of making a choice and taking action, especially when we feel stuck between a rock and a hard place. Further, it helps us realise that we often don't move until we have to—or until we have a real crisis on our hands. I am confident that Andy would not have made the fifteen-story jump into the cold water were it not for the imminent threat to his life.

So let's jump right in.

THE CONSEQUENCES OF
THE GREAT ACCELERATION

"The Great Acceleration of the world economy over the last 70 years has brought an unprecedented increase in output and human welfare. Human population grew from 2.5 billion in 1950."
WORLD ECONOMIC FORUM[55]

Over the past century, the world has seen unprecedented economic development and an exponentially growing population. Industrialization and globalization have led to wealth and prosperity; they have increased our lifespan by decades and brought billions out of poverty across the globe. Figure 4 illustrates the GDP development over the last two millennia.

The exponentially growing GDP has simply created a brand new world over the last century. When my own grandmother was born in 1908, most Swedish households still had no electricity and none had the modern appliances that we take for granted today. Lacking a good Swedish example, Figure 5 shows the diffusion of innovation in US households from 1900–2005, which is representative of her lifetime.

When my grandmother passed away in 2005, a lot had happened during those good 95 years. In fact, in less than a century, the world had in many ways completely transformed. This unprecedented development improved quality of life and made it less cumbersome in many ways. Just imagine having to wash your clothes by hand, having no shower, no refrigerator, no TV, no holiday in an exotic country, and not even a car or a telephone—much less today's mandatory smartphone.

Better economic conditions and ground-breaking innovation improved living conditions, and a globalized economy led to reduced
child mortality and longer lifespans, but also to an exponentially growing global population. Figure 6 shows the world population
growth over the past 12,000 years.

So, what is wrong with this? Higher GDP and more people on this
planet bring increasing potential for products and services, which in
turn means a flourishing economy. All good for business, right? Unfortunately not, as the amazing developments of the past century also
brought a lot of unintended consequences. It is widely recognized today that the unprecedented population growth coupled with unsustainable production and consumption practices upon which we have
built our modern society is putting the planetary systems and life as
we know it under significant stress.

In the report, *The Trajectory of the Anthropocene – The Great Acceleration* (2015), researchers zoomed further in on the development and
summarized their observations and conclusions with the insight that
the period from about 1950 until today is unique in human history:
"The second half of the twentieth century is unique in the entire history of human existence on Earth. Many human activities reached
take-off points sometime in the twentieth century and have accelerated sharply towards the end of the century. The last 50 years have
without doubt seen the most rapid transformation of the human relationship with the natural world in the history of human-kind."[59]

Figure 7 shows a number of socio-economic and earth system trends,
published in the report above, which helps visualize this development. It is not only GDP and population that have skyrocketed; several indicators point in the direction of exponential growth.

WORLD GDP OVER THE LAST TWO MILLENNIA

Total output of the world economy; adjusted for inflation and expressed in international-$ in 2011 prices.

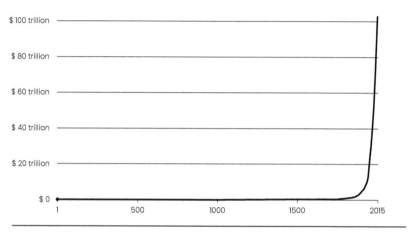

FIGURE 4

Global prosperity in terms of GDP (Our World in Data). [56]

THE SIZE OF THE WORLD PUPULATION OVER THE LAST 12.000 YEARS

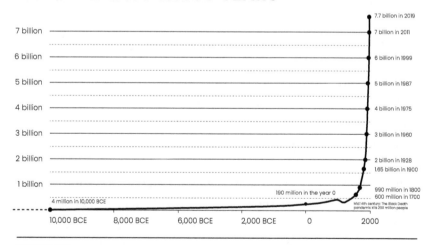

FIGURE 6

The size of the world population over the last 12,000 years (Our World in Data). [58]

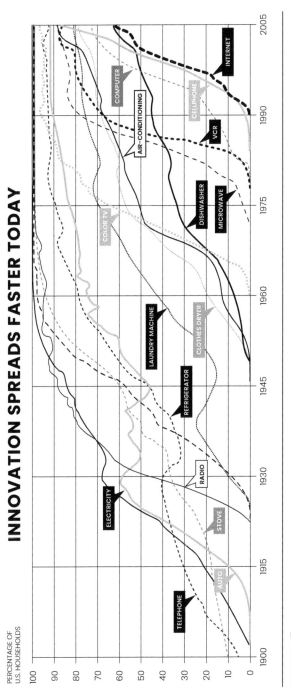

INNOVATION SPREADS FASTER TODAY

PERCENTAGE OF
U.S. HOUSEHOLDS

FIGURE 5

The diffusion of innovation in U.S. households 1900–2005. From "The 100-year march of technology in one graph" (TheAtlantic.com).[57]

SOCIOECONOMIC TRENDS

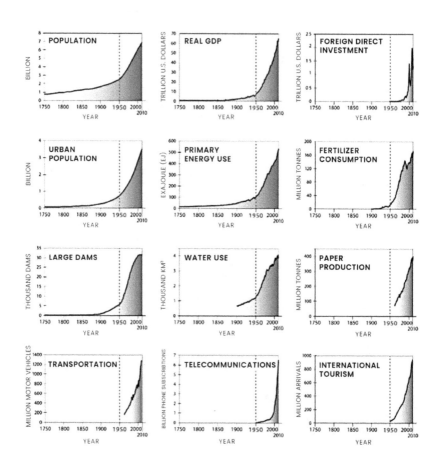

FIGURE 7

Trends from 1750 to 2010 in globally aggregated indicators for socio-economic development, and trends from 1750 to 2010 in indicators for the structure and functioning of the Earth System.[60]

EARTH SYSTEM TRENDS

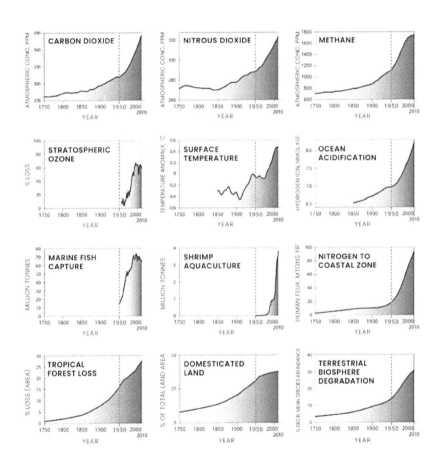

Even though the pace of change has been rapid over the past decades, futurists Ray Kurtzweil and Peter Diamandis claim that we will never experience a change and development this slow again and that we are already facing exponential growth in a vast number of technological areas. According to Diamandis, over the next 100 years we will experience as much change as we have over the past 20,000 years. The futurist Chris Luebkeman supports this claim, saying that "The changes we have witnessed during our lifetimes will pale in comparison to those which lie before us."[61] Others speak about system and paradigm shifts beyond capitalism, or even about new portals opening to other dimensions.

"Over the next 100 years we will experience as much change as we have over the past 20,000 years."

PETER DIAMANDIS

In my first book, *Navigera in i Framtiden* (2018), I set out to explore this concept of accelerating exponential change and what business leaders can do to surf its waves rather than become its victims. The unprecedented advances in technology and digitalization seem to have led to a human attention span shorter than that of a goldfish. This means that we now tend to focus on what is immediately in front of us rather than addressing brutal facts and what matters most in the long term, not only due to the short-sightedness of the quarterly economy but also due to our natural cognitive limitations. This short-sightedness is, however, not a completely new phenomenon. In 1972, authors of *The Limits to Growth* described a world where only a few have the luxury—or capability—of taking a long-term global perspective, while the majority are fully preoccupied with everyday life and the coming weeks and years.

A brutal fact that we cannot afford to ignore, however, is that we are currently consuming more than is sustainable on this planet. This is not only important but now also urgent, and something we must deal with now. There is simply nowhere to hide. The Stockholm Resilience Centre has illustrated this urgency in their *Planetary Boundaries* model, visualizing that several of our planetary life-sustaining systems are currently challenged and that we as humanity need to take action to continue to develop and thrive for generations to come.[62] Or, as said on their website: "We must stop considering nature as something separate from society because people and nature are truly intertwined... Development can no longer be done without an increased understanding of nature's role for our own survival and well-being."

For a non-scientist, this model may be easier to review in the simplified version presented in Figure 8, where Planetary Boundaries are connected to Sustainable Development Goals. This creates a visualization that helps us understand that the biosphere and the connected Sustainable Development Goals (SDGs) are the foundation for life and society on this planet and that economic prosperity and business are completely dependent on biosphere and society thriving.[63]

The *biosphere* is the regions of the atmosphere and surface of the earth that is occupied by living organisms. An *ecosystem* is "all the plants and living creatures in a particular area considered in relation to their physical environment" within the biosphere.[65]

Today, the health of the biosphere and the ecosystems that we rely on are deteriorating more rapidly than ever before in human history. In the words of the UN IPBES Global Assessment Report on Biodiversity and Ecosystem Services, "The health of ecosystems on which we and all other species depend is deteriorating more rapidly than ever. We are eroding the very foundations of our economies, livelihoods, food security, health and quality of life worldwide." There is still hope, however, "Through 'transformative change', nature can still be conserved, restored and used sustainably – this is also key to meeting most other global goals. By transformative change, we mean a fundamental, system-wide reorganization across technological, economic and social factors, including paradigms, goals and values."[66] The report's four key messages for policy makers are:[67]

1. "Nature and its vital contributions to people, which together embody biodiversity and ecosystem functions and services, are deteriorating worldwide."

2. "Direct and indirect drivers of change have accelerated during the past 50 years."

3. "Goals for conserving and sustainably using nature and achieving sustainability cannot be met by current trajectories, and goals for 2030 and beyond may only be achieved through transformative changes across economic, social, political and technological factors."

4. "Nature can be conserved, restored and used sustainably while other global societal goals are simultaneously met through urgent and concerted efforts fostering transformative change."

Kate Raworth, a recognized economist, have integrated the social and planetary boundaries in her book *Doughnut Economics* (2017), where she pointed out that humanity's challenge of the 21st century is to meet the needs of all within the means of the planet and its life-supporting systems, such as a stable climate, fertile soil and a protective ozone layer.[68] Her visualization, shown in Figure 9, also illustrates that some systems are clearly beyond the boundaries of what is sustainable. Furthermore, in connecting the model to our social foundation, she shows that planetary boundaries are completely interconnected with our societal wellbeing.

Adding to this complexity is that we, as a humanity, are currently consuming ecological resources equivalent to 1.6 Earths per year. There is even a name for the day that we consume more than the planet can cope with: Earth Overshoot Day. In developed countries, this day occurs in the first half of the year. In less developed countries it occurs in the second half.[70] Few manage to live below what is the Earth's capacity and as the global middle class is expanding and dreaming of more than they have today, this trend is obviously moving in the wrong direction.

/ We, as a humanity, are currently consuming ecological resources equivalent to 1.6 Earths per year /

The most urgent and important of all these issues may of course be climate change. Scientists today widely agree that the burning of fossil fuels has affected the concentration of CO_2 in the atmosphere. Before the Industrial Revolution, it was estimated that the concentration of CO_2 in the atmosphere was about 288 ppm (parts per million). We have now reached about 414 ppm and are on the way to doubling the amount of CO_2 in the atmosphere by the end of this century. In the latest IPCC report, the analysis is clear: "Observed increases in well-mixed greenhouse gas (GHG) concentrations since around 1750 are unequivocally caused by human activities." [71]

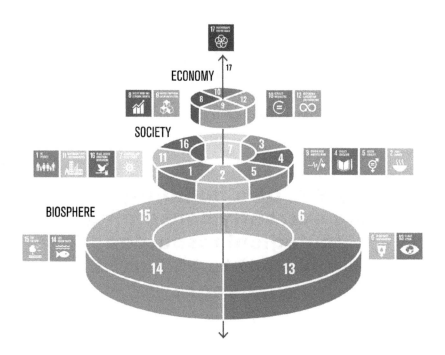

FIGURE 8

Connecting the planetary boundaries to the SDGs, by Stockholm Resilience Centre.[64]

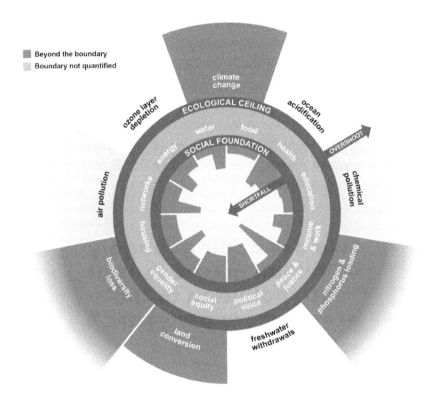

Beyond the boundary
Boundary not quantified

FIGURE 9

The Doughnut model of social and planetary boundaries,
by Kate Raworth.[69]

Scientists say that if CO_2 doubles, it could raise the average global temperature of the Earth between two and five degrees Celsius, which could bring devastating consequences for life on the planet.[72] In May 2021, we again saw the highest levels of carbon dioxide in the atmosphere since the measurements began 63 years ago. A senior scientist at the The National Oceanic and Atmospheric Administration's (NOAA's) Global Monitoring Laboratory noted that CO_2 persists in the oceans and atmosphere for thousands of years after it is emitted: "We are adding roughly 40 billion metric tons of CO_2 pollution to the atmosphere per year... That is a mountain of carbon that we dig up out of the Earth, burn and release into the atmosphere as CO_2—year after year. If we want to avoid catastrophic climate change, the highest priority must be to reduce CO_2 pollution to zero at the earliest possible date." [73]

"We are adding roughly 40 billion metric tons of CO_2 pollution to the atmosphere per year..."

NOAA RESEARCH NEWS

Going back 800,000 years in time, NOAA has of course seen fluctuations in CO_2 levels over time. There are however no other periods that even comes close to the atmospheric levels of CO_2 that are now being recorded (see Figure 10).[74]

The problems, however, do not stop here. And they are wicked indeed.

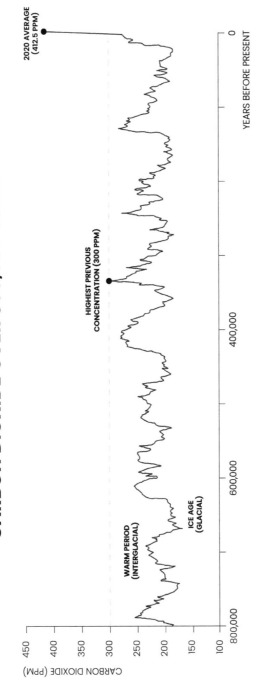

FIGURE 10

Atmospheric carbon dioxide concentrations (CO_2) in parts per million (ppm) for the past 800,000 years.[75]

SKOLSTREJK FÖR KLIMATET
#parentsforfuture
WARNING
WARNING
15.03. Klimastreik
MAKE THE PLANET GRETA AGAIN!

WICKED PROBLEMS AND SOCIAL TIPPING POINTS

"We cannot solve our problems with the same thinking we used when we created them."
ALBERT EINSTEIN

A *wicked problem* is a difficult problem to solve because of incomplete, contradictory, and/or changing requirements that are often challenging to recognize.[76] The world's unprecedented environmental and social challenges are indeed tremendously wicked. Seeing that climate change is striking harder and more rapidly than expected, the World Economic Forum's Global Risk Report, as well as many others, has stressed the urgent need to take action before 2030.[77]

Climate change is, of course, not the only wicked problem on the horizon. They are in plentiful supply. Wicked problems do, by the way, offer interesting business opportunities for those who dare to be visionary and go the extra mile.

The global challenges stretch from climate change and biodiversity loss to unsustainable consumption and production, filthy water and poor sanitation, inequality, poverty and hunger, war and corruption, and more. It actually does not take too much effort to realise what these problems are.

Elon Musk's Tesla is a great example of a visionary leader seeing the business opportunity in a wicked problem and ultimately challenging the whole automotive industry to transform. Why are more business leaders not following in his footsteps? We could argue that most business leaders lack Elon's entrepreneurial experience and perspectives, his visionary capabilities, and his ability to rally investors to buy into the vision and support the presented business opportunity. We could also argue that sustainability in the business world is still viewed as risk reduction and a dry topic reserved for experts, rather than as real opportunities that can enable companies to do well by doing good and integrating that thinking into their business strategies, business models and operating models. It could also be a simple question of a lack of awareness and knowledge. It may even be that business leaders on all levels are still stuck in delivering on the short-termism of the current capitalistic system, which favours quarterly results at the expense of long-term sustainable development, and that they have not been motivated to explore and understand the relevant fields. This is possibly because business leaders are still rewarded for focusing on short-term results rather than on the long-term horizon. It could also simply be that it is a bit uncomfortable and that it is easier to stay in the comfort zone, hoping that others will step up to take action. This time, however, there is nowhere to hide.

Instead, I believe we need to realise that we right now might be at not only a planetary tipping point, but a *social tipping point* that is putting things in motion whether we want it or not.

A *tipping point* can be described as the moment at which a series of small changes or incidents becomes significant enough to cause a larger, even more important change—a moment of critical mass, a threshold or a boiling point. It could also be explained as the exponential growth of a new idea or paradigm, where it suddenly starts to spread very quickly and gain real traction.

When Malcom Gladwell wrote his book *Tipping Point* (2001), he compared the emergence of social trends, such as fashion and word-of-mouth, and a vast number of completely unconnected changes in our society to that of an epidemic, saying that new ideas, products, messages and behaviours spread just like viruses do. It is slow at first, and then after a certain point, everything can change all at once.

In short, social conventions seem to determine which behaviours are seen as acceptable and which are not, but they can be changed. Malcom Gladwell was not the first to describe the phenomenon. In fact, the *theory of critical mass* argues that when a committed minority reaches a critical group size, the social system crosses a tipping point, triggering changes in behaviour that rapidly increase the acceptance of the minority view. These movements can have a rapid and dramatic impact on entire populations. Studies of social movements have, for instance, argued that a small group of activists can change the culture of an entire community. In some studies, activist groups at or above 25 percent of a population were able to change the social norms in their communities. At that point, their popularity and influence can explode, having a remarkable influence on the broader population and triggering a change in the rest of society.[78]

Hence, sustainability is no longer a 'nice to have'. It is a 'must have' and it is becoming mainstream. It is also increasingly becoming a stakeholder requirement, driven by consumers, activists, customers, investors and employees. Customer mindset now even seems to be changing from 'kudos for choosing eco!' to 'why are you NOT choosing eco?' This includes new values driving change in consumer behaviour, including social shaming, such as *flygskam* (flight shame), which became even more prevalent during the Covid-19 crisis. Lifestyle trends such as minimalism and zero-waste mindsets are also gaining popularity.

For example, once considered a niche market, Lifestyle of Health and Sustainability (LOHAS) consumers today make up more than 25% of shoppers in the United States, 20% in the European Union and an astonishing 40% in Sweden, which is the highest share in the world.[79]

BETTER FUTURE

LOHAS are driven by their values and beliefs and can be found across demography. They are known to be active, demanding, creative, well informed and influential.

Globally, it is not only LOHAS consumers who are increasingly demanding that companies provide information. There has, for instance, been a rapid rise in calls for higher transparency and ethical production by consumers in the clothing industry.[80] According to Statista, organic and fair-trade label marked consumer goods have grown substantially with 9 percent and 18 percent yearly growth rates between 2005 and 2017. This is to compare with a fast-moving consumer goods market with a yearly growth rate at approximately 5 percent globally. Another study shows that 31 percent of consumers today prefer organic food, and that 29 percent prefer fair trade goods.[81] Many consumers long for the responsible, fair, just and sustainable.

Another sign of this development is the result of a recent survey of 27,000 people in the general public that was conducted across 27 countries around the globe, where an overwhelming percentage of participants wanted governments to take stronger action to protect nature, even if that could mean restricting business activities. Hence, there is a public desire for governments to act. Another recent study by GlobaScan shows that consumers throughout the world increasingly feel a need to consume less to preserve the environment for future generations. The prediction is that people everywhere will be looking for more sustainable solutions to eleviate the increasing unease attached to the current levels of consumption.[82]

Investors are also realizing the urgency and need for a more long-term and sustainable approach to business. Mostly as a very rational means to protecting their investments, but still. This will ultimately have a large impact on how CEOs and management teams are incentivised and how businesses are run.

These strong trends and social movements have, of course, been picked up by our policy makers. In December 2019, the European Commission presented the *Green Deal,* which provided "an action plan to boost the efficient use of resources by moving to a clean, circular economy, restore biodiversity and cut pollution". It also outlined investments needed and financing tools available to ensure a just and inclusive transition to a green economy.[83] One part of this is the aim for the whole EU to be climate-neutral by 2050. This is not only a political goal. Reaching this target alone will require action by all sectors and include investments in environmentally friendly technologies; supporting industries to innovate; rolling out cleaner, cheaper and healthier forms of private and public transport; decarbonising the energy sector; ensuring buildings are more energy efficient; and working with international partners to improve global environmental standards. This political commitment is now also being translated into legal obligations, ensuring that the minimum level increases and forcing businesses to step up to the challenge. The *EU Taxonomy* is just one of the initiatives underway. In order to put pressure on industries outside the EU and to ensure fair competition, companies that import climate-damaging products to the EU will have to pay duties. This will most probably have an impact on products imported from countries that still cover the majority of their energy requirements with coal-fired power, such as China. As stated in a recent article in *Fast Company,* "The way you change corporate behaviour... is to change the law, and then enforce that law strictly."[84] The European way of life and economy will most probably also have to change significantly over the next decade.

With these changes in their business environment, many business leaders are already realizing the potential threats to their current business models, but also the need to focus on evolving consumer values in order to help their company stay relevant and attractive in their markets. Consumer values and behaviours are, however, not

BETTER FUTURE

something we leave at home in the morning. It is something that we bring with us to work. Hence, this development not only impacts our private shopping preferences and behaviours, but also spills over to our professional lives—in our expectations of employers as well as suppliers. Ultimately, it will infuse all of society and become the new normal—our dominating way of thinking and our dominating paradigm.

Driven by both business opportunities and risk mitigation, quite a few business leaders and companies worldwide are already rethinking business and riding the waves of sustainability transformation. Some are even taking drastic measures to deal with the climate emergency. Many are becoming aware that a failure to do so will lead to serious consequences for the survival of business, from reduced competitiveness and lost reputation to affecting financial performance and access to capital.

There is at least an urgent need to move beyond business as usual. Or as IMD Business School president Jean-Francois Manzoni has said, "In the new decade, it will not only be possible to do well by doing good; it will **only** be possible to do well by doing good."[85]

STUCK IN PARADIGM PARALYSIS?

**"All truth passes through three stages.
First, it is ridiculed. Second, it is violently
opposed. Third, it is accepted as self-evident."**
ARTHUR SCHOPENHAUER

Change and disruption may seem to be new characteristics related to our modern world but are in fact not new phenomenon. They have been with us since the beginning of time, and some patterns seem to be repeated continuously.

Following her studies of change throughout human history, Connie Gersick described what change as a pattern has looked like throughout history on a multitude of different levels—from organisms to organizations and civilizations. The identified change pattern is characterized by long periods of stability where existing systems and structures prevent change, followed by periods of revolutionary change where the prevailing systems and structures are broken up and replaced.[86]

Hence, systems and structures provide stability as well as rigidity but can only prevent change for limited periods of time until the external pressure to change and adapt becomes so large that the system is torn apart during a more chaotic and revolutionary period of time. This period is again followed by a new period of stability and then a period of revolutionary change. And so on. Throughout time. Interestingly, this is similar to the *S-curve* of innovation first described by Everett Rogers in the 1960s, which is how academics describe *paradigm shifts* (see Figure 11).

Each curve on the *S-curve* can be said to represent a generation of technology, idea or way of thinking—or simply a new paradigm.

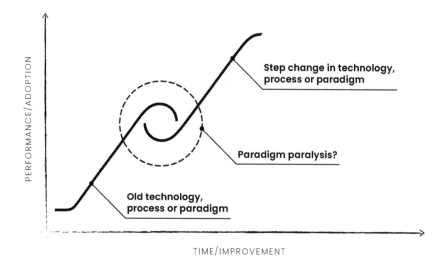

FIGURE 11

The S-curve of innovation.[87]

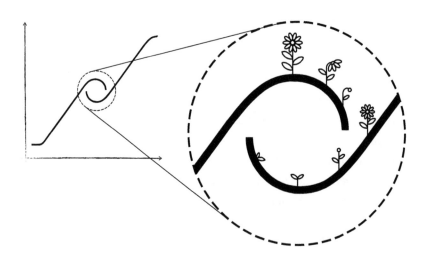

FIGURE 12

A paradigm shift—one paradigm crumbling and being replaced by another emerging paradigm.[90]

OLD BUSINESS PARADIGM	PARADIGM PARALYSIS	EVOLVING BUSINESS PARADIGM
Short-termism driven by financial markets with a focus on optimizing short-term profits		Long-termism encouraged by financial markets to protect long-term investments
Purpose of business is to maximise short-term profits for shareholders		Purpose of business is to advance the prosperity of humanity within the boundaries set by nature
"Take-make-dispose" logic		Circular, regenerative and more equitable business and operating models
Traditional Corporate Social Responsibility practices an add-on to reduce risk and safeguard reputation		Sustainability is a fully integrated part of purpose, strategy, business models, value chain and offering
Collaboration in industry associations		New models for collaboration based on mutual interest and the higher good

TABLE 2

The old and evolving business paradigms, and the paralysis that can appear in feeling stuck in the middle, with both new and old mindsets and practices co-existing at the same time.

As the dominating way of thinking and doing things ages, it can best be described as gradually losing its relevance. At one point or the other (when its relevance, usefulness or competitive advantage has been eroded), it is then replaced with a new generation of technology, or a new way of thinking resulting in a new S-curve. How does this work?

As a paradigm grows and matures, different alternatives—new ideas, technologies and ways of thinking—pop up. Some never spread or gain traction in relevant parts of society, but some do—even though they tend to be ridiculed at the outset by those representing the dominating paradigm. As Arthur Schopenhauer famously put it, "All truth passes through three stages. First, it is ridiculed. Second, it is violently opposed. Third, it is accepted as self-evident." Hence, what is today evident was not so evident just a few decades ago and will not be so evident in another few decades from now.

Again, for an idea to evolve into a new paradigm, it needs to gain traction in relevant parts of society. And as the old pattern of thinking reaches maturity, it sooner or later starts to collapse. In parallel, however, isolated alternatives have slowly begun to arise and give way to the new ideas, practices and/or technologies that are evolving by those exploring and pioneering the future. This new curve develops slowly in the early beginnings, accelerates quickly, matures and, finally, stabilizes and comes to a flattening and decline of the curve, as it is again replaced by a new paradigm—i.e., new ideas, practices and/or technologies.[88]

The process in which the dominant paradigm gives way to new paradigms to emerge and grow is simply called a *paradigm shift*, which is "an important change that happens when the usual way of thinking about or doing something is replaced by a new and different way".[89] See Figure 12.

Paradigm paralysis can then best be described as being 'stuck in the middle' between the old thought pattern and the new one that is trying to emerge, especially when the new pattern is not completely clear yet.

What if this describes our current situation? The new is emerging, but we still seem to be stuck in the past view of 'how things are done'. Let us imagine that we are evolving from a maturing and declining paradigm where the sole purpose of business is to create and maximise its short-term profits, into a new paradigm where long-term stakeholder value and more sustainable (and even regenerative) business practices seem to be the cornerstones of the new dominating thought system. In this development, a sense of being stuck in the middle—in paradigm paralysis—is, in my experience, what many business leaders currently experience as they stumble on the edge between the old paradigm and the emerging future. See Table 2.

This is, of course, especially challenging for business leaders who have been "brought up" and fostered in the old paradigm and see a huge gap between the old and the new. The good news is that even those stumbling between the different paradigms have a lot to learn from those companies and business leaders who are already in the frontlines.

NOTE TO SELF

CHAPTER 2

IT'S TIME TO MOVE BEYOND BUSINESS AS USUAL

"Business as usual will not save the planet."

HARVARD BUSINESS REVIEW[91]

Technology and innovation—mainly driven by the business community—have helped us leap forward and transform the world in ways that were previously unimaginable. But again, this has come at a great cost to our planet. Over time, it has also become increasingly clear that business as usual will not save the planet. Neither will the Sustainable Development Goals (SDGs) [92] if we do not act on them. But are things moving?

A Harvard Business Review study unfortunately found that most corporations seem to be addressing the SDGs on a superficial level.[93] Most simply connect what they are already doing to one or a selected set of these goals.

A study of 1,000 sustainability reports in the EU (2019) also revealed some interesting data.[94] In short, the study found that most companies, even those who set their objective high (e.g., "the wellbeing of our people, the community and the environment is considered in everything that we do") only use warm words rather than concrete targets and actions. Looking at the hard data, only 22 percent of the studied companies, for instance, provided Key Performance Indicators in summarised statements; 10 percent did not provide any at all; and 68 percent provided them scattered across the narrative, making it difficult for the reader to capture the overall picture and understand whether the company is moving the needle or not. In regard to climate change, 82 percent of the companies claimed to have policies, but only 35 percent had targets, and only 28 percent actually reported on their outcomes. Furthermore, only 15 percent reported a link between sustainability objectives and executive remuneration (which may help explain the poor transparency and performance).

/ Only 15 percent reported a link between sustainability objectives and executive renumeration /

Or as Paul Polman put it in a *Fortune* article, "The proliferation of corporate decarbonization plans and sustainability initiatives has now reached an impressive crescendo. But regrettably, the same can also be said of greenwashing, which is when a business presents itself as environmentally friendly in an attempt to obscure its past or current practices that are harmful to the environment... So far, corporate ESG data has been lacking in quality, consistency and comparability, which makes it difficult for asset managers to determine where to direct investments. Creating baseline social and environmental standards would help to unblock a vital pool of liquidity that is ready to back companies focused on long-term value creation."[95]

In their 2021 annual report, The State of Green Business,[96] the research team also observed a lack of action: "Despite the disheartening headlines, action on ESG concerns has continued relatively unabated in corporate C-suites and boardrooms." An uptick in the ambition level on corporate sustainability issues could, however, be noted: "Net-zero became a key commitment during 2020—goals that aim to eliminate, at least on paper, a company's greenhouse gas emissions, water extractions, fossil-fuel use or deforestation activities by a given date. And while those target dates are typically decades hence, they set the stage for activists, investors and other self-appointed watchdogs to monitor corporate progress towards their stated goals." They also noted an increasing interest in "restorative" and "regenerative" practices at the very frontline: "...the leading edge of sustainable business is shifting from companies having inadvertently negative impacts to having deliberately positive ones. And while most such corporate statements are still more aspirational than actionable, they signal a critical shift in thinking about the role companies can play in the years to come."

Finally, they also noted that a company's sustainability profile is now increasingly baked into its stock price and creditworthiness and that it could potentially affect the cost of capital it may need for growth going forward.

Other than that, few companies still seem to be moving anywhere beyond business as usual. In words yes, but not in terms of real action. Why? Possibly because the world's problems are still seen as something to be solved by governments, NGOs, scientists and other actors, rather than seen as the business opportunities that they really are. Or perhaps simply because they are so wicked and hard to understand.

AT AN INFLECTION POINT

"We are at an inflection point in history."

JOEL GARREAU

To put this in business lingo that you may be more comfortable with, your business and industry may already be at an *inflection point,* as described by renowned business strategist Rita Gunther McGrath in her book *Seeing Around Corners* (2019).

An inflection point can be defined as a moment in time where a certain change in your business environment will mean dramatic change to your business.[97] Over a company lifetime, several inflection points can occur as the business environment evolves. To use the language of the book so far, it could also be explained as the S-curve of a business reaching a point where an intentional strategic transformation will be necessary for the long-term health and survival of the company. See Figure 13.

As such, an inflection point represents both opportunities and threats. Even though it feels like this change is sudden, it has most probably been gestating for some time. It normally develops gradually—out of scope for many—and then suddenly seems evident. Hence, for those who scan the horizon and can pre-emptively make sense of what is happening, it can be spotted early and in time to react.

Used strategically, this turning point can poise your business for bigger things and has the power to bring about exponential change and growth. It can create new spaces—*blue oceans*—and destroy outdated technologies and business models. Inflection points may, however, also mean that you need to change the very assumptions on which your company was founded in the first place. In this light, strategic

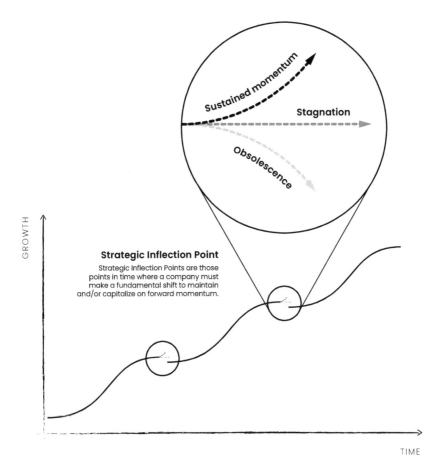

Strategic Inflection Point

Strategic Inflection Points are those points in time where a company must make a fundamental shift to maintain and/or capitalize on forward momentum.

FIGURE 13

Strategic inflection points along the S-curve.[98]

renewal is vital for any business to survive inflection points long-term. Without strategic renewal, a company is destined for decline, as it fails to remain relevant and value adding to its stakeholders. The most important question that you need to answer right now is whether you are at an inflection point or not. And if so, what are you going to do about it?

Some companies have seen the sustainability revolution coming faster than others and can be considered leaders in this race, and consumers and investors are now rewarding them for it. Sustainability disruption is now spreading more quickly than most probably expected. With one hand on your heart, could you have envisioned ten years ago that the electric car would disrupt the automotive industry at the pace that it has, that Oatly (oat-based milk and foods) would be a serious challenger to the dairy industry, or even that the plant-based Impossible Burger would be sold alongside Burger King's iconic Whopper? [99] See Figure 14.

/ Without strategic renewal, a company is destined for decline, as it fails to remain relevant and value adding to its stakeholders /

MANY CATEGORIES ARE BEING DISRUPTED BY SUSTAINABILITY TRENDS

Over the past five years (2014–2019)

ENERGY	PROTEIN	TRANSPORTATION	INVESTING
Global renewal capacity has grown by:	UK sales of meat subsitutes have grown by:	Global electrical stock has grown by:	Global sustainable debt issuance has grown by:
	MORE THAN:	MORE THAN:	MORE THAN:
50%	85%	900%	1,000%

FIGURE 14

Many categories are being disrupted by sustainability trends.[100]

There are also many signs across industries of increased focus on solutions to solve environmental and social challenges, from 'sustainability as a service'; to circular solutions and business models with a focus on repair, reuse and zero-waste; to apps tracking everything from CO_2 impact to health indicators. Open innovation and open-source solutions to collaborate to solve society's biggest problems have also appeared over the past decade in parallel to green tech solutions for alternative energy sources, carbon capturing and much more. Green tech and circular business models are mentioned in several trend reports as key elements in the trend landscape.[101]

As the first wave of innovators in this field seemed to be mainly activist-driven (e.g., Patagonia, The Body Shop and Ben & Jerry's), there now seems to be a second wave of innovators to be found at the intersection of tech startups and finding solutions to wicked problems. Norrsken Foundation has, for instance, identified its own top 100 list of impact startups.[102] These early-stage companies are hardly focused on ESG compliance, but rather driven by entrepreneurial spirit, personal values and conviction, purpose, cool technical solutions, innovation, impact business models, scaling to solve relevant wicked problems, and doing well by doing good in the process. Many impact startups are backed and supported by corporate new venture arms and impact investors. A few of these will eventually scale and become future unicorns and, as such, will hopefully contribute to a transformation towards a more sustainable and equitable society. The substantial inflow of entrepreneurial activity and capital will most likely also increase the speed of change within the field and the level of what is considered common practices versus strategically differentiating practices. This is a process that will, in many cases, very likely start with low-end disruption in market segments underserved by the incumbents and a series of acquisitions—as was the case in the preceding digital transformation.

No matter what, history has proven that sooner or later some new actor will disrupt your current business model and eventually make it irrelevant through new business models, new technology, or clever solutions that are perceived as good enough to your customers. Or as Michael Tushman, professor at Harvard Business School, puts it, "Disruption often strikes when a firm is at its weakest, when all resources are diverted to sustain core operations. That is what makes today's market uncertainty so dangerous. And while postponing investment in the future or funding a more comfortable present would be the easier path, you need to both fund the present and the future."[103]

/ History has proven that sooner or later some new actor will disrupt your current business model and eventually make it irrelevant /

In this context, disrupting your own business while you still can—while you still have a positive cashflow and good profitability—most probably means that you proactively move on to the next level of technology and business models (before you must) in order to safeguard your relevance and attractiveness and to continue bringing value to your ecosystem. Why wait?

THE ROLE OF NEW AND
EXPONENTIAL TECHNOLOGY

**"Technology made large populations
possible; large populations now
make technology indispensable."**
JOSEPH KRUTCH

You could argue that the industrial revolutions and increased use of technology are what got us into these problems in the first place. New technology is, however, neither good nor bad, exponential or not. It all depends on how it is used and on the intent of the user. Even an old-fashioned tool like a hammer has two sides: is very useful when we need to build things, but it can also be used to hurt people. The same is true for exponential technologies, such as AI and robotics. When used with malignant intent, technology can cause great damage and even a complete destruction of the world as we know it. Applied in a way that supports humanity and helps us solve problems in a smarter or more effective way than we currently do, new and exponential technologies can add great value and help us solve the wicked problems of the world. Also, having studied exponential innovation and technologies at Singularity University, this is an area that I feel warmly about.

Already in *Abundance – the Future is Better than You Think* (2012, 2014), Peter Diamandis and Steven Kotler showed us how progress in artificial intelligence, digital manufacturing, synthetic biology, nanomaterials and many other exponentially growing technologies can help us meet and exceed the basic needs of every human on this planet and that abundance for all is within reach. In the book *Ett Jordklot Räcker* (or *One Earth is Enough*, 2016), Rune Westergård, an engineer and business leader with extensive experience in solving wicked problems, argues that technology will help us solve the wicked problems that we have caught ourselves in and that it will help us live and prosper within the planetary boundaries. Johan Norberg, in his book *Progress: Ten Reasons to Look Forward to the Future* (2017), also highlights that the progress of past decades has been unsurpassed by anything in human history, and that the future looks promising, given that we deal with the problems proactively. These are principles that players like Singularity University and the World Economic Forum also seem to agree on. Similarly, I do not believe that the solution to our wicked problems is to stop consuming and go back to a pre-industrial society where our lifespans were shorter and poverty was widely spread. Instead, I believe that we need to use technology and business in combination as a force for good to create the future that we want for ourselves, our children and the coming generations.

As we speak, disruptive technology shifts are occurring in several industries. Let us take a brief look at what is happening in the energy industry—at the very core of the sustainability vortex.

THE ENERGY INDUSTRY EXAMPLE

The energy industry is one that was instrumental in creating the amazing economic growth and prosperity of the last century, but that has also contributed heavily to the climate change, pollution and health issues of this planet, mostly because of burning fossil fuels.

In my work as a consultant with a focus on strategy, innovation and transformation, I have been able to observe this development from within—with insights from Sweden, Denmark, France, Germany and Great Britain.

This started in 2015 when I was invited to deliver a speech at an energy conference at the Royal Academy in London. These were the days before Zoom, so I had to be at the venue in real life. After having delivered my shortest and fastest speech ever (the thirty minutes that I originally had at my disposal had, step by step, shrunk to five minutes), I concentrated on my next task of supporting participants from different parts of the industry in creating scenarios for the future, together with a group of facilitators gathered by Imperial College London. Now, this is when things got interesting. New technology was of course already available in 2015, but the current industry infrastructure—and especially the mindsets and skillsets of people in the industry—were far from prepared for the changes already in motion. The 'stickiness' of the old energy industry paradigm and 'the way we are used to doing things around here' simply surprised me, as did the lack of sense of urgency. The development has since accelerated and is now widely recognized as an industry-wide transformation—despite far too many incumbents protecting the status quo for far too long. So, what has happened?

Let us take a few steps back in time. Fossil fuels (coal, oil and gas) have, as you already know, been instrumental to the industrial revolution and to a large extent have enabled the living standards that we have today. Energy production—globally still mainly the burning of fossil fuels—has, however, come to account for around three-quarters of global greenhouse gas emissions and is far from sustainable. Today, it is considered the largest driver of climate change and a serious pollutant.

As you can see in Figure 15, fossil fuels still dominate the scene. Coal seems to have peaked already in 2013, while peak oil may take until 2040, at least if you listen to some observers within the industry. Also, the use of natural gas is still increasing. This is something that might seem both strange and controversial in these times of climate change, where atmospheric carbon has reached an all-time high and where the atmosphere and oceans, according to scientists, more or less have run out of capability to absorb additional carbon.

Rapid technological development within the field of renewable energy, however, provides hope for future generations. Renewable energies, such as hydropower, solar, wind, geothermal, wave and tidal and bioenergy, are picking up pace. To a large extent, this is driven by the increasingly effective solar and wind power solutions, but also by strengthened regulations and a growing awareness about the potential future risks of fossil fuels in the investment community, which is now less motivated to invest in fossil fuels and more motivated to invest in renewable energy solutions.[105]

To understand the impact of the ongoing technological developments enabling this change, let us review Figure 16, which shows the price of electricity from new power plants over a 10-year period (2009-2019). As you can see, the price of solar photovoltaic dropped by 89 percent over the period.

Why is this? And why is the same thing (i.e., rapid price drops) not happening to more mature energy technologies, such as nuclear power? In short, because old technologies depend on the price of the fuel that they burn and the power plant's operating costs. Renewable energy plants are completely different. Our World in Data means that: "Their operating costs are comparatively low, and they don't have to pay for any fuel; their fuel doesn't have to be dug out of the ground, their fuel—the wind and sunlight – comes to them."[107]

To understand why solar *power* got so inexpensive so fast, we need to understand why solar *technology* got cheap in the first place.

Even at very high price points, solar technology found use early on in highly specialised and advanced applications. As so often, the space industry was first out in 1958, when solar power was simply considered a good solution to supply a satellite that required electricity.

BETTER FUTURE

GLOBAL PRIMARY ENERGY CONSUMPTION BY SOURCE

Primary energy is calculated based on the 'substitution method' which takes account of the inefficiencies in fossil fuel production by converting non-fossil energy into the energy inputs required if they had the same conversion losses as fossil fuels.

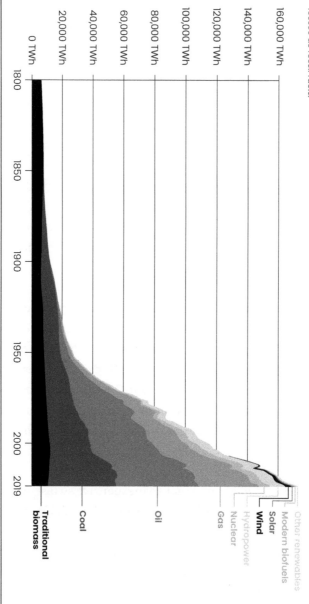

FIGURE 15

The development global energy consumption from 1800 through 2019 (OurWorldInData).[104]

THE PRICE OF ELECTRICITY FROM NEW POWER PLANTS

Electricity prices are expressed in 'levelized costs of energy' (LCOE). LCOE captures the cost of building the power plant itself as well as the ongoing costs for fuel and operating the power plant over its lifetime.

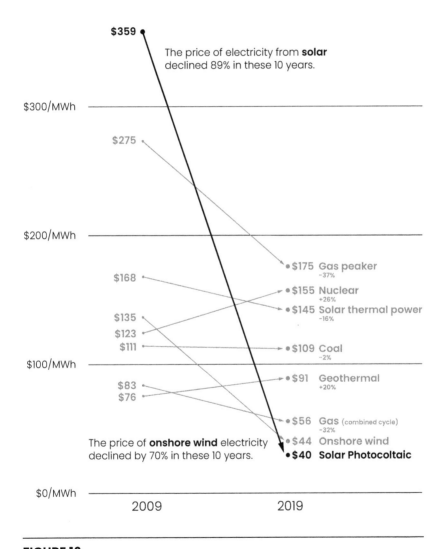

FIGURE 16

The price of electricity from new powerplants (OurWorldinData).[106]

The prices of solar modules then declined with increasing use and number of applications as volumes increased. More production volume gave producers the chance to learn by doing and to understand how to improve the production process further, which started a cycle of increasing demand and falling prices. Based on this spinning wheel, the technology became more and more cost efficient over time, which, in turn, further increased the demand. Figure 17 visualizes this development, where any technology become cheaper with increasing production and enter a virtuous cycle.

This is both about scaling technology per se and learning how to produce it more effectively and efficiently while identifying and adding new applications and markets. It is, however, also about applying new business models and safeguarding future investments into the new technologies rather than continuing to support the old, less efficient and environmentally hazardous technologies—in this case oil and gas.

What is happening in the energy sector is not unique and old technology becoming outdated is nothing new. This cycle has been found to be a natural part of the earlier industrial revolutions and was described decades ago by Joseph Schumpeter as *creative destruction*—or as a necessary means for societal renewal and progress. In this sense, the old inferior technologies simply give way to the new superior technologies emerging as they reach the end of their lifecycle (remember the S-curve).

But can something similar—a huge technology shift in the direction of more sustainable business—really happen to your own industry? I am here to say yes, it can, and you need to understand the up-and-coming technologies that have a potential impact on your own industry and ecosystem, because the sustainability revolution is already here. So, what do you do if you are part of an unsustainable industry?

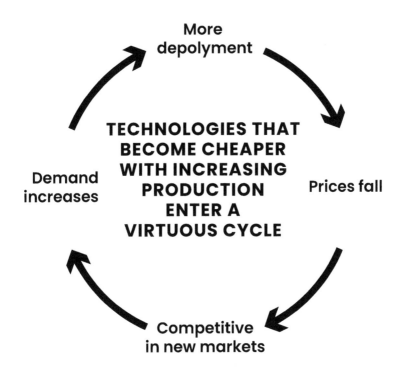

FIGURE 17

A simplified process of scaling technologies and becoming more efficient and effective.[108]

In short, you will need to proactively explore opportunities and gradually transform your business or risk becoming increasingly irrelevant to your stakeholders and ultimately fall into oblivion.

Our burning platform—based on a fundament of accelerating climate change, rapid loss of biodiversity, spiced up by Covid-19 and its economic impact across the globe—may still not feel imminent enough for you. It may even still feel like a potential distant threat to where you are today. Make no mistake. This is a very real challenge, and we all risk being slowly boiled as a collective of frogs without seemingly understanding the urgency of the situation. This is unfortunate because it is what we do today that co-creates the future. Also, because, as you will see in the book, these challenges present us with the possibility for an unprecedented green recovery for the benefit of future businesses, future generations, and our planet.

Let us briefly return to the frog analogy. This story is often used as a metaphor for the unwillingness of people to react to threats as they arise gradually rather than with a sudden impact. The story tells us that if a frog is put in tepid water that is very slowly brought to a boil, then it will not perceive the danger and be cooked to death. Some last century real-life experiments, however, seem to have shown that this is not true. The frog is smart enough to jump out when the water is gradually heated.[109] I personally find that to be a good sign. I believe that we, as entrepreneurs and business leaders, will step up before it is too late. We just need the inspiration and motivation to dare to rise to the challenge and a better understanding of our options based on some solid strategic thinking.

And what could be more appealing than a promising vision of the future? The next chapter will help you imagine just that.

REIMAGINE THE FUTURE

**"Before we want to build the world
we want to live in, we have to imagine it.
Greatness starts with a clear vision
of the future."**
SIMON SINEK

Let us imagine the future 30 years from now. What will the world be like in 2050? Being 51 as I write this, I will be 81 at the time, and my children Saga and Axel—now 11 and 19—will be 41 and 49 years old.

As a business leader with a three to five years perspective on your current position, you may wonder why this is relevant here and now. But bear with me.

I would like to ask you to bring out a pen and paper and find a nice, quiet place to sit. Now please write a letter to a future grandchild in 2050. Write about your hopes and the concerns that you have for the future, and about the life that you truly hope that he or she will be able to live. Think big picture: What does the world look like in 2050 and how did we as humanity get there? Write about your fears and what you are hoping for from the bottom of your heart.

When you are finished, take a deep breath and read the letter out loud to yourself. As you read, take in what this may mean to you as a business leader—and to your business—starting today. Because you will be part of co-creating this future, whether you do it intentionally or not. All decisions—big or small—that you make going forward will have an impact on what the future will bring because the future is co-created. With the resources and influence we wield as business leaders, we are particularly impactful.

A more systematic way to imagine possible and plausible futures is to work with trends and critical uncertainties to build future scenarios. I have personally found one of the more interesting 'scenario 2050' attempts to be that of Arup, a British design and engineering firm that has aspired to shape a better world since 1946. Considering the current polarization between our natural systems and our societal systems on the planet, they juxtaposed these two systems to explore the future. In their report *2050 Scenarios: Four Plausible Futures,*[110] they present four scenarios that we can use to spark our imagination. All but one of the scenarios, however, look pretty gloomy. See Figure 18.

Let us take a quick look at their gloomiest scenarios first: the one that we definitely want to avoid for our children and grandchildren at all cost.

"**EXTINCTION EXPRESS** depicts both declining planetary health and societal conditions. It is questionable how much longer humanity can survive." In this scenario, climate change and relentless consumption have resulted in ultimate destabilization, which has undermined the natural systems. The Amazon is almost entirely cleared, and space and deep-sea mining have become common to compensate for the increasing resource shortage on planet Earth. Clean water is a regulated resource with major corporations controlling its supply. Clean air is a luxury. Agricultural systems suffer from extreme weather and soil degradation. Mass climate migration and resource wars are common. As if that were not enough, in this scenario, most countries have adopted a protectionist, nationalist and isolationistic agenda and put themselves first. There is a large difference between those who have and those who have not—on global and local scales. Goods are easily accessible, but only to those who can afford them. Since AI and social scoring systems have resulted in a new type of global caste system, very few can choose the jobs they want, and the lower classes are increasingly without work, with few rights and little protection. Drugs

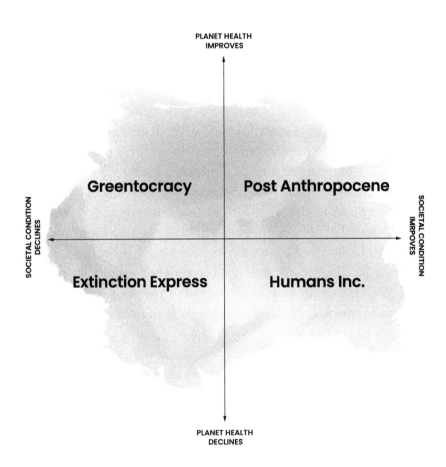

PLANET HEALTH
IMPROVES

Greentocracy

Post Anthropocene

SOCIETAL CONDITION
DECLINES

SOCIETAL CONDITION
IMRPOVES

Extinction Express

Humans Inc.

PLANET HEALTH
DECLINES

FIGURE 18

Four scenarios for 2050, by Arup's Foresight, Research and Innovation
team (2019).[111]

that manipulate the brain and make people smart and "happy" are more and more common for dealing with the challenges of daily life. Declining health makes the population susceptible to new types of resistant bacteria, which is an overwhelming challenge since few have access to healthcare.

The next two scenarios are not as dark but still do not encompass both planetary and societal health, but rather either or.

"HUMANS INC. represents our current trajectory, a world in which societal conditions advance at the cost of planetary health." In this scenario, human life is pretty good. The planet, however, is critically unhealthy, as we have strived to improve our living standards at the expense of the environment. Economical and societal well-being have been put first, and climate issues and environmental considerations have not been prioritized. Governments and companies have hesitated or delayed the necessary large-scale actions to mitigate the challenge. Some countries have attempted to change the increasingly dire situation, but most simply continue to exploit our planetary resources in their attempts to improve living conditions and provide access to resources, jobs and education to their populations.

The **GREENTOCRACY** scenario "describes an improvement in planetary health which has been enabled by severe restrictions on human society: restrictive living conditions, conflict and authoritarian regimes prevail." In this scenario, authoritarian regimes have taken the lead and climate action as well as biodiversity have become the top priority across national, as well as transnational, agendas. People have had to adapt to an increasingly top-down green agenda to save the planet at all cost. Taxes has severely slowed down consumption and the prices for carbon-intensive products have increased by 500 percent since 2020... and it gets worse. But I will just stop here.

What really piqued my interest when reading their report was the **"POST ANTHROPOCENE"** scenario, as it integrates planetary and societal health. In short, it "shows how societal conditions and planetary health might exist in a harmonious relationship, fortifying each other for mutual progress and benefit." In this scenario, we are on a path to a regenerative economy, where we consume resources only at the rate at which they can be replenished, and our societal structures are well balanced. All as a result of working together to solve the global challenges, global biodiversity loss has stopped, and ecosystems have recovered. Humanity has understood that production and consumption need to be linked to the natural environment and all waste is taken care of. We use 50 percent reused materials in all new products and repurpose 90 percent of all waste. Everything is simply considered a resource. Cities no longer live in conflict with nature but rather in something similar to symbiosis. We are seeing advances in agriculture and innovative dynamic organic farming, which have already improved biodiversity and soil quality. Tech companies and others contend for leadership in this green economy, driven by the vast opportunities in green technologies and shifting consumer values. The "we-economy" enables assets to be better utilized and we have finally managed to decouple GDP growth from resource consumption. This is just a short summary, but still a promising one in my view.

Now, stop for a minute and take it all in again. In these four future scenarios, my own children—today aged 11 and 19—will be 41 and 49 years old. How old will your children and grandchildren be in 2050? And what is the future that you want to leave for them?

When studying scenario planning for Professor Rafael Ramirez at Oxford Saïd Business School, I learned that a golden rule is not to reuse someone else's scenarios, since those will normally have been built for a specific purpose. Considering Arup's ambition to explore the current polarization between our natural systems and our societal systems on the planet, their approach is, however, tempting to continue exploring. If you do not have the resources to explore scenarios on your own, why not build on the "Post Anthropocene" scenario to at least try and create a vivid vision of a future worth investing in for future generations to help others see what you see. Because it is not enough to build scenarios for the future. We will also need to decide what future we intentionally work to co-create.

/ A burning platform without a vivid and hopeful vision simply leaves people in dispair /

Under the current circumstances, I realise that we need to highlight the negative scenarios to build a burning platform and get traction in the right direction. We however also need to be mindful of the power of hopeful, inspiring visions that pull us into a future that we want— not only as business leaders but as humanity. A burning platform without a vivid and hopeful vision simply leaves people in despair. A vivid vision of a promising future can indeed provide the hope needed to help us step out of our comfort zones and dare to make a difference.

Today, the UN Global Goals is an attempt to reach the promise of a fair, just and sustainable world by 2030. Their share volume (17 sustainable development goals and 169 targets to be monitored and reviewed) is, however, far too much for most people to digest. Scenarios and vivid visions—conveyed through short and compelling stories and visualizations about the future – could for sure be convincing complements. A simple conclusion could also be that the world needs more leaders that can step up to the challenge, navigate its complexity and help people envision a better future—where they are at. As Simon Sinek puts it, "Before we want to build the world we want to live in, we have to imagine it. Greatness starts with a clear vision of the future."

Overall, the increased focus on sustainability needs to be based on the simple realization that we, as a species, created this whole mess in the first place and that we now need to clean it up, intentionally and consciously, and develop it into something different and better. Otherwise, we will put the dire consequences of our actions in the laps of the next generations to come—with an even more limited timespan to act than we have today. As Albert Einstein insightfully said, "We cannot solve our problems with the same thinking we used when we created them".

Apart from the opportunity to restore the planet, our biodiversity and atmosphere, as well as safeguarding the future of humanity, these challenges also come with vast business opportunities. Let us take a look at those in the next section.

THE BUSINESS OPPORTUNITY

"If you don't even try, there is no opportunity for success."
KATIE LIME

Only treating the ongoing climate and biodiversity crisis as a threat will bring fear and block our brains from thinking creatively. If we can instead see the underlying opportunities, we are likelier come up with creative and impactful solutions to these extremely wicked problems.

The renowned management consulting firm Roland Berger has done an ambitious mapping of business opportunities unfolding in the sustainability space from an Environmental, Social and Governance (ESG) perspective: short-term (2020-2025), mid-term (2025-2035) and long-term (2035-2050). What they found is illustrated in Figure 19 and presented in their report *Sustainarama–How sustainability will change the world in 2050.*[112]

The short-term opportunities unfolding in *the environmental field* are described as CO_2 reduction in the supply chain; increased use of recycled materials; and designing for circularity. Identified mid-term environmental opportunities include eliminating use of rare metals; zero waste; waste blockchain and corporate environmental tracking apps. And some long-term opportunities unfolding in the environmental space are CO_2 negative value chains; zero pollution; sub-zero emission products with a negative footprint; corporate biodiversity strategies; and close the loop solutions.

From a *social perspective*, their report highlights gender diversity, eliminating child and forced labor, and animal welfare programs for the short term. As mid-term opportunities they mention sustainabil-

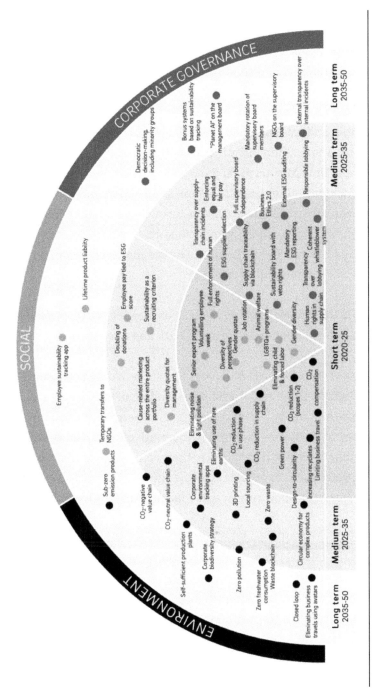

FIGURE 19

Roland Berger's trend map of sustainability 2020–2050.[113]

ity as a recruiting criterion, and employee pay tied to ESG scores. As long-term opportunities they among other things highlight lifetime product liability and employee sustainability tracking apps.

From a *governance perspective* the report indicates human rights in supply chain and transparency over lobbying as short-term opportunities, as well as sustainability boards with veto rights, and mandatory ESG reporting. Mid-term they see transparency over internal and external incidents along the value chain as an opportunity and having NGOs on the supervisory board. Long-term, they highlight democratic decision making, artificial intelligence on the management board (programmed to represent the needs of the planet), and bonus systems based on sustainability tracking.

So where is the money, you may ask? Let us look into some of the estimations of World Economic Forum, UNDP and Accenture.

In *the Future of Nature and Business* report, the World Economic Forum highlighted three major systems—food, land and ocean use; infrastructure and the built environment; and energy and extractives—that are key to the future as they together with climate change have a massive impact on biodiversity. As to their analysis, a number of transitions in these socio-economic systems could deliver USD 10 trillion of annual business opportunities and 395 million jobs by 2030.[114]

According to the UNDP and the *Better Business Better World* report, achieving the Global Goals could potentially open USD 12 trillion in market opportunities in four economic systems: food and agriculture, cities, energy and materials, and health and well-being.[115] These four systems are critical to deliver on the United Nations Sustainable Development Goals (SDGs) and represent approximately 60 percent of the real economy. See Appendix 1 for an overview of the largest opportunities defined in the report.

The transition towards a circular economy, according to Accenture, also represents USD 4.5 trillion global growth opportunity by 2030.[116] The circular economy is already opening vast new opportunities for businesses within repair, waste recycling and waste recovery. Many are already realizing the potential and are developing new business models and solutions that fit the future requirements. Several market leading companies, such as MARS, Pepsi Co, The Coca-Cola Company, and Unilever, have already pledged to use 100% reusable, recyclable or compostable packaging by 2025.[117]

/ Achieving the Global Goals could potentially open USD 12 trillion in market opportunities /

As to The Global Commission on the Economy and Climate's *New Climate Economy Report,* a transition to a more just, green and regenerative economy could, already by 2030, generate USD 26 trillion in financial value and could globally create more than 65 million new green jobs.[118]

THE ROLE OF PEOPLE AND PURPOSE

Growth does, however, not necessarily need to happen though new market entry or new products; it can also happen through a focus on doing good for people and the environment, even with the basic tools and approaches of corporate responsibility that have been well documented over the past decades. Already in 2015, a meta-analysis of more than 300 studies in the field of Corporate Responsibility showed a positive relationship with financial performance: it can add strategic business value through protecting the company's licence to operate and reducing risk, as well as through protecting, nurturing and growing brand and reputational values. It can boost how shareholders view the performance of the firm and enhance the share price and total market value. It can also help increase the commitment, affinity and engagement of employees. This in turn can enhance job performance, increase productivity, reduce turnover, lower absenteeism, and reduce the incidence of employee corruption. In addition, employee engagement links to corporate responsibility in some sort of virtuous cycle. Together they supposedly reinforce one another and then enhance the financial performance, sales revenue, brand and reputation value, and innovative capability of the firm. [119] In a world where the majority of employees are "just coming to work" and only 16 percent are fully engaged,[120] this is for sure be a true win-win-win – for people, profit and planet. See Figure 20.

According to Gallup, disengaged employees mean 15 percent lower profitability, with 37 percent higher absenteeism, and 18 percent lower productivity. Translated into dollars, this is equivalent to 34 percent of a disengaged employee's annual salary, or $3,400 for every $10,000 they make.[122]

As a consulting firm with a focus on employee retention, productivity and engagement puts it on their blog: "On average, a person will waste over 30 years of their lives in workplaces where they don't have a sense of purpose and don't reach their full potential. When we feel unfulfilled by the work we do, we don't feel accountable. We don't do our best or go above and beyond. We feel lonely. This affects our physical and psychological well-being to the point that the risk of cancer, heart disease, diabetes and addictions significantly increase. Essentially, we are literally working ourselves to death." [123]

THE SAD STATE OF EMPLOYEE ENGAGEMENT

The vast majority of employees globally aren't fully engaged with their work.

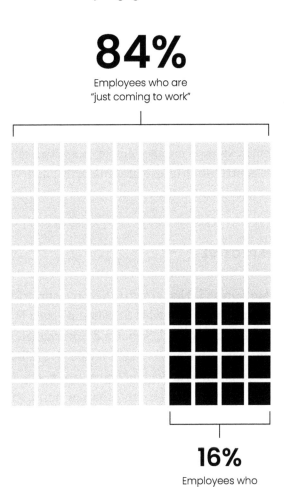

84%
Employees who are
"just coming to work"

16%
Employees who
are fully engaged

FIGURE 20

Harvard Business Review, The power of hidden teams, 2019.[121]

Corporate social responsibility programmes have, however, over the past decades shown to be more of an "add on", rather than being truly integrated in the core business. An integrated purpose has, however, explicitly been found to help companies overcome the challenges of slow growth and declining profits, as it supports the people side of the business: "Many high-growth companies use purpose to generate sustained profitable growth, stay relevant in a rapidly changing world, and deepen ties with their stakeholders".[124] *Sustainability purpose-led* companies, such as Patagonia and Unilever, have taken this even further, as they have put sustainability at the very of the core of the business while building a more meaningful business for all. In my view, the potential value of engaged employees with a sense of meaning and higher contribution is an extraordinarily important opportunity to capture in this context.

AN ESG PERSPECTIVE

In the corporate word, ESG has grown to become a priority. Let us just briefly remind ourselves about what ESG is and how it is used.
ESG is short for Environmental, Social and Governance. ESG ratings (or scores) have been developed to help investors evaluate the long-term risk of investing in a particular company or portfolio of companies. ESG investing is rapidly becoming the new norm, sped up by the pandemic and climate-change.

In short investors increasingly assess factors that can have a material impact on a company, or a portfolio of companies. Companies and portfolios with higher ESG ratings are considered to imply lower risk. Also, for companies to access capital, the incentives to disclose and manage ESG and climate-related risks have increased dramatically since banks have become more focused on ESG as they have come to realize that climate-change is a financial risk to the entire global financial system.[125] This also means that good ESG ratings are becoming increasingly critical to listed corporations in order to remain attractive to investors and to access capital.

As to the SustainAbilty Institute, the number of data providers, ESG standards, ratings and rankings has, however, expanded rapidly over the past years, with more than 600 ESG ratings and rankings existing globally.[126] These data providers use slightly different methodologies and consequently also produce slightly different ratings. Hence, it has become a bit of a jungle. The top ESG rating providers that carry most weight however seem to be MSCI, Sustainalytics, ISS, Bloomberg, FTE Russel, S&P Global and Moody's.

ESG ratings in general focus on material risks and the way a company is operated in the three dimensions of Environment, Social and Governance rather than on the impact of a company's products and services, which is harder to measure. Ratings normally also include the general risk of the industry that a given company is in, as some industries are considered more exposed to risk than others.[127] ESG ratings can be described as aggregations of a wide range of direct and indirect signals or indicators, often based on large number of sources. As such, an ESG rating is far from perfect.

A relevant note is that large cap companies generally have a better average ESG rating than small cap.[128] Anna Lundén, the Managing Director, Equity Portfolio Manager at Wellington Management has explained it well: "Small- and mid-sized companies have less public information and, given the lack of disclosure versus large-cap companies, reliance on ESG data from third-party providers may lead to an incomplete picture that would penalise these smaller companies..."[129]

With all its imperfections, ESG ratings however still have meaning. A closer look at the ESG ratings of sustainability leaders for instance reveal that they in general are highly ranked compared to their industry peers. With a few exceptions, most today reach the highest percentile ranks of their industries. This is also true for most of the companies in the study of sustainability leaders for this book where ESG rating is available (see Appendix 2 and 3).[130]

No matter what, we can expect high ESG ratings to be increasingly important for listed companies to access investor interest and capital going forward. In parallel, a strong focus on sustainability will be increasingly important to remain relevant and attractive to consumers, customers and employees. Ultimately this is largely about being relevant to different audiences in your communication, and about who is involved in this work from the inside of your organization. Figure 21 illustrates this in a good way.

/ A strong focus on sustainability will be increasingly important to remain relevant and attractive /

In the next chapter, we will learn from those on the frontlines of Better Business. Most of these companies also achieve ESG ratings that outperform their peers.

DO YOU PURSUE SUSTAINABILITY COMMUNICATION, ESG COMMUNICATION OR BOTH?

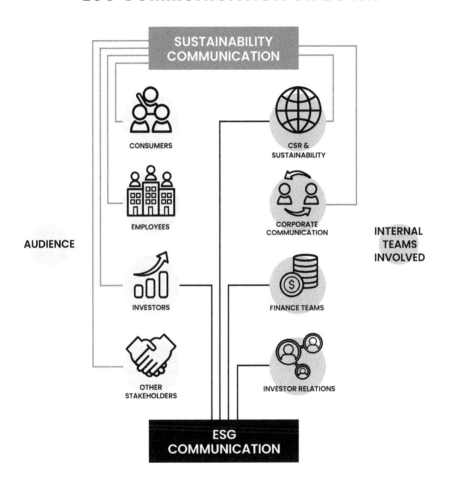

FIGURE 21

Sustainability communication, ESG communication or both.[3]

 **NOTE TO SELF**

CHAPTER 3

LEARNING FROM THE FRONTLINES OF BETTER BUSINESS

"The future is already here – it's just not very evenly distributed."

WILLIAM GIBSON

We have so far learned that sustainability and Better Business is not only urgent, but also a window of immense business opportunity and a potential competitive advantage. Why? Because social and planetary tipping points are being reached, technology development is accelerating, inflection points are imminent in many industries, too few have chosen to act on the opportunities so far, and many wicked problems urgently need innovative solutions. These are solutions that the world of business is particularly well equipped to solve through the ingenuity, creativity, collaboration and resources that it can so often call forth more effectively and efficiently than other human organizations.

With this in mind, let us learn from those who have come far on their Better Business journeys. Or as William Gibson said, "The future is already here, it is just not very evenly distributed," meaning that those who have gone before us are, in a sense, already in the future.

Well-known pioneers in the field are consumer-goods companies and brands like Patagonia, Ben & Jerry's and The Body Shop—all Certified B Corporations adhering to the highest standards of social and environmental performance (even though two of them have been acquired by big corporations). They have all become known as activist companies and brands challenging the commercial and societal contexts of their time, with social and environmental responsibility at the core of their very purposes. From an environmental perspective, their original focus however mostly seems to have been supporting conservation of natural habitats; fair trade, natural and organic ingredients; and working against animal testing.

/ How might your company take the next steps to transform into a Better Business —and beyond? /

Nowadays, many companies are already capitalizing on this moment to become a force for good, and not only in the fast-moving consumer goods field. However, many more need to start considering the opportunity. So where might you start? How might your company take the next steps to transform into a Better Business—and beyond?

SIX JOURNEYS

As part of the research for this book, good practices of 40 organizations have been studied. To encourage you on this transformation towards Better Business and beyond, we will start this chapter by taking a closer look at the evolutionary journeys of six of these companies that have, in different ways, been recognized for their efforts in this field. Please note that these six companies all started their journeys from 'business-as-usual'.

First up are the journeys to Better Business integration of two globally recognized sustainability champions from the very frontlines: Patagonia and Interface. Ørsted, the praised sustainability leader within the energy industry is our next milestone. Then, we will look into the relevant journey of Unilever, a global fast-moving consumer goods multinational with a leading edge in their sustainability focus. We next zoom in on IKEA, the global market leader in home furnishing, aiming to become People and Planet Positive. Oatly, the rebellious oat milk company, marks our final stop.

Why these six? Most importantly, five of the six corporations (Unilever, Patagonia, IKEA, Interface and Ørsted) have been repeatedly recognized as global leaders when it comes to integrating sustainability into their business strategy, most recently by 700 experts in 70 countries as presented in GlobeScan's yearly Sustainability Leaders Report 2020 and 2021. In relative terms, Oatly is still a newcomer in this crowd, but has already been recognized by TIME Magazine as one of the top 100 influential companies of 2021 and as an important contributor to the growing interest in plant-based foods across the world. Oatly, together with Patagonia, also represents some of the more rebellious thinking that I call for in the preface of the book.

In the beginning of each case presentation, you will find a fact box with key elements of each company summarized. The build-up of the journeys themselves are based on available facts and stories from an array of different sources and are unique for each company. As I have attempted to go back to the place in time when the respective journeys started – in some cases more than 25 years ago – the reconstruction of the journeys have been challenging, albeit not impossible. Due to this reconstruction, these stories may from time to time sound anecdotal rather than factual, especially as parts of the journeys are be based on interviews with key individuals – and as such also highly dependent on their individual long-term memory. Even so, these stories still provide a unique insight in what a transformation from business as usual to Better Business can look like.

After the case presentations, I will summarize the key takeaway of the chapter with a few thoughts about the evolution of Better Business.

We will then explore the Three Levels of Better Business and the StepUp Framework together with 14 good practice examples to help you accelerate your company's strategic journey towards Better Business and beyond.

We have a lot to learn. Let us begin.

"There must be a better way
to make the things we want,
a way that doesn't spoil
the sky, or the rain or the land."

PAUL MCCARTNEY

PATAGONIA

"We are in business
to save our home planet."

RYAN GELLERT

FACTS

Start of company	1973
Start of Better Business transformation	Following a 1991 growth crisis, where the company had to lay off 20 percent of its staff
Type of transformation	What started as a crisis was followed by a strategic shift, and then an evolutionary journey with purpose and values in focus rather than growth
Ownership	Privately held
Industry	Apparel for outdoor sports
Revenue (est 2020)	$1 bill USD (est €850 mill Euro)
Number of employees (est 2020)	3,000

Learning about Patagonia just makes you feel good. Maybe this is because they have since long been an impact-driven frontrunner in one of the world's most polluting industries: apparel.

Over the past decades, the rise of fast fashion has encouraged completely unsustainable consumption behaviours, with cheap and quickly replaceable garments produced and consumed along a traditional take-make-dispose logic. This is not to mention the mountains of waste for incineration, as very little fabric can be recycled at all.[132] In an era when fast fashion gradually had become the norm, Patagonia had already chosen a completely different route, which they stuck to. Their committed approach to sustainability now acts as an inspiration to many others within and outside of their industry.

Patagonia is a privately held American clothing company that markets and sells minimalist, colourful, high-quality outdoor clothing around the world. Over the years, the company has earned recognition for the quality of its clothes as much as for its ground-breaking environmental and social practices, all supported by masterful storytelling and brand-building practices. After quite a lot of hype, Patagonia was named the coolest company on the planet by *Fortune* in 2007. Today, it is widely recognized as one of the most socially and environmentally responsible companies in the world. This is quite impressive for a company with only about 3,000 employees and a turnover of approximately $1 billion USD.[133] Their journey and learnings are well documented and generously shared by the company online, as well as by their founder, who has authored several books on the topic.

What few may know is that Patagonia started out as a very ordinary company and that it has taken them decades to transform into the responsible company that they are today. A passion for the outdoors, however, seems to connect its products with the social and environmental initiatives they pursue. Let us take a look at the unfolding of their journey.

Patagonia was founded in California, USA, in 1973, by Yvon Chouinard, who can be described as an American rock climber, environmentalist and fly-fishing enthusiast. Today, he is a billionaire businessman in his early 80s who is still a strong believer in doing well by doing good. The history of Patagonia is actually impossible to separate from that of its founder.

It all seems to have begun in Yosemite, where the young Yvon Chouinard and his friends hid from the rangers as they spent a lot of their time climbing rocks and icefalls, feeling like rebels. Over the years, his climbing interest grew and eventually materialized in a company selling climbing equipment. Vincent Stanley, who was one of Yvon's first employees, and still holds a position as Director of Philosophy at Patagonia, describes the climbing-business as "a solid business, with a large percentage of the global market share in rock-climbing equipment. The size of the total market was however tiny. So although the business was self-supporting, profits were marginal." After a trip to Scotland in the beginning of the 1970s, from whence Yvon Chouinard brought home a quality rugby shirt that his friends liked, a collection of 'rugged technical clothing' was established and Patagonia Inc. came to life. At this time, however, Patagonia was not intended to become a responsible company. Rather, it was seen as a way to provide some cushion for the equipment company.

As things developed, Patagonia became something much more than it was originally intended to be. Chouinard believes that the fact that they started out as a team of California climbers and surfers who spent a lot of time in nature may have helped them spot the unintended environmental consequences of industry and commerce earlier than others. Wanting to make a difference, they started supporting local activism with a focus on the protection and conservation of nature. Vincent Stanley remembers the days: "from the beginning we supported small, local grassroots environmental organizations who tended not to receive help from foundations or individual charitable funders."

Due to the founder's unconventional background and approach, the company also developed into a place of personal growth with space for attaining personal goals. In 1984, they opened an on-site cafeteria offering mostly vegetarian, healthy foods and started providing on-site childcare. Also, the employees were given time to work on their activist callings.

/ They realised that they had become dependent on a growth that they could not sustain /

In their early days, the mountaineering community relied on traditional materials such as cotton, wool and down for protection. Patagonia, however, looked for fabric properties better suited for mountaineering and started to use synthetic fibres that insulated well and dried quickly—although they were not optimized from a sustainability perspective. And at a time when outdoor products were mostly forest green, they soon started making their line in vivid colours. This was a huge hit, and they began growing at a rapid pace, adding new people without proper introduction and training. This came to a halt during a 1991 crisis in which they had to lay off 20 percent of their work force. This also came to mark a huge shift, as they realised that they had become dependent on a growth that they could not sustain and that they themselves had contributed to some of the problems in the world. This made them contemplate what kind of business Patagonia should be going forward and why they were in business at all.

Out of this deep and insightful work came a set of philosophies wherein they described who they wanted to be and how they wanted to behave. What they presented was a company wanting to design and produce high-quality, long-life products, responsibly sourced and manufactured, while doing as little environmental harm as possible. All in all, how to do well by doing good.

In his book *Let My People Go Surfing*, Yvon Chouinard describes these philosophies as an expression of the values that applied to the different parts of the company: "We knew that uncontrolled growth put at risk the values that had made the company succeed so far. Those values couldn't be expressed in a how-to operations manual that offers pat answers. We needed philosophical and inspirational guides to make sure we always asked the right questions and found the right answers. We spoke of these guides as philosophies, one for each of our major departments and functions."[134] Based on this work, the company developed integrated philosophies regarding customer, design, production, distribution, marketing, finance, human resources, management and environment, mainly to help guide their team members on the way. To me, these later philosophies represent not only their values, but an integrated set of strategic choices, clearly defining where to play and how to win.

One of the decisions coming out of these new philosophies had to do with the use of organic cotton. By 1996 they decided to go 100 percent organic, fully well knowing that there was not a large market for it (yet)—neither on the supply nor the demand side. As part of this journey, Patagonia started sharing and exchanging learning and stories with other companies with the same concerns as they had about the social and environmental responsibilities of business, such as the founders of Ben & Jerry's and The Body Shop. Their circle later widened and came to include conversations with REI, The North Face and other leading companies in the outdoor industry—something that in

BETTER FUTURE

1989 led to the creation of the Conservation Alliance, a non-profit organization working "to fund and advocate for the protection of North America's wild places", and envisioning "a planet where wild places, wildlife and people thrive together."[135] In line with their convictions, Patagonia also started its own Environmental Grants Programme to support environmental organizations with bold, direct-action agendas and a commitment to long-term change. This all stemmed from a belief that the best way to create real change is through grassroot movements. They still support innovative work with a focus on addressing the root causes of the environmental crisis and seeking to protect both the environment and affected communities.[136]

In 2002, the focus on environmental activism led to the founding of the "1% for the Planet" foundation, where other companies were also invited to commit one percent of their revenue to environmental action. Yvon Chouinard explained, "The intent of 1% for the Planet is to help fund these diverse environmental organizations so that collectively they can be a more powerful source in solving the world's problems."[137]

When they realised that they had to tackle their own and their suppliers' operational practices in a more structured and systematic way, they again sought out others who were willing to offer advice—from Levi Strauss to Nike to Timberland. They even spoke with the carpet-tile manufacturer Ray Anderson, called 'America's greenest businessman' and the founder of Interface, a company that we will learn more about in our next case.

To formalize their efforts and legally preserve their values and philosophies for the future, in 2011, they decided to amend their articles of incorporation and register their business in California as a Benefit Corporation (December 2011). They also became a Certified B Corporation (January 2012). As Yvon Chouinard said, on the day they amended their articles of incorporation: "Patagonia is trying to build a company that could last 100 years... Benefit Corporation legislation creates the legal framework to enable mission-driven companies like Patagonia to stay mission-driven through succession, capital raises, and even changes in ownership by institutionalizing the values, culture, processes and high standards put in place by founding entrepreneurs."[138]

Going back to their initial certified B Corporation assessment in 2012, the company initially scored 107 points out of a total of 200 (80+ points make a company eligible for the B Corporation certification). Instead of being satisfied with their ratings, they set even higher targets. And after a series of ongoing improvements and hard work, they reached 154 points in 2019, one of the highest scores ever in the history of the B Corporation certification.

Through the B Corporation assessment and related audit processes, Patagonia has been able to identify both strong and weak spots and to further improve its business in a more systematic and transparent fashion. Patagonia has been particularly recognized for providing consumers with products that embody "the highest standards in sustainable sourcing and publicly shares values with stakeholders" and for their "commitment to source the most environmentally responsible materials available... beyond the product and into the supply chain itself."[139]

But the devil so often lies in the details. And of course, Patagonia has had its challenges along the way, such as formalizing environmental metrics data collection and internal operational policies. As to their B Corporation certification assessment in 2014: "Patagonia should develop comprehensive systems for collecting environmental impact metrics (water use, waste, energy use and CO_2 emissions) for corporate and supply chain operations as well as integrate more life cycle assessment measurements into data collection practices."[140] Hence, it is not enough to have the ambition to save the world through grass-roots movements if you have not cleaned up your own back yard. This is something that Patagonia has long since realised, and proactively and transparently worked to change. In this work, they have not only continued pushing the boundaries throughout their own supply chain, but have also started offering services for repair and reuse ('Worn-Wear') that prolong the life of already worn Patagonia garments. In 2018, they even engaged in identifying better practices for regenerative organic farming. And in 2019, they launched a programme called ReCrafted, with clothing made from fabric scraps from old Patagonia gear.

It is also worthwhile to say a few words about their pilots in regenerative organic farming. In 2018, Patagonia partnered with other actors to form a coalition called the Regenerative Organic Alliance. This became a team dedicated to setting new standards and a certification—The Regenerative Organics Certification—for practices of regenerative organic agriculture. The approach was created to help support farmers, ranchers, brands and non-profits harness regenerative organic practices and support their business ecosystems in the development towards regenerative practices. This would ultimately mean not only better crops but also healthier soil with better carbon capture properties. If widely spread, these practices could actually help relieve the climate crisis.[141]

In the last publicly available B Corporation assessment (2019), Patagonia clearly stood out for its best practices and seemed to really live as they learn. Between 2012 and 2019, they were recognized as the Best Overall company three years in a row: 2017, 2018 and 2019. They were also recognized for Best for Environment six out of seven years and twice for Best for Community. But with 151.4 points out of a possible 200, there is still room for improvement.[142] In a recent comment on this journey, their current CEO, Ryan Gellert, said, "This made us better in so many ways. Using the B Impact Assessment and being part of this community have really dimensionalized us on social issues and in thinking more broadly about our responsibilities… We are so often held up as this example of sustainability, particularly in the business sector. And the reality is, we're 48 years into this and we're not a sustainable company. If anything, we're a responsible one in that we really try to be clear-eyed about our impacts, and we're really deeply committed to not only trying to work through the biggest issues in our supply chains and elsewhere but also scaling solutions and open sourcing them to industry and beyond. But there is a tremendous amount of work to be done still, and I think often what we're reminded of is that the reward for solving one problem or challenge is an invitation to a bigger one. That's been our journey."[143]

"We're 48 years into this and we're not a sustainable company. If anything, we're a responsible one."

RYAN GELLERT, PATAGONIA CEO

It may come as no surprise that 91 percent of Patagonia employees feel that this is a Great Place to Work.[144] One of Patagonia's most important insights is that people and culture matter. So, what are the policies that support its employee engagement? Perhaps the biggest success comes from the belief that employees also have a life outside of work. They are encouraged to pursue an active outdoor life and to support the causes they believe in. Patagonia also spends around $1 million USD every year subsidising onsite childcare facilities for employees to enable both family and work, which is a big thing in the US.[145]

Going forward, Patagonia aims to continue to use their voice to stay successful. Ryan Gellert asserts, "Our ambition is to be in business 100 years from now on a living planet with healthy customers. That's the goal and that's also how we frame our decision-making. One of the other things that we're really focused on internally is creating different ways for customers to interact with Patagonia. That's product repair. It's also allowing customers to sell product that is still usable, but they're done using, so that we can offer it for resale at more approachable price points. Rental I think is an opportunity in the future, as is taking responsibility for every product we've ever made. Ultimately the big idea there is a relationship between us and our customers where we're collectively trying to accomplish the same things, and we're enabling that on our side."[146]

The lessons of the Patagonia case are both simple and powerful. It all started with the making of high-quality products that last and a passion for the outdoors. A crisis forced them to rethink their approach, and they then gradually moved to integrating sustainability practices into the core of their business as they decided to take responsibility—for their own value chain, their business ecosystem and beyond. All this while being transparent and generously sharing their practices along the way.

It feels truly promising to see other companies across the fashion and apparel industry—and beyond—be inspired by this amazing pioneer. To Patagonia this means that they will need to continue developing their approach going forward to keep their leading edge. Hence, even in the field of sustainability, competitive advantage is merely transient.

With this, we will move on to our next case—Interface—who's founder Ray Anderson rightfully has been mentioned as a source of inspiration to Yvon Chouinard.

"Our ambition is to be in business 100 years from now on a living planet with healthy customers. That's the goal and that's also how we frame our decision-making."

RYAN GELLERT, PATAGONIA CEO

INTERFACE

"We have a choice to make
during our brief visit to
this beautiful blue and
green living planet:
to hurt it or to help it."

RAY ANDERSON

FACTS

Start of company	1973
Start of Better Business transformation	A customer question in 1994 lead their founder Ray Anderson to read a ground breaking book and have an epiphany
Type of transformation	A strategic shift followed by an evolutionary journey
Ownership	Listed
Industry	Carpet tile
Revenue (est 2020)	$1.3 bill USD (est €1,1 bill Euro)
Number of employees (est 2020)	4,000

As I sat down for the Zoom call with Nigel Stansfield, a long-time member of the group executive management team at Interface, I knew that this B2B company had long been highly recognized for its accomplishments in the environmental sustainability field. But I still had not understood the extent of their efforts and was blown away by our conversation. Here I was talking to this insightful man, who had been on a more than 25-year journey of Better Business. Who could be better to learn from?

In pure facts and figures, Interface is a US-based worldwide leader in the design, production and sales of commercial flooring, such as carpet tiles, luxury vinyl tiles, rubber tiles and sheet products. They have been in business since the 1970s, are a listed company (Nasdaq), and have the commercial vision of becoming the most valuable interior products and services company in the world. Over twenty years, Interface grew to become a leading US-based company in the carpet tiling industry and made its founder, Ray Anderson, a wealthy man living the American dream. Their business model primarily targets architects and building contractors with design support and a direct selling approach. In 2019 they had about 4,000 employees and a revenue of US$1.34 billion (up 13.9 percent from 2018). Geographically, they have a presence in 110 countries across the globe, even though most of their revenues still stem from the Americas (57 percent).

What does this have to do with sustainability and Better Business, you may wonder? Well, what if I tell their story like this instead ...

For their long-term and groundbreaking work on sustainability, Interface was announced as a UN Global Climate Action Award Winner in 2020. They have also been recognized as a top five global sustainability leader in the GlobeScan SustainAbility survey for 18 consecutive years (1998-2020). Further, they have the ambition to ultimately become a fully regenerative company.

Let us go back to the mid-1990s to understand their journey. In 1994 one of Interface's more important customers asked Ray Anderson (the founder, who was by then in his 60s but still their CEO): "What is your company doing for the environment?" Ray could not really answer the question, and the best he came up with was simply, "We comply with legislation." As it was a large and important customer asking the questions, he soon set up an internal task force to approach the question in a better way. In preparing a speech for the kick-off meeting of the same task force, he read the book *The Ecology of Commerce* by Paul Hawken and was deeply moved. He suddenly saw the consequences of commerce and what his business was doing to the environment and future generations. In what can best be described as an epiphany, his perspectives on business and sustainability were completely changed. Deeply taken by this experience, he immediately started an internal crusade to change his company. He shook the foundations of the petroleum-intensive carpet manufacturing industry by declaring a Moonshot (an audacious corporate goal): Interface was committed to becoming the world's first environmentally sustainable and, ultimately, restorative company.

Ray Anderson then went to Wall Street to share his newfound epiphany with analysts and investors. If this was well received? Not really. At first, his management team literally thought that the old man had gone mad. And Wall Street rewarded his awakened perspectives with a dramatic drop in share price. His deep conviction, however, soon spread good vibes internally, and the company decided to continue working on these challenges from the inside, rather than talking so much about it on the outside. And as they were a 'bunch of engineers', they started looking at how to approach the area in a structured and scientific way. For several years, they did not really talk openly about their journey but made tremendous progress.

What they did? As no one had really done something like this before, there was no McKinsey team standing ready to fly in and help out, or any benchmarks to draw from. Instead, their own engineering team got together and decided to tackle the challenge, which started by setting baselines on seven fronts. They did so with the support of what grew to become their 'Eco Dream Team': specialists, academics and thinkers from different fields, including the amazing author of the previously mentioned book, Paul Hawken, himself an American environmentalist, entrepreneur, author and activist. Hawken had by then already authored articles, peer-reviewed papers and several books. All certainly influenced the work of Interface.

/ No one had really done something like this before, there was no McKinsey team standing ready to fly in and help out, or any benchmarks to draw from /

Forming a high-profile dream team around the environment was not considered common practice for a carpet tile company in those days, and their approach was completely ground-breaking in the manufacturing sector. Together with 'the Eco Dream Team', they agreed to tackle seven fronts, where they set baselines to enable ongoing follow-up and measurements. And with this work, an ambitious programme called 'Mission Zero' unfolded. It aimed at zero negative impact on the planet by 2020 and aggressive zero targets in several areas: zero waste to landfill, zero fossil fuel energy use, zero process water use and zero greenhouse gas emissions. In this process, they looked at the material and energy flowing in and out of the company—what they took in and what they took out in the form of products and waste, including waste reduction, energy use, renewable energy, carbon emissions and water use. Much of the same things are still measured today, as several of the goals have been reached.

This was, of course, an extremely bold step for a carpet tile manufacturer that had never before given any thought to the environment. It was quite before anything of its time. We are still in 1994, by the way, the same year that Ray had his epiphany.

So, how did it go? Working in the background, the well-structured efforts of the engineering team laying the foundation not only proved to be good for the environment, but also soon saved the company hundreds of millions of dollars in costs. And people slowly started to realise that what they were doing made real sense. Their work also opened up new and sincere conversations with key customers, as well as new business. The late Ray Anderson, who became one of the first corporate sustainability evangelists in the US, was driven not only by doing good, but also by doing good business. In 2007, he said, "I always make the business case for sustainability. It's so compelling. Our costs are down, not up. Our products are the best they have ever been. Our people are motivated by a shared higher purpose—esprit de corps to die for. And the goodwill in the marketplace—it's just been astonishing."[147]

Even though some of their ambitious goals remain to be reached, they accomplished the most relevant by 2020 or even before. They for instance realized in 2019 that their net emissions of CO_2 were extremely low and took the decision to offset the small remainder. This helped them reach their bold target of Zero Carbon one year before target. Today, they offer their customers flooring that is not only well-designed and has good acoustics, but also has Zero Carbon properties.

This makes them attractive and well positioned to their customer base, as large construction companies and commercial building owners are increasingly interested in lowering carbon in their projects.

Keeping momentum, their latest environmental initiative, 'Climate Take Back', was launched in 2016. Despite not having the resources of companies like IKEA and Unilever, Interface now seeks to take a step forward and dares to inspire a world-changing sustainability movement catered around climate take back. It encompasses four areas:[148]

1. Live Zero
2. Love Carbon
3. Let Nature Cool
4. Lead the Industrial Re-Revolution

'Live Zero' means aiming for zero negative impact on the environment. 'Love Carbon' means to stop seeing carbon as an enemy and instead start using it as a resource in their production. 'Let Nature Cool' means supporting the biosphere's ability to regulate the climate. And 'Lead the Industrial Re-Revolution' means transforming industry into a force for the future that we want. And they are already well underway. More about this can be found on their website.

Still today, Interface remains modest about their accomplishments and seems to prefer to be somewhat of a silent hero. Looking at their website, there is still a lot of potential in bringing their hearts into their brand identity and out to the wider public, as well as to the slowly awakening investor community—who is, by the way, taking sustainability far more seriously than they did 25 years ago.

Internally, however, their people are long since well aware of the higher purpose at the very core of the company: "To lead the industry, to love the world", as well as their supporting values, which are:

'designing a better way', 'inspiring others', 'being genuine', 'connecting the whole', and 'embracing tomorrow today'. The purpose as well as the values all surfaced through internal workshops with their own people. And as Nigel said at the end of our Zoom-call, "It is amazing what happens when you start putting purpose into a business and it starts to touch people... Our purpose has helped us continue forward. And it has helped us to open an amazing international talent pool that never would have been accessible to us as just a traditional carpet tile manufacturer."

Interface—this pretty extraordinary carpet tile and flooring company—has certainly learned to balance the interests of their different stakeholders and made sustainability an integrated part of their core, and they have made it really good business.

What started with a simple customer question and an epiphany for Ray Anderson in 1994, ultimately completely transformed Interface and put it at the very frontlines of Better Business, well underway to becoming a regenerative business. It is an example that we can all learn from. With an ambition to become fully regenerative and to lead what they call the Industrial Re-Revolution, I am convinced that we will see more of Interface going forward.

ØRSTED

"Replacing fossil fuels with green energy is the main lever to combat climate change."

WWW.ORSTED.COM

FACTS

Start of company	**2006 as a merger of six Danish oil and gas companies following the deregulation of the Danish energy market**
Start of Better Business transformation	**2008 as part of a strategy process with the ambition to identify ways to differentiate the business**
Type of transformation	**A strategic shift and an evolutionary journey based on the testing and experimentation of new business models for renewable energy**
Ownership	**Listed**
Industry	**Energy**
Revenue (2020)	**52.6 bill DKK (est $8,5 bill USD)**
Number of employees (2020)	**6,420**

Ørsted, the Danish renewable energy company, came to life as late as 2006. Today, they are a world leader in offshore wind parks and are acknowledged as one of the most sustainable companies in the world in Corporate Knights' Global 100 index (#1 in 2020, and #2 in 2021). They currently have among the highest ESG ratings in the energy industry globally. They have also been acknowledged for their impressive transformational journey by Innosight.

Ørsted is the result of a 2006 merger of six Danish oil and gas companies that went back to as early as 1857, and was called DONG Energy (short for Danish Oil 'n Gas) after the merger. In 2006, the company had the leading coal technology in Europe. At the time, the company earned most of its revenues by selling heat and power, with an 85 percent share from coal. In 2009, top management announced a major strategic shift, as the company would now seek to generate 85 percent of heat and power from renewable sources by 2030. The strategy was to invest aggressively in offshore wind and phase out coal. At the time, this strategy was not completely well-received by their employees, as the vast majority had their key competence in old technologies.

In 2016, after a major business model transformation towards renewable energy with a particular focus on offshore wind parks, DONG Energy had one of the highest valued IPOs in Europe. And in 2018, the company finally decided to change its name to Ørsted to break free from its fossil fuel heritage. By 2019, Ørsted had already become the world's largest producer of offshore-wind energy. It had also increased its renewable-generation share to 86 percent, which meant reaching its target from 2009 to generate 85 percent of heat and power from renewable sources by 2030—21 years ahead of schedule.

How could this happen in such a traditional industry, which still today sees so many companies struggling to adapt to a society in change?

In researching this company, it is not hard to find articles describing their journey, albeit from slightly different perspectives and with slightly different twists. I have, however, had the privilege of talking to Anders Eldrup, who was the CEO of the company from 2006–2012, and Thomas Ollendorf, who was the CEO of their Swedish subsidiary at about the same time.[149] These dialogues have been particularly interesting because this was the time when the first big shift in their strategy happened. This shift would ultimately lead to the transformation of their whole business and make them one of the world's most recognized sustainability leaders, with Henrik Paulsen as the CEO who ultimately enabled them to reach their goals.

In short, their transformation was initiated by a visionary leader, a formal strategy process applying future scenarios, and a potential acquisition that led to the difficult decision to explore the opportunities of renewable energy and new business models, rather than investing heavily in old technology.

To understand the context, let us first go back to the inception of DONG Energy. The merger that created DONG Energy in 2006 was a result of the increased competition in the deregulated and liberalized Danish energy sector of 2000-2004. This dramatically changed the rules of the game, opened up for international competitors and led to increasing price pressure in a highly commoditized market. This, in turn, led to an increasing interest among Danish industry players in differentiating their offerings and exploring new opportunities.

Anders Eldrup, the company's first CEO after the merger, told me that the story of their transformation really started in 2008, the year before the painfully unsuccessful climate conference in Copenhagen. At that point, one of the companies in the merger had already started experimenting with offshore wind. Two smaller parks had already been built with good results and created a lot of interest and good will. Instead of being paralysed by the very mixed political messages of the time, the leadership team sat down to review their strategy and realised that their current portfolio—based on fossil fuels—included some challenges and that off-shore wind parks and renewable energy could actually offer a unique opportunity going forward.

In their analysis, they saw a sinking price and margin on gas, which at the time was an important and considerable part of their portfolio. Listening to stakeholders, they also realised that coal could become more regulated and more taxed in the future. They also realised that there was a large societal resistance to coal itself, as it was already considered harmful to the environment. This led them to question whether coal would be an acceptable energy source in the future, which in turn helped them make the difficult decision to pull back from what would have been their largest investment so far: building a large coal plant in Germany—an investment with a life span of 50 years.

Interestingly, very few energy companies seem to have come to similar conclusions at around the same time, in spite of the available information and in spite of the long return on investments. So, why did Anders Eldrup and his team reach these conclusions and dare to make such controversial decisions at the time?

In our dialogue in 2017, Anders told me, "The analysis showed us that there was a large societal resistance towards an investment in the German coal plant. And I personally got more and more doubtful as to if it would be defendable to do. Would coal really be an accepted energy technology so far into the future (50 years)? Our conclusion after reviewing the scenarios was that it would be a higher risk to invest in a new coal plant—even if it was a well-established technology—than it would be to invest in off-shore wind, which was at the time still considered a new technology... So, we decided to test building new offshore wind parks. We were already in the field—a field that represented high entry barriers to other potential newcomers—and saw a potential to become a leading player... Of course, there was doubt, and we only decided to build one more offshore wind park at the time in some sort of a trial-and-error approach, where we tested and learned one step at a time. The experiences, however, taught us that the risks were relatively small, that the technology worked, that the costs were reasonable and that the facilities operated well from a maintenance point of view. We had also negotiated guaranteed prices on the generated electricity with the relevant states. Everything combined with the "free fuel" (i.e., wind) made this an interesting business case that also attracted investors."

/ Interestingly, very few energy companies seem to have come to similar conclusions at around the same time /

Anders Eldrup also engaged in the UN Copenhagen Climate Conference (COP15) during 2009, and there became even more convinced that they had chosen the right path, which accelerated their transformation away from fossil fuels even further. There, close to 115 world leaders attended the high-level segment, making it one of the largest gatherings of world leaders ever outside UN headquarters in New York. In total, more than 40,000 people participated, representing UN agencies, governments, nongovernmental organizations, intergovernmental organizations, media and faith-based organizations. This was a crucial event in the global negotiating process, and some progress was made. It has, however, also been described as a huge failure since it did not produce the desired outcomes. Anders Eldrup, in his role as the CEO of what was back then called DONG Energy, was there, advocating for an ambitious, predictable and transparent climate deal that would make it possible for the energy industry to invest in renewable technology. In our dialogue, he described how his participation had a big impact on him personally.

"You have to be a little bold when you make these kinds of decisions and you need to set a clear vision."

THOMAS BROSTRØM

Enabling this transformation was also their early experimentation with new financial models, where they offered investors the opportunity to invest in their new offshore wind parks. This was something that early on attracted the Danish pension funds. They also experimented with their go-to-market model and directed their new sustainable offering to large companies with a potential gain in a strengthened sustainability profile. In these 'Climate Partnerships', the company helped their customers reduce their carbon emissions. NovoNordisk was first out. This was quite different from their existing sales process, involved the executive level and put completely new demands on their sales teams, which ultimately also had to transform their way of working.

In spite of this early success, Anders Eldrup, whom I have heard being described as an extraordinary visionary compared to other business leaders in the energy industry, left his assignment six years into the journey. However, the transformation he had initiated prevailed.

As margins continued to decrease in the company's traditional business (making its old business model even less attractive), the company found itself in a liquidity crisis in 2013. At that point, the new top team decided to accelerate the transformation further by selling off old technology and increasing the speed of its transformation to renewable energy.

As their President of North Americas, Thomas Brostrøm, in hindsight said in an interview, "I think the biggest takeaway is you have to be a little bold when you make these kinds of decisions and you need to set a clear vision, which we did. We basically said we believe in a world that runs entirely on green energy. And we basically believe that this is the way the world is going. So we better get started early on."[150] Or as Martin Neubert, Executive Vice President and CEO of Offshore Wind, put it in a 2020 interview with McKinsey: "The ability to reinvent ourselves has proven to be key. In 2006, DONG Energy consisted of some oil and gas licenses. Then it reinvented itself through the merger of six domestic energy companies. A few years later, the company reinvented itself again by establishing a wind-power business unit that became a global leader within a few years. Scanning new horizons and spotting new business areas are essential to Ørsted's strategy and our ambition to become a global renewable-energy major."[151]

This, of course, sounds really easy and convincing. Anders Eldrup painted a more realistic picture. He told me that their journey took a lot of testing and experimentation to get right and that it was built on learning from 'trial and error'. And, as they in the beginning only added one new offshore wind park at the time, they limited risk and learned a lot along the way. Further, Eldrup said, "These experiences taught us that the risks were relatively small, that the technology worked, that the costs and level of maintenance were reasonable."

BETTER FUTURE

Today, Ørsted is the world leader in offshore wind, and is run in three entities: Offshore, Onshore and Markets & Bioenergy. Since 2006, they have more than halved their carbon emissions, and now target a 98 percent reduction by 2025. They have also reduced their power stations' coal consumption by 73 percent as they decided early on to use sustainably sourced wood chips and wood pellets to convert their coal- and gas-fired power stations. In 2023, they plan to completely stop using coal. On their website, we can read: "We're committed to renewable energy, enabling people, businesses and communities to lever its potential without having to worry about causing a negative environmental impact or limiting the opportunities of future generations. Therefore, it's also our ambition to build enough renewable energy to supply green power for 30 million people by 2025 and 55 million people by 2030."

To me, the strategic decision point of Anders Eldrup and his team in 2008-2009 summarizes the power of envisioning and reimagining the future. All based on future scenarios and trying to understand your role and relevance to your future ecosystems already today— even though the rest of your industry does not yet seem to understand what is going on (and governments fail to act). Their transformational journey also gives us a hint as to why testing and experimentation are important keys to learning fast and limiting risk. Their offshore wind parks simply would not exist without it.

When today looking back at their journey, Anders Eldrup told me: - "In a world that must change drastically due to the climate crisis it is crucial as a business leader to look closely into the risk analysis. Often business-as-usual will come out as more risky."

Food for thought.

"In a world that must change drastically due to the climate crisis it is crucial as a business leader to look closely into the risk analysis. Often business-as-usual will come out as more risky."

ANDERS ELDRUP

UNILEVER

"We can no longer pretend that business is immune from the rising tide of environmental or social challenges or that companies can create value in isolation from the communities of which they are a part."

PAUL POLMAN, UNILEVER CEO 2009–2019

FACTS

Start of company	1929
Start of Better Business transformation	**Not completely clear, but probably around 1995 to mitigate risks in supply chain**
Type of transformation	**Evolutionary approach, accelerated with a strategic shift during the period with Paul Polman as CEO (2009-2019)**
Ownership	**Listed**
Industry	**Fast moving consumer goods**
Revenue (est 2020)	**50.7 bill Euro (est $60 bill USD)**
Number of employees (est 2020)	**149,000**

Unilever is a large multinational with roots all the way back to the 1880s. The company is the result of a long journey of mergers and acquisitions, divestiture, brand building, innovation, category and market development. And as a large multinational, Unilever understood early on that it has a large footprint, a large potential impact on consumers worldwide through their brands, and a large responsibility. This is something that they have been able to turn into a competitive advantage, especially over the past decade.

Today, the company has a leading market position in all key categories, €51 billion in turnover (2020), 155,000 employees, worldwide representation in terms of production and sales facilities, more than 400 brands—of which most still are local, and a massive supply chain with more than 100,000 suppliers. On an annual basis, 2.5 billion people worldwide use their products to feel well, look good, and get more out of life. Many of their brands are familiar all over the world, while the vast majority are still local brands that meet the specific needs of consumers in the markets where they are sold. From 2014 to 2019, this giant delivered an average underlying sales growth of 3.3% per year. The largest part of their growth today comes from their purpose-led brands.

Unilever grew to fame as a global leader on sustainability under the leadership of their former CEO Paul Poleman (2009–2019), who became known as something of a corporate CEO activist on the global stage in roles as Chairman of the World Business Council for Sustainable Development, a member of the International Business Council of the World Economic Forum, a member of the B Team, and vice-chair of the Board of the UN Global Compact.

We will start our story back in 1995, when I happened to work as a market research officer in one of Unilever's Swedish subsidiaries (Van den Bergh Foods) on my first job after university. Because in 1995, Unilever published its first Code of Business Principles. And, in the same year, the company formed the Marine Stewardship Council together with World Wide Fund for Nature (WWF) to support sustainable fishing. This arrangement was initiated in the wake of the collapsed cod fishery in Canada in 1992, where 35,000 fishermen and plant workers lost their jobs—an event that highlighted the global issue of overfishing and the importance of sustainable fishing. For Unilever, it was surely driven at the time by their need to protect and safeguard their supply chain and long-term licence to operate in the field. But also, by its long commitment to being a responsible business.

The WWF partnership ultimately brought very positive implications, not only for Unilever but also for other parts of their business ecosystem. And the idea of safeguarding relevant supply chains soon generated new initiatives in other parts of the business. One of the more well-known and documented cases was their Lipton tea brand, where the team started working on ensuring more sustainable farming practices through education and support for a large number of small farmers. Another well documented case relates to palm oil, an often criticised but cheap commodity used in many consumer products, and an important ingredient to many of Unilever's products. Their significant dependency on palm oil, combined with the increasing societal pressure against the unsustainable production of the same, was most certainly also why they became a founding member of the Roundtable on Sustainable Palm Oil in 2004. In 2008, they further announced a commitment to draw all palm oil from certified sustainable sources by 2015. This was ultimately a result of Greenpeace activists dressing up as orangutangs and storming their headquarters in London. Needless to say, with all of these experiences behind them, Unilever truly understood that long-term sustainable value chains and ecosystems were critical to their business.

One year after the Greenpeace action, their new CEO, Paul Polman, entered the company. He was by then already convinced that running

BETTER FUTURE

a business in a sustainable and responsible way was key to long-term growth in a volatile world of finite resources, and that it would mitigate risk and reduce costs. On his first day as CEO, he ended the quarterly reporting to FTSE shareholders by saying, "Unilever has been around for 100-plus years. We want to be around for several hundred more ... if you buy into this long-term value-creation model, which is equitable, which is shared, which is sustainable, then come and invest with us. If you don't buy into this ... don't put your money in our company."[152] In doing so, Paul Polman seemed to have already decided to build a long-term focused, sustainable and purpose-led company.

The same year, their new strategy, Compass, was launched to prepare the corporation for the next decade. The target was to double the size of the business while reducing their environmental impact and to create long-term value for the company's stakeholders. About one year later, in 2010, the company decided to accelerate its transformational journey further with the launch of the Unilever Sustainable Living Plan, their sustainability strategy. The Unilever Sustainable Living plan set out hundreds of targets and commitments under three overall key goals (see Figure 22):

- We will help more than a billion people improve their health and well-being.
- We will halve the environmental impact of the making and use of our products.
- We will enhance the livelihoods of thousands of people in our supply chain.

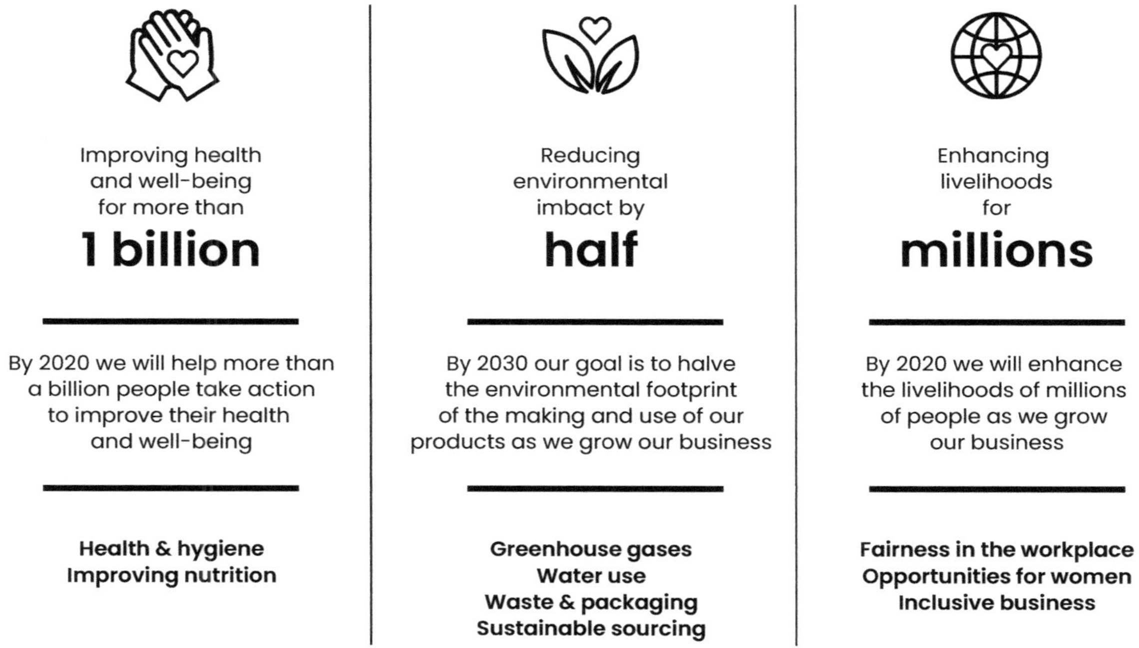

Improving health
and well-being
for more than

1 billion

By 2020 we will help more than
a billion people take action
to improve their health
and well-being

Health & hygiene
Improving nutrition

Reducing
environmental
imbact by

half

By 2030 our goal is to halve
the environmental footprint
of the making and use of our
products as we grow our business

Greenhouse gases
Water use
Waste & packaging
Sustainable sourcing

Enhancing
livelihoods
for

millions

By 2020 we will enhance
the livelihoods of millions
of people as we grow
our business

Fairness in the workplace
Opportunities for women
Inclusive business

FIGURE 22

An overview of the Unilever Sustainable Living Plan as of 2021.[153]

At the time of its inception, the Unilever Sustainable Living Plan was one of the most ambitious sustainability plans ever created by a corporate multinational. Paul Polman was soon deeply engaged in getting other companies to step up to the challenge—a mission that seems to have intensified in the wake of the 2015 launch of the UN Global Goals, to which Unilever and Paul Polman also somehow contributed. Today, the Unilever Sustainable Living Plan continues to focus on decoupling the company's growth from its environmental footprint while further increasing its positive social impact and contributing to the UN's SDGs.

"B Corp companies come with many of the attributes that fit with our long-term goals and our culture."

PAUL POLMAN

An important part of Unilever's transformational journey has not only been the Sustainable Living Plan but also their Sustainable Living Brands. An ever-growing number of their leading brands have now integrated sustainability into the contribution they make to the world and into their products' ingredients and lifecycle. Still, many remain. Of their total brand portfolio, which includes more than 400 brands, the Sustainable Living Brand portfolio still only includes 41 brands. To speed up the transformation, they have in parallel acquired some of the very pioneers in the sustainability field: Ben & Jerry's (2010), Seventh Generation (2016) and several other B Corporation Certified companies. As Paul Polman said in an interview, "When we look at any of our acquisitions, one of the main considerations is always whether it is a good fit to Unilever. We look for companies that have similar vision and values to ours. That is critical to the success of the partnership. B Corp companies come with many of the attributes that fit with our long-term goals and our culture, and therefore it is no surprise that some of our recent acquisitions, such as Seventh Generation, Pukka Herbs and Teas, and Sir Kensington, have been B Corps."[154] All in all, the Unilever Sustainable Living Brands represent half of the company's growth today and they grow twice as fast as their other brands. It is also a prioritized and integrated part of their future strategy.

For Unilever, this journey is not only about environmental sustainability. It is also about being a good corporate citizen, a good employer and a trusted supplier. And doing business with integrity and responsibility has been an integrated part of their values and culture since long. Today, Unilever identifies as a purpose-driven rather than profit-driven multinational. Their CEO since 2019, Alan Jope, is committed to continuing their journey: "I intend to build further on Unilever's century-old commitment to responsible business. It is not about putting purpose ahead of profits, it is purpose that drives profits."

And I will for sure continue using some of Unilever's many Sustainable Living Brands at home. Probably in the shower tomorrow morning and maybe already when cooking dinner tonight.[155]

IKEA

"Waste of resources
is a mortal sin at IKEA."

INGVAR KAMPRAD, FOUNDER

FACTS

Start of company	**1943**
Start of Better Business transformation	**Frugality and resource efficiency has been core to company culture since inception. Sustainability a strategic priority since 2012 (launch of first sustainability strategy).**
Type of transformation	**Evolutionary, sped up with strategic shifts in 2012 and 2018**
Ownership	**Foundation since 1982**
Industry	**Furniture and home accessories**
Revenue (est 2020)	**€40 bill Euro (approx $47 bill USD)**
Number of employees (est 2020)	**200,000**

When Ingvar Kamprad, the founder of IKEA, passed away in 2018, he left behind a vast business empire with an extremely successful and scalable business model. By then, IKEA had come a long way since the company was founded in 1943. From being a small, frugal, entrepreneurial business in Småland in southern Sweden to soon selling flat-packed furniture through a mail-order catalogue, IKEA had indeed grown to become one of the most successful home furnishing brands in the world. But the world had changed, and in 2018, IKEA had just initiated a reinvention of the company. Conversations with Torbjörn Lööf, Inter IKEA Group's CEO (2013-2020), and Lena Pripp-Kovac, currently Chief Sustainability Officer at Inter IKEA Group, helped me better understand the company, their focus on integrating sustainability into the core, and their challenges going forward.

Torbjörn told me, by 2016-2017, the management team had come to understand that they were at a crossroad with their current way of operating, and they realised that they needed to reinvent themselves. This reinvention would be driven by changes in their business environment, such as digitalization, an increased focus on sustainability and rapidly changing consumer values, beliefs and shopping behaviours. As stated in their strategy, "Today, we see societal changes that are changing people's behaviour and as a consequence the retail industry as a whole. It is the biggest revolution to have happened since IKEA was founded and it is clear that we have come to a crossroad. The time has come to create the conditions for the next big IKEA era, a period that will encompass our future where we will reinvent ourselves as we continue to grow and develop."[156]

This was simply based on the important insight that what got IKEA to where they were would not be what would get them into the future. IKEA's "Direction 2025, Three Ways Forward—Our To-Do List" is actually a great example of just that. It included three simple priorities:

1. Make IKEA affordable for people who cannot afford IKEA today.

2. Reach and interact with many more of the many people, where they are.

3. Create a positive impact for people, society and the planet.

Make no mistake. Even though simply expressed above in only three sentences—and even though the strategy tied their past to their present and their present to their future—these three statements were deeply rooted in the global megatrends and indeed required a transformation of the company. It required IKEA to move from a traditionally successful retail company based on a mega store concept into e-commerce, digitalization and other types of store formats to reach and interact with many more people where they are. And from being the furniture world's answer to fast fashion—and based on an unsustainable 'take, make and dispose' logic—IKEA would have to move into offering sustainable and circular solutions with a positive impact for people, society and the planet. All this while making IKEA even more affordable for people who could not afford it yet.

IKEA's sustainability journey started around 2000 with the launch of IWAY, a code of conduct for suppliers across its value chain. Most possibly it had by then already been a since long integrated part of the company's purpose and culture, since its founder, Ingvar Kamprad, was notoriously known for his frugal manner and for not wasting anything.

When IKEA published its first sustainability strategy in 2012, the company already understood the potential in using its size to do good. Today, IKEA's sustainability strategy is still based on the same fundamental insight, i.e., that a balance between environmental, economic and social impact will help more people live better lives within the boundaries of our planet. This will also potentially help IKEA flourish as more people are lifted out of poverty and into the middle class across the world. See Figure 23.

In line with these insights, by 2013, IKEA had already produced renewable energy equivalent to one-third of their total energy consumption through their own photovoltaic panels on more than 100 stores and 96 wind turbines in seven countries; less than 15 percent of the waste generated in their stores went to landfills; and they used recycled waste wood for the production of new wardrobes and bookshelves.[158] Today, IKEA has even started selling home solar solutions to democratize clean energy. They simply want to empower as many people as possible to produce and use clean energy and play a part in creating a better future for the planet. They have of course not developed the original technology. They have simply applied it and found a viable and attractive way to package the value proposition and go to market with an interesting business model.

More recently, IKEA has also accelerated its efforts with an investment of €600 million to become People and Planet Positive by 2030, all aiming at speeding up the transition to a net-zero carbon economy. According to Financial Times, this brought their total investments into sustainability to an impressive €3.8 billion EUR,[159] all in parallel to heavy investments into digitalization.

Considering that IKEA is a brand acting as an umbrella for a large number of companies and operating units, its current sustainability strategy is surprisingly simple and accessible, acting as a guideline across its entire value chain. Its aim is to inspire, activate and lead decision-making and goal-setting to help achieve the big positive changes that they want to see in the world and throughout the IKEA

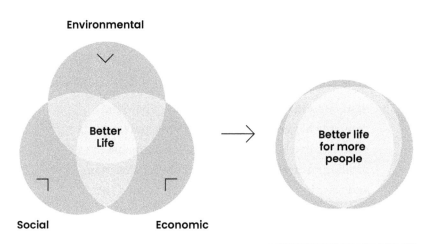

Environmental

Better
Life

Social   Economic

Better life
for more
people

*The better balance between
environmental, economic and
social impact, the more people
will have the chance at
a better life within the
boundaries of the planet.*

FIGURE 23

The foundation of IKEA's sustainability strategy, with the goal of
creating a better life for more people.[157]

ecosystem. They hope to achieve this in a collaborative way while being transparent about what they learn. The current version is now set for 2030 and reviewed annually, in line with the UN Sustainable Development Goals.[160]

As in their overall business strategy, where sustainability is an integrated part, the IKEA sustainability strategy today has three parts, based on the three global challenges that they want to address on a higher systemic level: unsustainable consumption, climate change and inequality. The strategic initiatives they have chosen to focus on can be described as follows (see Figure 24):

1. **HEALTHY AND SUSTAINABLE LIVING,** where the company has committed to inspiring and enabling people to live healthier and more sustainable lives, promoting circular and sustainable consumption, and creating a movement in society around better everyday living.

2. **BECOMING CIRCULAR AND CLIMATE POSITIVE,** IKEA has chosen to focus on transforming into a circular business, becoming climate positive, regenerating resources, protecting ecosystems and improving biodiversity.

3. **BEING FAIR AND EQUAL,** where the company will work on providing and supporting decent and meaningful work across the value chain, being an inclusive business and promoting equality.

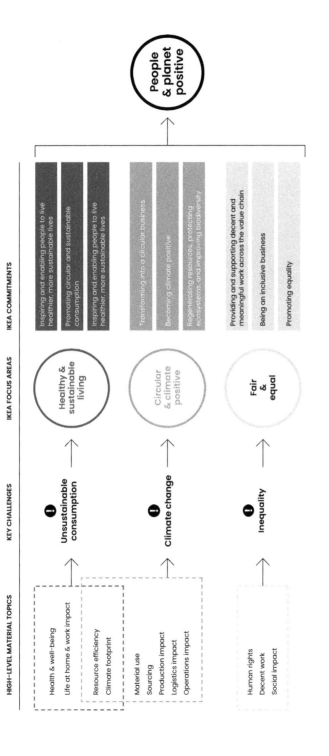

FIGURE 24

An overview of IKEA's sustainability strategy.

"Most things remain undone.
Glorious future."

INGVAR KAMPRAD

In going about this reinvention, IKEA has chosen to be collaborative and to drive change through extensive testing and experimentation in many different parts of the group. It has activated its whole ecosystem, including innovation hubs, suppliers and the IKEA Foundation. They have since come to realise that their future success is tightly intertwined with the development of society as a whole and the everyday lives of many people. With this insight, it is not surprising that in 2012 their sustainability strategy already showed spiring aspirations to change the world for the better: "IKEA can be a small but significant force in helping to create... a more sustainable world."[161] This ambition could very well go all the way back to Ingvar Kamprad's heritage from the earlier so harsh and poor province of Småland, where waste should be minimized and all resources utilized in the best way possible, in combination with their strong corporate culture and values, where cost-consciousness and accepting responsibility still seem to be strong drivers.

In a later section of the book, we will return to IKEA and explore how it has started to work in co-creating a circular economy, and in exploring opportunities for breakthrough innovation.

As I write this, IKEA is still in the midst of this important transformation, and a lot of work remains. As their late founder Ingvar Kamprad might again have chosen to express himself, "Most things remain undone. Glorious future."

OATLY

"We didn't know
it was going to explode
the way it did."

TONI PETERSSON, CEO

FACTS

Start of company	**1994**
Start of Better Business transformation	**2012 as part of a strategic renewal and repositioning of the company**
Type of transformation	**A strategic shift followed by an evolutionary journey**
Ownership	**Listed since May 2021**
Industry	**Plant-based foods and drinks**
Revenue (est 2020)	**€355 mill Euro (approx $421 mill USD)**
Number of employees (est 2020)	**800**

If you have not heard of them, Oatly is a rapidly growing Swedish food company that has become well-known for both its oat milk and its odd, rebellious and fearless lifestyle approach to market communications that fundamentally challenges the traditional dairy industry. It is not without reason that they call themselves 'fucking fearless' and have chosen their own path. Their style has attracted hordes of Millennials and Generation Z—as consumers, as well as prospective employees—even though the company's slightly unorthodox initiatives and communication have not seldom been perceived as politically incorrect by outside observers.[162]

What most people do not know is that Oatly was founded as a very ordinary company called Ceba Foods in southern Sweden in 1994. As Oatly say in their latest sustainability report: "It all started in the late '80s in the south of Sweden. A group of scientists at Lund University were exploring the mechanisms and effects of lactose intolerance. They looked around and decided it might also be cool to develop a plant-based food that people could use as a substitute for cow's milk. They wanted this new food to be the perfect combination of nutritional value and sustainability, and it would have to taste good enough to make people consider switching from dairy. The bar was set high, so it didn't happen overnight, but in 1990, the big day finally arrived. The scientists discovered that natural enzymes could break down fiber-rich oats into a liquid food." [163]

The founders were a team around the passionate inventor of oat milk, Richard Öste. What they founded was a company offering a healthy oat-based milk substitute for people who could not tolerate traditional dairy products due to allergies or a sensitive stomach. The founders came to realise early on that oat-based milk was a far better environmental alternative compared to dairy milk and a potential lifestyle product, rather than the medical health care positioning that they started out with. After their first decade, the company name was changed to the easier-going Oatly in 2006. When it still did not take off, the board of directors decided to bring in a new CEO in 2012 to shake things up. At the time, the company only had 50 employees and a revenue of 198 MSEK, or approximately €19 million.

"We recognized that if people drink our products, they're doing something good for themselves (...) but also for the planet."

JOHN SCHOOLCRAFT

In came Toni Petersson, an unconventional and entrepreneurial leader bringing creativity, vision and inspiration, and challenging the team to think far outside the box. He brought with him a creative team that he had collaborated with earlier, who soon got to work. John Schoolcraft, Creative Director, who was responsible for the brand's repositioning, remembers the time: "As in lots of conceptual development, we initially looked at the origins and roots of the brand. We recognized that if people drink our products, they're doing something good for themselves in terms of their health but also for the planet in terms of the carbon emissions and land usage from production."[164] In parallel, the team wanted to validate their hypothesis that oat milk would be far better for the environment than cows-milk, so they conducted their first Life Cycle Assessment (LCA), a methodology for assessing the environmental impact associated with all the stages of the life cycle of a commercial product, process or service. This confirmed their hypothesis.

BETTER FUTURE

Armed with a superb sense of spotting trends, a strong conviction, the LCA that supported their claims, and an active board of directors fully supporting the transformation, Toni and his team managed to completely re-envision the company's purpose, strategy, brand and marketing communication. The strategic intent behind the repositioning was to move from being a process-focused company with a limited target audience with certain pinpointed health issues to a lifestyle company targeting value-driven and trend-sensitive consumer groups outside of the traditional health segment. The overall ambition was to become a value-based and purpose-led company and a leader within sustainable health. Their approach and positioning at the time were, however, more that of a rebellious challenger to the dairy industry.

The strategy implementation started during 2013. In 2014, their brand was relaunched in Sweden with a rebellious communication style that at the time spoke to the rapidly growing vegan movement. At about the same time, the company also realised that it needed to create its first sustainability roadmap.

To support this ambitious journey, they launched a book called *Change* as an internal guide. It presented the company vision, goals and strategy. The main goal, according to the book, was to create global change. It also formulated 14 statements of change to clarify how the company wanted to pursue this ambitious agenda.

These change statements were, to a large extent, focused on brand repositioning but also aimed to move their own culture, and as a start helped build change internally—a movement that soon spread externally as the brand caught fire.

By 2015, Toni and his team had managed to reposition the Oatly brand in its core markets to ride the waves of change in society and truly hit

OATLY'S

14 STATEMENTS OF CHANGE

1. We are totally new and totally relevant, finally.
2. We are perfectly positioned for change.
3. We won't offer change; we offer an upgrade.
4. Start small, but start somewhere.
5. The product as the hero.
6. The product can get better.
7. Focus on occasions where we fit into people's lives.
8. People buy the stuff they notice …
9. … for personal reasons…
10. … or because they want to eliminate badness from their lives.
11. Be a human, not a logo.
12. Be red bull in the market.
13. Be totally fearless.
14. Be sustainable.

SOURCE
Change 2012 (internal Oatly document).[165]

the trend-sensitive younger generation with a growing preference for authentic brands, 'good companies' and plant-based foods. This was supported by the launch of a creamy Barista version that was a big hit in the rapidly growing coffee chain concepts at the time, through which parts of their new and enlarged target group could be reached. It was also backed by a challenging and rebellious communication style and transparent sustainability reporting that not only helped create millions of fans, but also challenged the Swedish dairy industry. They used a multitude of communication channels from product packaging to sponsorships, social media, ads, videos, talk-shows and different sustainability projects to test out and explore new agricultural practices with local farmers. They also worked with public affairs to positively influence questions of political relevance, especially in relation to plant-based foods and oat milk. All in all, this helped transform their value proposition from a low-engagement product into a high-engagement lifestyle brand charging a premium price. The cooperation with local farmers and different research projects also helped them learn about their own ecosystem and how to not only become more sustainable, but to start exploring more regenerative practices.

In the first year after the relaunch (2015), sales grew by 40 percent. The repositioning of the brand, however, was only a first step on this journey. The growth continued in market after market throughout Europe and the company doubled its sales on a yearly basis. Pretty impressive, and good for the climate too, as every glass of Oatly oat milk produces about 75 percent less CO_2 compared to dairy milk.

The already ambitious plan for geographic expansion gained even more traction with the renewed mission of spreading Oatly's change agenda to the world—now the US and China. This was supported by several investor rounds necessary to fund the heavy investments needed to support their mission and rapid growth towards a more sustainable world. In 2016, state-backed China Resources, for instance, took a majority stake in the company through a joint venture with Belgium's Verlinvest. In 2020, Blackstone invested an additional $200 million in the company, giving the firm a stake of about 10 percent. Blackstone was seen as an especially controversial move by climate and political activists who felt this left a sour taste.[166] Oatly instead saw it as a great way to reroute 'old' capital into where it is most needed in building a better future.

/ Oatly was acknowledged by TIME Magazine as one of the top 100 influential companies of 2021 /

You may wonder why investors have been key to this transformational journey in the first place? Well, even though sales soared and Oatly's revenue reached approximately €400 million by 2020, the company the same year reported a net loss of approximately €60 million as it continued to focus on rapidly entering new markets and growing exponentially through building brand awareness and expanding production. Without their investors, Oatly would not have been able to scale exponentially and would not have afforded to create the spin that has helped people discover plant-based alternatives (which happens to be one of the keys to dealing with climate change globally). In early May 2021, Oatly was even acknowledged by TIME Magazine for just this—as one of the top 100 influential companies of 2021 and as an important contributor to the growing interest of plant-based foods across the world. And of course, with the increasing surge for plant-based options, if Oatly had not moved as fast as they did, someone else could have stepped into their place with copies instead

BETTER FUTURE

(something that is already happening). This is a situation they have wanted to avoid—as they proudly see themselves as the original inventors of oat milk.

As Oatly started growing exponentially with the help of investor infusions and rapidly added on new team members, their culture started to wobble. A challenge that most business leaders in exponentially growing companies will recognize. At this stage, the CEO wisely brought in an experienced senior leader to support the leadership team and organization on the journey. In came Christel Kinning, with a strong focus and interest in building conscious organizations and platforms for human growth. At Oatly, she took the role of Chief Transformation & People Officer, after many years as CEO and as a non-executive board member in other exponentially growing companies. She brought maturity and experience that now helps the company build more conscious leadership, beginning with a further clarification of the company's purpose and values, a solid strategic scaffolding, upgraded people practices (such as their new employee on-boarding experience) and leadership development.

Still, neither exceptional marketing communication nor people and culture development come for free. To enable their continued expansion and change agenda, Oatly went public at the end of May 2021. Their initial public offering was priced at $17 per share, giving the company an implied valuation of $10 billion.[167] This was an amazing development for a small Swedish company having started in a lab at Lund University in the mid-1990s. But will their playful and rebellious spirit survive the demands of the stock exchange? I know that they are working very hard at not becoming just another large corporation and in keeping their uniqueness. Let us hope that the increased access to capital will help them soar rather than restrain their ambitions going forward, as they risk moving from being a challenger of the system to just another integrated part of it.

You may, of course, also wonder what happened to their focus on sustainability in the midst of this massive expansion and hype. Well, health and sustainability are at the very core of who they are, and they have put a lot of energy not only into dreaming about how to create a better future but also into laying a solid foundation. By scaling fast, the big challenge is how to proactively mitigate the unwanted consequences of rapid growth. And it is not enough to have good intentions—you need to live as you learn. Here, Oatly has had some challenges on the way. Even though they have managed to decrease the average per-litre climate impact in Sweden, their total climate impact has, for instance, increased due to more litres sold—something they have been very transparent about. To address these issues and more, Oatly now works in a systematic manner to improve issues of materiality. They have, for instance, decided to partner with a leading supply chain sustainability rating and evaluation tool and to collaborate more actively with their suppliers. They have also identified a partner that will help them become one of Europe's first companies to digitize and deploy a fleet of electric trucks. The company has also continued its pilots with farmers in Sweden and the US to test cost-sharing incentives and market opportunities for farmers to incorporate oats into their farm rotations. While safeguarding a healthy oat supply for Oatly, added crop diversity will help break up pest cycles, increase agrobiodiversity, reduce the use of nitrogen-intensive fertilizers, and provide additional markets to farmers for new crops. Also, healthier soil will help bind more CO_2. A win-win for all.

Going forward, Oatly continues to invest in innovation for plant-based solutions and has the ambition to help people become healthier and help make the planet more sustainable. Their updated sustainability strategy also shows high ambitions in relation to their own organization, the business ecosystem and the world and society:

"We are a sustainability company, and through this plan we aim to drive a systemic shift in society — in the ways people eat, food is produced, and the planet is treated — where people can make small changes, like switching to plant-based foods, that improve their lives and ensure a healthy planet for future generations... Our mission can only be realized if we take action in every part of our organization... Our success is dependent on all of us taking ownership and implementing the actions necessary in our daily jobs."

As part of this plan, Oatly has launched four ambitions in three key strategic areas going forward.

EXCERPT FROM OATLY
SUSTAINABILITY STRATEGY 2029

KEY STRATEGIC AREA:

WE WILL DRIVE A FOOD SYSTEM SHIFT

AMBITION

AMBITION 1: By 2029, Oatly's food system will give back to nature and communities where we source by restoring carbon, improving biodiversity, and boosting farmers' income.

TO-DO LIST

- Establish an Oatly "Restoration Farming" system that supports farmers with restorative and regenerative agricultural practices to produce climate neutral oats and help farmers transition from livestock to more diverse plant-based farming, with well-researched, locally appropriate solutions.
- Source 100% of our strategic direct materials using tailored solutions that represent the most sustainable available option for each material, practice or region.
- Launch lighthouse partnerships with communities and other supply chain stakeholders to improve livelihoods and promote equity, fair working conditions and human rights—while restoring the natural environment and biodiversity."

KEY STRATEGIC AREA:

#2

WE WILL SET THE EXAMPLE AS A FUTURE COMPANY

AMBITION

AMBITION 2: By 2029, we will reduce our climate footprint per liter of Oatly produced by 70% from a 2019 baseline of 0.48kg per produced liter and align that ambition with a 1.5 degree C climate pathway.

AMBITION 3: By 2029, all facilities that produce our products will meet "Future Factory" criteria, which we will define in line with the principles of sustainable, efficient, safe and inclusive, and we will support our production partners along the journey.

TO-DO LIST

PLANET	*PEOPLE*
• Develop criteria for making sure our factories are sustainable, efficient, safe and inclusive. • By 2029, source 100% renewable energy (both heat and electricity) for our production from a 63% baseline in 2019 and reduce energy consumption from 0.4 kWh per liter produced in 2019. • By 2029, shift to 100% sustainable ground transport (inbound and outbound) for our products and materials, employing electric vehicles, rail or vehicles using renewable fuels. • By 2029, reduce our water withdrawal by at least half from 4.3 liters per liter of Oatly in 2019. • By 2029, eliminate production waste to landfill – reducing waste, repurposing fiber residues for food or feed, and composting or converting the rest to energy.	• Create a safe and equitable arena for personal growth, thought leadership and transformational change. That means zero discrimination, universal fair compensation and benefits, safe and inspiring workplaces, and an inclusive business that reflects the world around us. • Maintain sustainability as our core value, helping our co-workers feel committed and understand how they can contribute toward sustainability. • Incentivize our leaders to prioritize sustainability by making it part of their performance expectations.

KEY STRATEGIC AREA:

#3

WE WILL LEAD THE CHARGE TO EMPOWER A PLANT-BASED REVOLUTION

AMBITION

AMBITION 4: By 2029, mainstream plant-based diets by leading a shift from dairy, with a milestone to shift 2.9 billion litres from dairy to Oatly by 2025, saving up to 2.5 million tonnes of CO_2e.

TO-DO LIST

- Take a stand on climate change and sustainable food systems in key public forums to demand climate action in the markets in which we operate.
- Empower consumers to make sustainable food choices by publishing the climate footprint for 100% of our products, calling for mandatory climate footprint declarations for food in our top markets, and building awareness of the health and other impacts of a transition to a more plant-based, sustainable diet.
- Mobilize and inspire a movement of baristas, chefs, healthcare professionals, retailers, decision-makers, community leaders, youth, scientists, and consumers to support people in their shift to plant-based diets.
- Challenge outdated rules and regulatory barriers to level the playing field for plant-based diets and activate grassroots action to change the policy landscape.
- Support the shift of capital to more sustainable ventures by engaging the finance community and showing that new investments in sustainable solutions add value and performance.

TABLE 3
Oatly Sustainability Strategy 2029.

Note that all goals in Oatly's Sustainability Strategy are set to 2029, instead of the more conventional 2030. Again, Oatly is doing things its own way, and aim to be one year ahead of everyone else in reaching their ambitious sustainability targets for the end of this decade. That is for sure another story to tell. And as they say in its latest sustainability report: "By scaling our business sustainably, supporting responsible and restorative food and agricultural practices, and empowering people around the world to shift to plant-based diets, we can drive the global shift toward a sustainable food system."[168]

This finalizes the six case descriptions from the frontlines of Better Business. We will in the next section draw on these cases to reflect on the journey of sustainability within a corporation over time. Let us continue.

REFLECTIONS ON THE JOURNEYS

"Time is change, transformation and evolution."
I.L. PERETZ

Our six case descriptions highlight a diverse group of companies and an equally diverse set of journeys towards Better Business. These six sustainability leaders however also have a few things in common, such as:

- They have a long-term view.
- They are guided by a higher purpose.
- They continuously work to reduce their footprint, and some even explore regenerative practices.
- They to a large extent pursue meaningful innovation, integrating insights into wicked problems into their solutions and market communication.
- They have integrated their higher purposes throughout their cultures and organizations, as well as into their offerings, business models and operating models.
- They work to challenge and support their industries and business ecosystems to elevate their practices.
- They aim to change the world, e.g., with the support of systems thinking, different types of collaboration, and donations to grass-root movements.

Now, our six sustainability leaders have all been through an unfolding and development of their practices over time, even though all journeys seem to have been sparked by either a strategic insight, a crisis, or even an epiphany.

THE DEVELOPMENT OF SUSTAINABILITY OVER TIME

Several researchers have already captured the development of sustainability within organizations over time.[169] They generally describe an evolutionary approach from an initial sense of denial and rejection to the idea of sustainability, via a focus on legal compliance and philanthropy, to realizing that a focus on sustainability can help reduce cost and become a competitive advantage, to finally integrating sustainability into the core and transforming the organization.

Suzanne Benn, Professor of Sustainable Enterprise, and her colleagues, suggest three waves of change.[170] See Figure 25. The First Wave is described as a state of opposition and ignorance, where the concept of sustainability initially is rejected and business as usual prevails. The Second Wave is described as a journey from compliance (focus on reducing risk) to efficiency (cost reduction through environmental management), and finally the realization that sustainability can bring competitive advantage. In The Third Wave, there is a transformation to a sustainable business. All our case companies above are currently in this third wave.

In contrast to the Three Waves of Sustainability model above, as observed in the six selected case descriptions above there seems to be a unique evolutionary journey for each organization, rather than a one-size-fits-all pattern. This is possibly because the journey unfolds in different contexts, and at different speeds, as does change in general. Let us shortly revisit the journeys again below.

Patagonia supported activist causes and different types of conservational projects in California to protect natural habitats early on, all based on their founder's interest in outdoor sports and relationship to nature. Along the journey they experienced an existential crisis and came to realise that they themselves were not as innocent as they

	FIRST WAVE		SECOND WAVE			THIRD WAVE
	Opposition	Ignorance	Risk	Cost	Competitive advantage	Transformation
	Rejection	Non-responsiveness	Compliance	Efficiency	Strategic proactivity	The sustaining corporation
	› Highly instrumental perspective on employees and the natural environment › Culture of exploitation › Opposition to government and green activists › Community claims seen as illegitimate	› Financial and technological factors have primacy › More ignorant than oppositional › Seeks, business as usual, compliant work force › Environmental resources seen as a free good	› Focuses on reducing risk of sanctions for failing to meet minimum legal and community standards › Environmental management seen as a source of avoidable cost for the organization	› HR systems seen as means to higher productivity and efficiency › Little integration between HR and environmental functions › Follows route of compliance plus proactive measures to maintain good citizen image	› Focus on innovation › Seeks stakeholder engagement to innovate safe environmentally friendly products and processes › Advocates good citizenship to maximize profits and increase employee attraction and retention	› Reinterprets the nature of the corporation to an integral self-renewing element of the whole society and in its ecological context
	Value destroyers	Value limiters	Value conservers	Value creators	Value creators	Sustainable business

FIGURE 25

Waves of sustainability model (Benn et al., 2020).[171]

had thought, but rather part of the same system that contributed to the environmental problems that they detested in the first place. One thing led to another, and as they crafted their guiding principles, they also stepped up to take a more systematic responsibility and evolved into what is considered one of the most sustainable companies in the world. Today, Patagonia is both a Benefit Corporation and a highly rated Certified BCorp experimenting with regenerative practices. Along the journey, they have also transparently and generously shared their insights and efforts inside and outside of their industry while continuously and strategically building their brand.

And remember **Interface**: their transformation was sparked by a simple question from a customer and the epiphany of their founder, which caused them to set extremely ambitious long-term targets and fully focus on systematically reducing the impact of their environmental footprint. This helped them build a solid foundation over time, which became the basis for continuous innovation and ultimately turned into a full integration of sustainability—and even regenerative practices—into their core identity. They also generously shared their learnings within and outside of their industry early on and now aspire to lead the Industrial Re-Revolution to transform industry as we know it into a force for good.

Ørsted's transformational journey, on the other hand, started out with a more traditional strategy process, in a situation where incumbents were looking to differentiate their value propositions and business models in the wake of the deregulation of the Danish energy industry. In this process, the company (named DONG Energy at the time) identified a long-term business risk in coal, saw decreasing margins in gas and an interesting business opportunity in offshore wind. Their CEO became even more convinced that renewable energy was the right path ahead after his participation in the Copenhagen Climate Conference in 2009. Decreasing margins on their old, commoditized business and a liquidity crisis in 2013 accelerated the change as they gradually transformed their value proposition, business model and modus operandi. This has made them the most sustainable energy company in the world and the #1 global player in offshore wind.

Looking at **Unilever**, their journey instead seems to have been sparked by a focus on reducing risk and safeguarding future supply throughout their massive supply chain. This work seemingly developed into two streams—building resilient supply chains and building brands that are relevant in today's and tomorrow's society. With more than 400 brands, of which only 41 can be considered purpose-led, they have an active brand portfolio strategy to support their transformation, including acquisitions of sustainability brands (e.g., Seventh Generation). Their former CEO, Paul Polman, also successfully utilized the company's size and influence to spread his mission about building a better business and a better future, e.g., through the World Economic Forum and different UN bodies.

For **IKEA**, frugality with resources has, on the other hand, been part of their genome since their inception. Their systematic focus on sustainability seems to have started with risk mitigation associated with their supply chain (i.e., IWAY Code of Conduct for suppliers across the value chain around year 2000). With an increasing awareness about the need to revitalize their business model for the future, they also realised that their pure size could help change their business ecosystem and even the world to the better. This has evolved into today's strong focus on People and Planet and on identifying circular practices for a more regenerative future. This will help the company to become even more frugal in their resource use and to stay relevant and attractive going forward, as they test and experiment themselves into their next 100 years of business.

Finally, **Oatly** has been on an impressive transformational journey over the past decade. In their case, it started in 1994 with oat milk invented and developed for people with sensitive stomachs or a milk allergy, a hypothesis that oat milk was better for the environment than milk, and a new CEO coming in 2012 with the mission to build a lifestyle company. A bold strategic repositioning and transformation followed. Their approach, supported by an understanding of the importance of trends and the rise of the vegan movement, initially aimed to challenge the dairy industry. As their rebellious repositioning and communication style took off, the company started growing exponentially, driven by consumer demand and innovation and supported by somewhat controversial investors. Only one month before their IPO in 2021, they were recognized by TIME Magazine as one of the top 100 influential companies and as an important contributor to the growing interest in plant-based foods across the world.

A note to the journeys presented is that I may not have focused enough on balancing the journeys of these Better Business heroes in digging even deeper into the problems and challenges that they have experienced along the way. These journeys have of course not been a walk in the park, just as any other change and transformational journey. Problems have arisen. They always do when change, people and organizations are involved. This will however need to be the topic of another book.

THE CONTINUUM OF CHANGE

What I have found particularly interesting in this research is rather that the continuum of change observed in the six case companies can be described as stretching from disruption or crisis on the one end to long-term incremental evolution on the other end. In between shock and evolution there is a window of opportunity for a strategic shift or transformation. See Figure 26.

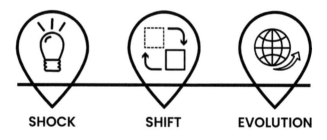

SHOCK　　　**SHIFT**　　　**EVOLUTION**

FIGURE 26

A continuum of change.[172]

This narrative is indeed helpful but does not give a complete picture of the journeys of our six case companies. Together with Three Wave Model of Sustainability by Susanne Benn and team (see Figure 25), it however provides some interesting reflections.

The journeys of Interface and Patagonia, who have both been active in this field for more than 25 years, may indeed seem evolutionary. The very start of their journeys was however sparked by rather different events–an epiphany by the CEO and founder of Interface, and a crisis with mass-layoffs at Patagonia. From these events came clear strategic shifts, followed by continuous evolution. As Susanne Benn points out in her model, this most probably started in ignorance, or at least in not being consciously aware of their own negative environmental impact. The respective events then jump-started their journeys into the second wave, and evolution over time brought them into the third wave, where they have continued evolving into sustainability companies, driven by their ambitious goals (especially Interface), their conscious awareness as well as their realized competitive advantages.

The starting points for Ørsted and Oatly have rather been driven by strategic insight, and a desire to reposition and differentiate their respective businesses. This has then been followed by what can be characterized as evolutionary journeys, based on continuous learning, testing and experimentation. Both transformations have increased their respective relevance and attractiveness in relation to their stakeholders. Ørsted has also managed to decrease its risk. In the case of Oatly their transformation led to an explosion of consumer interest and exponential growth. In the case of Ørsted net sales have remained been flat over time, while they have gradually and successfully phased out their old fossil-based technologies and replaced it with renewable technologies. A challenge in itself.

In the cases of Unilever and IKEA, our corporate giants, the starting points of their respective journeys seem to have been linked to risk mitigation in relation to their enormous supply chains. The journeys are characterized by a combination of evolutionary and strategic shifts over time that has helped increase their relevance and attractiveness to their stakeholders. A shift from 'merely' being responsible corporations towards being leading sustainability companies has also protected their licence to operate, especially considering the impact that their global businesses have across the world. They are for instance some of the largest buyers of palm oil (Unilever) and wood (IKEA) in the world.

The big question is, of course, whether the companies that start this journey today will have the luxury of incremental change and evolution. I believe that the longer you wait, the more disruptive the experience will be to your organization. You will, however, not need to start from scratch as many have already paved the path and learning from the frontlines of Better Business will help you accelerate your journey.

USING BETTER BUSINESS AS A BRIDGE

Going back to our definitions, a Better Business was defined in the beginning of this book as a for-profit organization that has a long-term perspective and is guided and inspired by a higher purpose that helps the organization create, deliver and capture value to stakeholders, while minimizing ecological and social costs, engaging its business ecosystem and reducing its footprint. It could be a Certified B Corporation or a Benefit Corporation, but it does not have to be.

With this definition, all our case companies can be defined as Better Businesses. Even so, all but Interface still have significant planetary footprints. Interface is currently also the only one with the outspoken ambition of becoming regenerative going forward. The others are, however, starting to explore the area: Patagonia, for instance, is currently involved in pilot initiatives for regenerative organic farming, and IKEA has set targets to become regenerative in some areas by 2030. This increased interest in regenerative business practices was also prevalent when I enlarged the study to a larger population of sustainability leaders across industries (see Methodology).

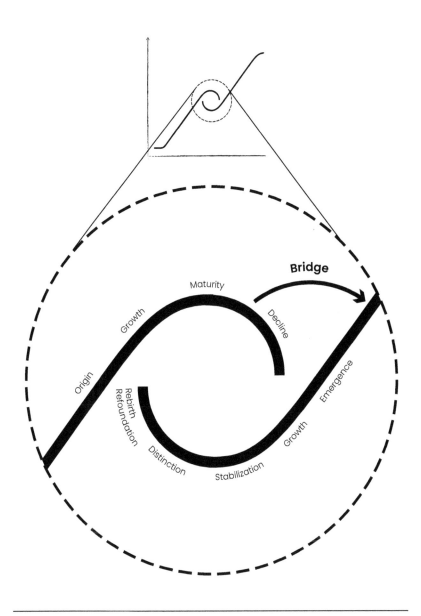

FIGURE 27

Bridging business as usual and the emerging paradigms of Regenerative Business through Better Business, inspired by Berkana's two loop model.

In the beginning of the book, I also mentioned that Better Business is most probably only part of a developmental trajectory towards regenerative business. As such, Better Business can act as a bridge in closing the seemingly massive gap between business as usual and regenerative business practices. There is simply so much to learn—and unlearn—to be successful in the paradigm that is evolving. And learning takes time. It is not only about skills. It is even more so about mindset, beliefs and habits about how things should be done and what we get rewarded for. And even more about what we value. In the situation that we as humanity—including the world of business—is in, we will need to question everything. Demanding anyone take a giant leap from one paradigm to another is probably not fruitful. Providing a bridge between the old and the new that is emerging is more helpful. Hence, the Better Business concept (see Figure 27).

A relevant question is whether additional case descriptions would present you with even more diversity than what you have seen in the case descriptions above? Yes, of course, they would—but not as much as you think. Instead, with every new case you would start seeing patterns emerge, as I did in my own research into sustainability leaders across industries. What are the emerging patterns?

In the next chapter, I will answer this question as part of three conceptual frameworks: The Playing Fields of Better Business, the StepUp Framework for Better Business transformation, and the Fit for Purpose Model. You will also be introduced to 14 good practice examples as part of the StepUp Framework. All models and examples are, of course, simplifications of a complex reality and never perfect, but they can help us organize thoughts and inform our decisions.

NOTE TO SELF

CHAPTER 4

THE STRATEGIC PLAYING FIELDS OF BETTER BUSINESS

"Where will you play?"

A.G. LAFLEY AND ROGER MARTIN

According to one of the world's top management thinkers, Roger Martin, an important rule of success is that strategy takes more than a big vision, no matter how brilliant it is. First of all, it takes defining the playing field.

The strategic playing field of a company normally includes its deliberate choices about targeted customer segments, its value proposition, its distribution channels and choice of geographic presence. It is normally highly dependent on the particular industry context. In the case of Better Business, however, three completely different playing fields seem to be particularly relevant for any company to take into consideration (see Figure 28):

- The organization itself,
- Its business ecosystem,
- The world and society.

These three levels are also commonly used for a strategic analysis of a company's situation and environment. In reality they are three different system levels that will help you identify your strategic ambition and set the scene for your potential impact and circle of influence. Let me explain.

According to systems theory, the world can be seen as a complex adaptive system of interconnected parts and subsystems. A system can be described as "a group of interacting or interrelated elements that act according to a set of rules to form a unified whole". Changes in one part of the system can create an unforeseen impact on any other. Changes outside of the system can, too.

We are actually free to define a system. We do that by specifying its boundaries, which in practice means choosing which entities are inside the system and which fall outside of it. This is how I have defined the three levels relevant to the book:

Your Organization

Since we are coming from a business perspective, we will put your organization at the very centre of our systems map (even if your business is really only a small part of your business ecosystem, and an even smaller part of the world and society; it is in reality also very far from the centre of the world—a fact that we sometimes tend to forget). Your business and organization are your formal responsibility as a corporate business leader. This is also the playing field where you, as a corporate business leader, have the largest impact and influence.

Your Business Ecosystem

Your business is part of a larger, human-made system that I have chosen to call your business ecosystem. Multinational companies with large and complex value chains, like Unilever, will most certainly be part of several different business ecosystems. Defining and understanding these business ecosystems is highly relevant.

The World and Society

Any business ecosystem is part of something even larger—ultimately our world and society, which encompasses a vast array of subsystems. To keep it simple, I include everything on this planet that is outside of your business ecosystem: the biosphere and humanity as a whole, including human-made systems, such as global institutions (e.g., the UN, IMF, iNGOs) and other types of organizations and infrastructures. Interestingly, as a corporate business leader you can have an influence on this level if you only know how to go about it—especially if you are a business leader in a large corporation like Unilever or IKEA. But even a smaller corporation like Patagonia and Oatly can aspire to change the world.

As with most system definitions, this is a simplification that is far from perfect—but it has a purpose. You may feel this is too theoretical and wonder how this possibly could be applicable for your business. Well, as we have seen in our six cases, organizations on the frontlines of Better Business do not play only on an organizational level. Instead, they collaborate with other stakeholders to improve conditions and upgrade their industry and business ecosystem. Some even aspire to change the world. Hence, as a Better Business, you need to know how to mobilize initiatives on all these system levels to make a meaningful difference beyond your own organization.

A challenge is that with each level, the complexity increases. Hence, the business ecosystem level is more complex than the organizational level and the world and society level is more complex than the business ecosystem level. This also means that they are uncertain and cannot be predicted or controlled.

BETTER FUTURE

The next challenge is that the natural playing field for us as business leaders is the organization and its immediate transactional environment (e.g., customers, suppliers and competitors). That is what we have been trained for. What we have not been trained for is how to manage increasingly complex and uncertain business ecosystems or global challenges. This makes the opportunity for Better Business a tricky one. It is, however, not optional going forward.

So, what is it that we need to master? Where should we start? There are a million questions that need to be answered. Before we rush ahead to answer any of those, we need to go from this high-level system approach to something more practical.

/ We have not been trained for how to manage increasingly complex and uncertain business ecosystems or global challenges /

THE STEPUP FRAMEWORK FOR BETTER BUSINESS TRANSFORMATION

As earlier explained, Better Business seems close to the description of what Susanne Benn calls the Third Wave of Sustainability (see Figure 25). As a consultant I however personally missed a more structured operational framework for this stage to help my clients shape their Better Business strategy. Hence, I utilized the observations from the frontlines of Better Business to design and refine a framework for just that (see Methodology for more information about the approach).

To develop a useful strategic framework for us as business leaders, I simply started out with the three playing fields described above, and then zoomed in on the organizational level and split that up into three different steps that are key in approaching Better Business. Based on observed good practices in the research for this book (see Methodology), those were:

- lay a solid foundation,
- explore and innovate,
- integrate into the core.

To that, I added the strategic intent of a Better Business leader at the business ecosystem level, which is to upgrade the business ecosystem. I also added the often-observed ambition to change the world. With that, we have a model that I simply call the *StepUp Framework* (see Table 4 and Figure 29). It is designed to help you understand your current situation, identify your strategic ambition and intent going forward and to help you accelerate your company's strategic journey towards Better Business and beyond.

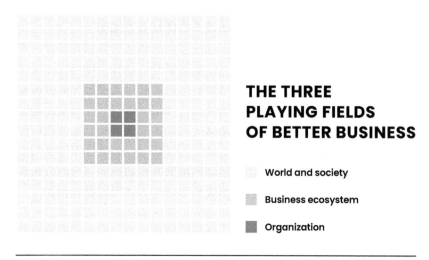

THE THREE PLAYING FIELDS OF BETTER BUSINESS

- World and society
- Business ecosystem
- Organization

FIGURE 28

The three playing fields of Better Business.

PLAYING FIELD	STRATEGIC INTENT
World and society	Collaborate to change the world
Business ecosystem	Upgrade your ecosystem
Organization	Integrate into the core
Organization	Explore and innovate
Organization	Lay a solid foundation

TABLE 4

The strategic intents of Better Business leaders on the three playing fields.

World and society

5 COLLABORATE TO CHANGE THE WORLD

This level is about collaborating to change the world, upgrading society, and building a better and more equitable future for humanity and the planet.

Business ecosystem

4 UPGRADE YOUR ECOSYSTEM

This step is about supporting and challenging your whole industry and business ecosystem to transform their practices in a way that supports sustainable development, outside of your direct control and outside of your immediate value chain.

Organization

3 INTEGRATE INTO THE CORE

In this step, sustainability becomes an integrated part of your core: why you exist as a company, what you want your role to be in society and how you aim to make a difference for your stakeholders. It also becomes fully integrated into your strategy, business model and operating model.

2 EXPLORE AND INNOVATE

On this second step, we focus on exploration, innovation and on capturing relevant business potential in relation to sustainability through the solutions that you offer your customers, i.e. your products, services and value proposition. This requires quite different competencies and capabilities than the first step.

1 LAY A SOLID FOUNDATION

This basic, foundational step encompasses the classical fields of sustainability, quality management, compliance and transparent reporting and has a focus on systematically reducing negative impact, decreasing risk, protecting your reputation from unnecessary missteps and safeguarding your social licence to operate.

FIGURE 29

The StepUp framework shows the strategic intents and good practices of Better Business leaders on the three playing fields.

What are then these different steps of Better Business? A short description and overview follow.

Lay a Solid Foundation

This basic, foundational step encompasses the classical fields of sustainability, quality management, compliance and transparent reporting and has a focus on systematically reducing negative impact, decreasing risk, protecting your reputation from unnecessary missteps and safeguarding your social licence to operate.

Explore and Innovate

On this second step, we focus on exploration, innovation and on capturing relevant business potential in relation to sustainability through the solutions that you offer your customers, i.e., your products, services and value proposition. This requires quite different competencies and capabilities than the first step.

Integrate into the Core

In this step, sustainability becomes an integrated part of your core: why you exist as a company, what you want your role to be in society and how you aim to make a difference for your stakeholders. It also becomes fully integrated into your strategy, business model and operating model.

Upgrade your Business Ecosystem

This step is about supporting and challenging your whole industry and business ecosystem to transform their practices in a way that supports sustainable development, outside of your direct control and outside of your immediate value chain.

Collaborate to Change the World

This top level of the framework is about aspiring to change the world for the better through cross-sectoral and global collaboration. It aims to upgrade society and co-creating a better, more sustainable and more equitable future for humanity and the planet.

To make the StepUp Framework more useful and easier to understand, I have in the coming sections included 14 examples of good practices to inspire you on your own journey going forward. Again, based on the research for this book (see Methodology).

/ To explore and innovate require quite different competencies and capabilities than laying a soild foundation /

GOOD PRACTICE EXAMPLE OVERVIEW

In identifying good practices, I performed a study of 30 for-profit organizations across different industries, sizes and backgrounds (see Methodology) – all in the process of moving beyond the business-as-usual paradigm, and most already to be considered a Better Business. I also added a scan of 10 non-profit organizations (foundations) in the search for inspiring good practices on the higher levels of the framework. In this study, I aimed at qualitatively identifying what could be considered good or evolving practice (and not to quantify any frequency of their occurrence). Table 5 helps provide examples of some of the observed good and evolving practices.

SYSTEM LEVEL	STRATEGIC INTENT	EXAMPLES OF GOOD AND EVOLVING PRACTICE OBSERVED
World and society	Collaborate to change the world	• Identifying and understanding the wicked global problems and related systems. • Building a Theory of Change. • Starting or supporting a foundation and selecting good causes in line with the systems change you want to co-create. • Cross-sectoral collaboration to solve wicked problems through unconventional partnerships. • Pursuing corporate activism. • Starting a think tank to impact policy makers through research, articles, books and reports. • Becoming an impact investor. • Building a global movement.
Business ecosystem	Upgrade your business ecosystem	• Becoming a thought leader and activist aiming to change your industry and business ecosystem. • Supporting the change of the ecosystem outside of your control through knowledge and financial means. • Cooperate within business associations and other key stakeholder groups to raise the ethics and practices of the industry, e.g., through self-regulation. • Build relationships with selected authorities to speed up the development in a direction that supports your vision, e.g., through laws and regulations.
Organization	Integrate into the core	• Having a long-term perspective. • Taking a stakeholder-centred approach of creating shared value. • Creating—and living—a higher purpose, supporting values, an energizing vision, and an integrated strategy. • Getting your people engaged and excited in shaping your future. • Actively building and managing a portfolio of sustainability products, brands, business models and business units. • Acquiring companies or brands to speed up your transformation. • Aligning your operating system while working in three horizons and distributing resources accordingly. • Becoming a certified B-Corp.

SYSTEM LEVEL	STRATEGIC INTENT	EXAMPLES OF GOOD AND EVOLVING PRACTICE OBSERVED
Organization	Explore and innovate	• Understanding and monitoring the trends, and societal and environmental challenges unfolding mid-term and long-term. • Understanding the opportunities connected to the Sustainable Development Goals. • Reviewing your current portfolio and identifying how it could be systematically revitalized from a sustainability perspective. • Developing sustainability brands. • Exploring your enlarged value chain to identify potential innovation areas. • Designing in sustainability and circularity into your products and adding maintenance services to support long-life. • Exploring impact and circular business models. • Being curious and embracing innovation. • Learning fast through collaboration, testing and experimentation. • Releasing fear, letting yourself learn and have fun to explore new ways forward.
Organization	Lay a solid foundation	• Identifying your relevant stakeholder groups. • Interviewing stakeholder representatives to understand their concerns and priorities in relation to your business. • Identifying and understanding the key challenges relevant to your business along your value chain. • Conducting life cycle analysis (LCA) to understand the challenges related to your products. • Mapping and calculating the footprint of your business along your particular part of the value chain. • Conducting a materiality analysis based on your findings to identify the most relevant challenges to address. • Setting relevant and bold long-term goals where it matters most and addressing these challenges systematically through programmes with a clear governance structure and a focus on continuous improvements. • Aiming to reduce or even terminate waste and emissions, e.g. science-based targets for CO_2 reduction. • Clarifying and safeguarding the necessary competencies, roles and responsibilities. • Conducting regular audits internally and among suppliers. • Using external and independent experts to audit your own progress towards your goals. • Transparent reporting on progress and challenges along selected goals, KPIs and standards (e.g., ESG, SDG, GRI etc). • Aiming at risk reduction, adherence to laws and standards and continuous improvements.

TABLE 5

The StepUp framework with good practice examples.

Not surprisingly, startups and small companies have few resources to systematically work on laying a solid foundation. Those that start out with an aspiration to change their ecosystem and the world will, however, ultimately need to deal with their foundational practices. And as they grow, it will be needed for them to be regarded as trustworthy among their stakeholders.

/ The most logical way to start the journey towards Better Business may seem to be to lay a solid foundation /

For a large company, the most logical way to start the journey towards Better Business may seem to be to lay a solid foundation. Because what you say to your customers and other stakeholders will need to be authentic and transparent. Otherwise, your efforts will easily be branded as 'green washing' or 'purpose washing' and quickly erode your credibility—especially if you aim to change the world, but do not have your own house in order, or if you claim to sell a sustainable product but have a large value chain in disarray behind the curtains.

Interestingly, the higher levels of the StepUp Framework seem to have a pull effect on the lower levels. Or, as Karen Hamilton, Global Vice President of Sustainable Business at Unilever, expressed it in our conversation around this model, "Being active on the higher levels can help transform the organization." Why? Because people are inspired by meaningful efforts on higher levels, for instance, an outspoken ambition to change the world for the better and a series of meaningful projects that are aligned with that ambition. Practically, this means that you can start laying your foundation and, in parallel, work on some of the upper levels to help mobilise your people internally on the transformational journey. Building a Better Business is, in this sense, more about learning to play the full piano than about taking a certain sequential approach.

Far from everyone will initially have an ambition—or mandate from their owners or board of directors—beyond laying a solid foundation to minimize risk. But do not mistake yourself. Even this basic level will need to evolve over time as pressure and demand from investors, regulators and consumers rise. Even this level is not a one-time effort but a continuous one. You can choose to be proactive or reactive, but the need to adapt and change the way you do business will come sooner or later. An important strategic choice is, for instance, whether to be a leader or a follower in this field within your industry. For your company to continue to be relevant and attractive as your business environment evolves, I recommend you start thinking in these terms here and now.

It is worth mentioning that I have noticed that the word *transformation* often implies something drastic and that it is not always well received throughout organizations. Also, the closer this transformation comes to the individual, the more stressful it is for people to handle. Instead, focusing on a higher purpose and how we as an organization want to make a difference in the world helps people see the big picture. Then we can start talking about how to get there.

Since the Better Business journey often involves a major transformation of the company, it is far from enough to do a few strategy sessions in an exclusive conference centre outside of the company to bring a Better Business into life. Instead, it is more fruitful to see this as a long-term transformational journey in several steps, as you are hopefully still in a position where you can paint the big picture and let your company evolve and transform over time supported by external collaborations, ongoing learning, testing and experimentation. Everything depends on the actual starting point of this process, your ambition level going forward and the maturity of your stakeholder and customer base. Remember the difference between the long-term evolution of Interface over a 25-year period and the comparably speedy repositioning of Oatly, which was orchestrated in less than a decade while cleverly surfing the waves of change in society.

/ Every small step in the right direction marks progress /

We all need to start from where we are and develop a clear vision of the future we want to create. Every small step in the right direction marks progress, even though we might not know exactly how to get there when we start out.

In the next section, I will describe each level more thoroughly to help you approach the challenge of building a Better Business. Sharing this (the whole book, actually) with your management team will help you better navigate your way forward as an organization, together.

NOTE TO SELF

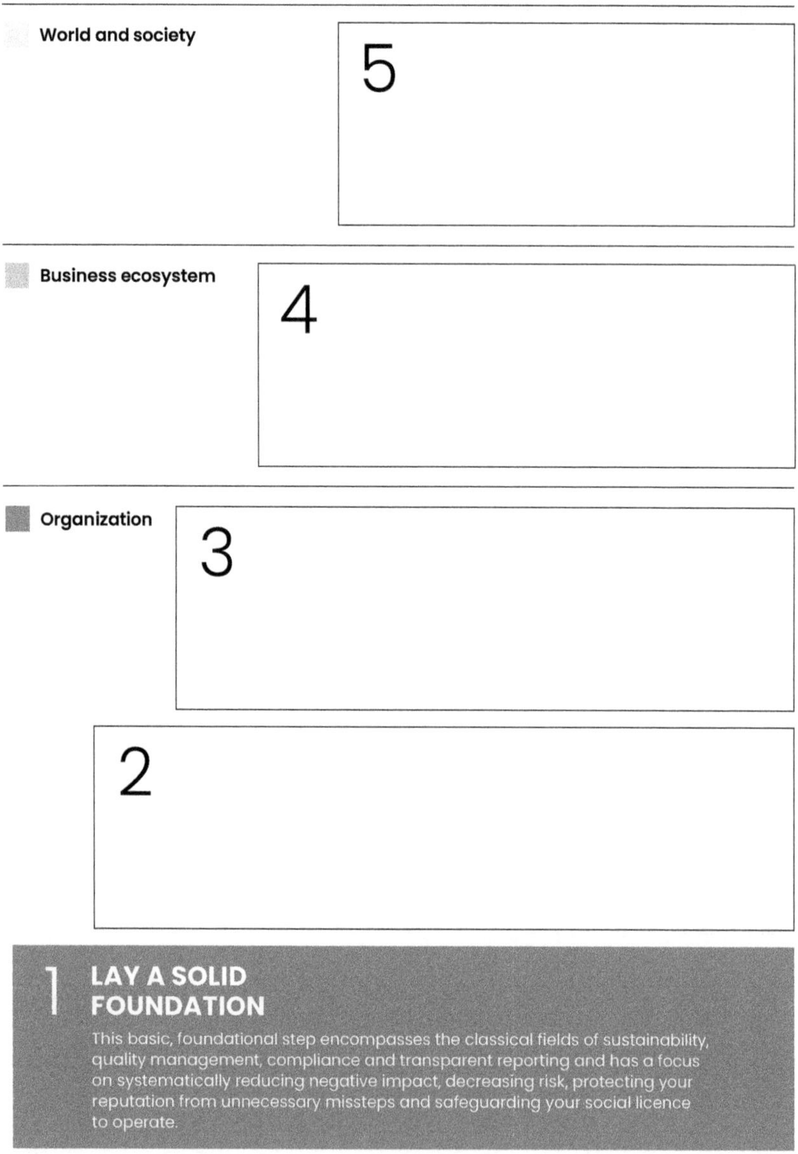

World and society

5

Business ecosystem

4

Organization

3

2

FIGURE 30

The StepUp framework's first step of Better Business transformation: lay a solid foundation.

STEP 1
LAY A SOLID FOUNDATION

This very first step of the StepUp Framework encompasses the classical fields of sustainability, compliance, quality management and risk reduction to proactively protect your company and reputation from unnecessary missteps and safeguard your licence to operate. As such, it is a step for the experts with the overall aim to understand and reduce risk, and transparently report and communicate your progress in the field as the responsible corporate citizen that you are.

In its essence, *laying a solid foundation* means striving for a systematic approach with clear goals and incremental yearly improvements in the field of sustainability. This does not mean that long-term goals have to be modest—on the contrary. Think about the amazing transformation of Interface, where their founder's Moonshot was brought to life in the arduous work and incremental improvements of their engineering team over a period of more than two decades. These extremely ambitious goals were, as you remember, 'zero waste to landfill', 'zero fossil fuel energy use', 'zero process water use' and 'zero greenhouse gas emissions' (goals set already in 1994 for 2020). All goals were related to their own facilities and operations as a first step.

BETTER FUTURE

Another example of bold goal setting is Microsoft's ambition to not only become carbon negative by 2030, but to remove from the environment the equal amount of carbon that the company has emitted since it was founded in 1975 by 2050. A bold goal that is now being followed by others, e.g., Velux, a manufacturing company especially known for its roof windows, who recently announced that they aim to become "lifetime carbon neutral" by 2041 in offsetting their carbon emissions from their last 79 years. [173]

Goal setting in the decade of action will also require you to adopt the SDGs. In *SDG Ambition: Setting Goals for the Decade of Action* – UN Global Compact has partnered with Accenture, SAP and 3M to help businesses do just that. They suggest an approach where goals go from being incremental to being science-based; where output-oriented goals are replaced by impact-oriented initiatives that drive change for business society and environment; where goals go from an emphasis on philanthropics and the direct operations to an expanded impact across global value chains; and where independent KPIs are replaced by interconnected systems of KPIs.[174]

If you are a corporate business of a decent size, you probably started working on this first step of the Better Business journey at least a decade ago and you most certainly already have specialists working on projects to identify and address your most material sustainability issues, goals and reporting. You may, however, still not be systematic or bold enough in your approach or have the necessary competencies across the organization. Training relevant stakeholders across the organization, making them accountable and responsible for implementing the relevant programmes, and simply safeguarding adherence to standards will help your sustainability team make significant progress and help your corporation advance on the journey. If you still have limited traction on this step, it may not primarily be about a lack of competencies in your organization, but about your priorities as a senior business leader. Good practices on this level are generally well known by the expert community working in the field. So, what can you do to give the sustainability team more traction across your organization?

Transparent communication and reporting is a skill in itself. An earlier referred to study of 1,000 companies in the EU (2019)[175] revealed that most companies use 'warm words' in their description of their aspirations rather than showing concrete targets and actions. As only large, listed companies were included in the study, it is quite surprising to see that only 22 percent of the companies provided Key Performance Indicators in summarised statements, that 10 percent did not provide any at all, and 68 percent provided them scattered across the narrative, making it hard for the reader to capture the overall picture and understand if and how the company was moving the needle. This hardy reflects good practice.

Among our six case companies the level of ambition as well as the level of transparency is high. So also, among the top 10 sustainability companies as to the GlobeScan SustainAbility Survey 2020. In Appendix 2 you can find a brief overview of a selection of metrics in relation to certifications and ratings as to information available on their respective company websites. As earlier mentioned, a private company like Patagonia has chosen to focus fully on living up to the highest standards of the B Corporation certification, while the large (stock-listed) multinationals seem to have a stronger focus on factors that are important for their ESG rating.

In general, good practice examples observed on this foundational step are:

- Identifying your relevant stakeholder groups.
- Interviewing stakeholder representatives to understand their concerns and priorities in relation to your business.

BETTER FUTURE

- Identifying and understanding the key challenges relevant to your business along your value chain.
- Conducting Life Cycle Assessment (LCA) to understand the challenges related to your products.
- Mapping and calculating the footprint of your business along your particular segment of the value chain.
- Conducting a materiality analysis based on your findings from the points above to identify the most relevant challenges to address.
- Understanding how your issues of materiality connect to the SDGs and identify in which of these areas – and how – that you as a company can make the biggest difference.
- Setting relevant and bold long-term goals where it matters most and addressing these challenges systematically through programmes with a clear governance structure and a focus on continuous improvements, e.g., science-based targets for CO_2 reduction.
- Highlighting how your sustainability goals contribute to the SDGs.
- Clarifying and safeguarding the necessary competencies, roles and responsibilities across the organization.
- Conducting regular audits internally and among suppliers.
- Using external and independent experts to audit your own progress towards your goals.
- Transparent sustainability and ESG reporting on progress and challenges along selected goals, KPIs and reporting standards.
- Where possible, including outcomes as part of remuneration, at least on the executive team level.

An important note to this step is that it never stops evolving. As stakeholder demands and regulations are expected to increase the pressure on organizations to become even more responsible and sustainable, this is an area that will need to be attended to on an ongoing basis going forward. This is true of all the steps, by the way. Already today however, this step most often cannot be considered strategically differentiating, but rather common practice. It is simply a must going forward. Including NetZero Carbon ambitions for 2050. Seeing that most smaller companies have not even identified risks in relation to sustainability—at least in Scandinavia—makes me think that there is still a lot to be done for many to just reach a minimum level.[176] For larger corporations this may provide a competitive advantage over smaller competitors, as a systemic focus on sustainability is increasingly a demand from customers and regulators.

Going forward, I believe this step—a solid foundation—will be considered your ticket to operate in society, and the minimum level accepted by society for large and mid-size companies. It will also be required and expected by your customers, consumers and investors, if it is not so already. Increasingly, it will also be a requirement for smaller companies to get their house in order. If not, they will simply not be relevant and attractive to larger customers.

In reviewing different cases for this chapter there are a few good practice examples that stand out. First out is an example of bold goal setting practices.

GOOD PRACTICE EXAMPLE:
BOLD GOAL SETTING

A group of corporate leaders within sustainability (UN Nation Global Compact members) have identified the following best practices for bold goal setting in the field: [177]

- **"FOCUS ON ISSUES THAT ARE STRATEGICALLY IMPORTANT TO YOUR COMPANY:** Start with where you believe the company has the most significant impact and where important business opportunities exist. This may mean going beyond operational boundaries. For example, you may want to set goals related to your supply chain or product use."

- **"SET STRETCH GOALS:** This means setting some ambitious goals, even if you don't yet know how to achieve them. This will stimulate innovation, investments, positive engagement and, ultimately, performance. Leading companies are setting science-based targets defined by what the external world requires, rather than by what seems easily achievable."

- **"CONNECT YOUR GOALS TO YOUR BUSINESS STRATEGY:** Link each sustainability goal to how it will support revenue generation, productivity and/or risk management."

- **"CONNECT YOUR GOALS WITH THE GLOBAL UNITED NATIONS SUSTAINABLE DEVELOPMENT GOALS:** Making your sustainability goals public as commitments to society can help you communicate to stakeholders the in-depth contribution your company is making to sustainable development."

- **"ENSURE SUPPORT AND OWNERSHIP:** You will need to secure and maintain broad organizational support for your company's sustainability goals. This includes internal and external support, both from the top down and bottom up."

This leads us to our next good practice example – Ørsted – and their systematic approach to identifying sustainability themes and building programmes to reach their goals.

GOOD PRACTICE EXAMPLE:
THE SYSTEMATIC APPROACH OF ØRSTED

Over the years, this corporation has developed a systematic approach to identifying sustainability themes, underlying challenges and developing programmes to approach them. They do this in five phases: mapping, prioritizing, anchoring, developing programmes, and realizing plans and reporting on progress (see Figure 31).

FIGURE 31

Ørsted's systematic approach to sustainability is a process in five phases. [178]

BETTER FUTURE

Great, but what does that mean to us? Below, I have summarized a few learnings from Ørsted's Sustainability Report 2020, where they share their approach in detail.[179] I am certain that your sustainability team can be inspired by their well-organized modus operandi. It can also be useful for you, as a business leader, to know how it can be done. Here it is:

1. **MAPPING SUSTAINABILITY THEMES**
   Ørsted's annual process starts out by mapping sustainability themes that are important to their business and to their stakeholders. For example, they clarify how regulators and NGOs see the challenges and opportunities for building renewable energy in balance with nature. This work then translates into an overview of sustainability themes that could affect their business and stakeholders.

2. **PRIORITISING SUSTAINABILITY THEMES**
   When the sustainability themes are mapped, they are then evaluated by importance from a stakeholder as well as a business perspective. This ranking of importance is most often a qualitative exercise and is based on different factors. The output of this work is a simple matrix of sustainability themes ranked based on importance to stakeholders and the business. This matrix is then used by the sustainability team to prioritize the themes that should be actively addressed going forward.

3. **ANCHORING THEIR SUSTAINABILITY THEMES IN THEIR BUSINESS**
   When a prioritized set of sustainability themes is defined, they are anchored in the internal governance structure. This gives their senior management and Board of Directors an overview of what is most important and enables them

to make decisions on how to address the identified themes. This anchoring in executive accountabilities and responsibilities also ensures that their initiatives are embedded in their business strategy as well as daily operations.

4. DEVELOPING AND UPDATING SUSTAINABILITY PROGRAMMES
Based on the above identified challenges, the team develops sustainability programmes for the most important themes. They currently have 20 sustainability programmes in their portfolio. Based on their annual evaluation process, they either update existing programmes or develop new ones.

5. REALISING AND REPORTING ON PROGRESS
Reporting on the progress of each sustainability programme and the challenges they face in relation to those is the very key to ensuring transparency and to giving their stakeholders an opportunity to scrutinize their performance and hold them accountable. Their reporting is also the basis for a continued dialogue with stakeholders on the sustainability themes that are material to their business. How? As Ørsted mentions in their Sustainability Report: "Each quarter, as part of our quarterly financial reporting, we publish a comprehensive ESG performance report with detailed updates on our performance across programmes and other sustainability performance indicators. Once a year, we publish our sustainability report where we address the broader sustainability agenda we work on and present the challenges and opportunities we see on the horizon. It also provides an overview of our sustainability performance for the year across our programmes." [180]

With systematic approach to sustainability, Ørsted aims to stay at the forefront of its industry and help the world to transition to green energy. But, as their current CEO, Mads Nipper, stated in their last sustainability report: "We don't have all the answers or full visibility of the journey we have ahead of us to create a sustainable society. That shouldn't prevent us from taking decisive action now to stop climate change and create a better tomorrow. After all, that's what leadership is about." [181]

In our last example in this section, we will take a quick look at a good practice regarding gathering your relevant data and transparently sharing it on your website.

GOOD PRACTICE EXAMPLE: UNILEVER'S SUSTAINABILITY REPORTING CENTRE

Transparent reporting is as you already know a key practice in the field of sustainability. Still, many companies struggle to get it right. Unilever has solved this with something that looks like a knowledge hub. First, they have structured their website so that their sustainability engagements are easy to find for employees, consumers and customers, as well as for investors.[182] Well there you can find rich and detailed information on Unilever's approach, goals and initiatives to contribute to a better world, all connected to the SDGs. Then, they have gathered and structured all data, policies and reporting regarding sustainability and ESG in what they call their Sustainability Reporting Centre.[183] There they present their approach to reporting, as well as vast amounts of data for further exploration in a structured and well packaged manner. This is presented in three sections, that all aim to support their credibility as a sustainability leader:

A) Sustainability data and metrics
B) Policies and management approach
C) Reporting, standards and archive

Sometimes it is easier than we think. Being well structured and trans-parent is a good start.

This closes the first level of the StepUp Framework and brings us to the next, which focuses on exploration and innovation.

 **NOTE TO SELF**

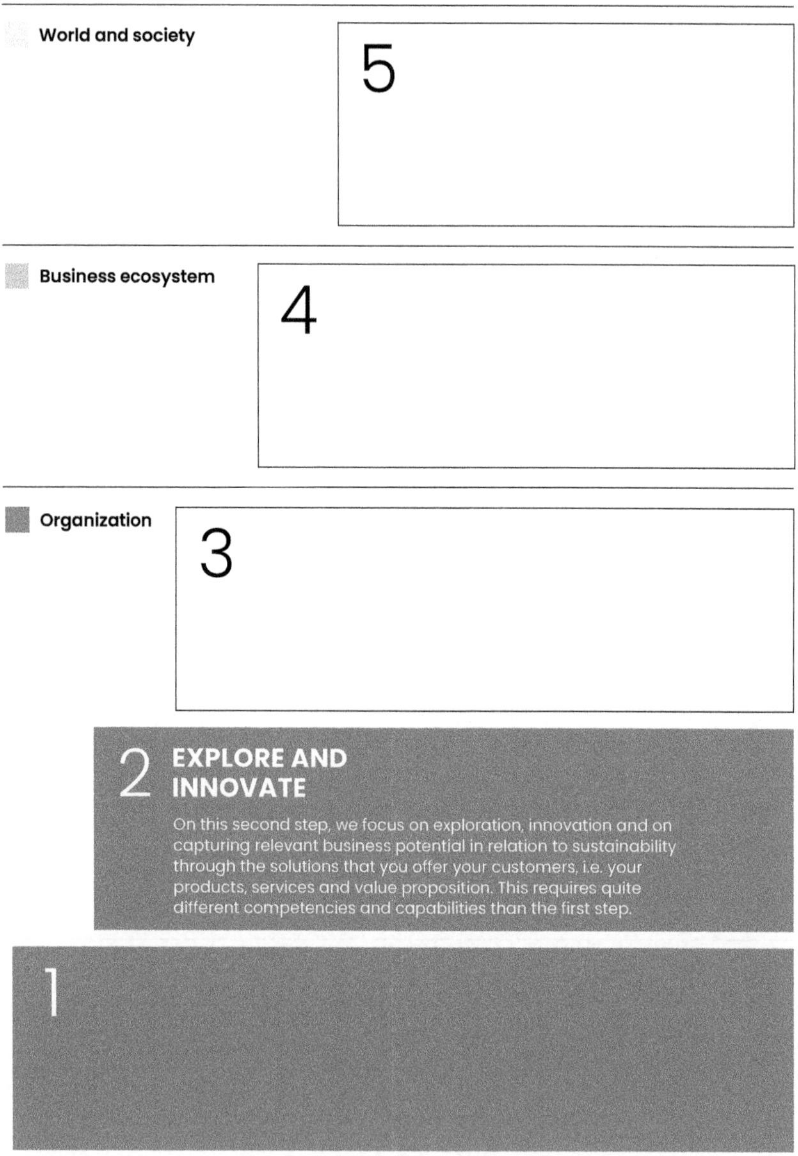

World and society

5

Business ecosystem

4

Organization

3

2 **EXPLORE AND INNOVATE**

On this second step, we focus on exploration, innovation and on capturing relevant business potential in relation to sustainability through the solutions that you offer your customers, i.e. your products, services and value proposition. This requires quite different competencies and capabilities than the first step.

1

FIGURE 32

The StepUp framework's second step of Better Business transformation: explore and innovate.

STEP 2
EXPLORE AND INNOVATE

On this second step of the StepUp Framework, 'Explore and Inno-vate', we focus on exploration, innovation and capturing relevant business potential in relation to sustainability through the solutions that you offer your customers, i.e., your products, services and value proposition. As such, this requires quite different competencies and capabilities than the first step, even though sustainability expertise is still an important enabler.

Innovation is about staying relevant and attractive and renewing your company over time. Innovation can be many things. It can be break-through innovation, disruptive innovation or sustaining innovation. It can be related to products, services or business models, but also to any other part of a business, such as brands (what you promise and how you communicate), process (the systematic activities that help deliver on the company's offering), structure (how you organize your company's assets and resources to create value) and profit models (how you make money).

But why focus on *exploration*? This is actually a prerequisite for in-novation. And exploration and innovation need each other—especial-ly in times of change and disruption. The first part of an exploratory journey may even take place before a clear company strategy is in place. It is simply about systematically scouting for, and understanding potential problems to solve, and identifying potential business opportunities and future bets.

In this step, your team will need to dig deeper into megatrends and other types of emerging trends, create an understanding of relevant wicked problems, and strive to understand your customers jobs-to-be-done, ideate and prototype new concepts, sketch out relevant business models, and run tests and experiments to validate them—most often long before they can define the actual business case.

Ultimately, exploration and innovation are the keys to corporate renewal and longevity. In fact, all companies need to optimise the core and explore the future in parallel. Ideally this is of course combined with a clear strategic direction. Think about Ørsted again. Their strategic decision to explore the business opportunities of offshore wind farms was indeed a brave move at the time that the decision was taken. Their innovation was not about the technology, however, but rather about the business model and the way they financed it.

Interestingly, most of the companies I have studied at the frontlines of Better Business are not regarded as world-class in rankings of the world's most innovative companies. Instead, the top 10 most innovative companies in 2021 (according to a study by Boston Consulting Group) had a distinctly digital feel and background, starting with Apple, Alphabet and Amazon.[184] Only Microsoft (#4), Tesla (#5) and IKEA (#32) match the criteria for this book. Apple (#1) has also come far when it comes to sustainability, at least according to their ESG ratings. This innovation gap most probably means that there is an opportunity to focus on exploration and innovation in this field.

Traditional product or technology-driven innovation will, however, not alone transform our world to the better. We will also need to look for new business models as the means to create the necessary transformations. As stated by Stefan Schaltegger and his colleges in a relevant research paper, "...the usual approaches to sustainable development of philanthropy, corporate social responsibility, and technological process and product innovation are insufficient to create the necessary radical transformation of organizations, industries, and societies toward genuine, substantive sustainable development." [185]

Today we do not only have a need for innovation and business model innovation, but for more *meaningful innovation* that helps solve the wicked problems faced by humanity. It is not enough to reduce harm, instead we need to start thinking about how to solve the really big problems. Tesla has understood this – which has sparked the wheel of change across the whole automotive industry. You could of course argue that small volumes of luxury electric cars are hardly any better for the environment than the alternative. But remember the technology cycle (see Figure 17): what starts out as being exclusive for only a few ultimately reaches scale effects which enables a mass-market approach. Replacing traditional cars with its electric equivalent will indeed need to be part of the solution to a wicked problem, i.e., climate change.

This is important. Because much of the innovation efforts of today, in reality, bring very little or no added value for the planet and humanity. The world is actually full of meaningless innovations and failed innovation efforts. Ideally, innovation would help remove problems and simplify life for its users in a meaningful way, reducing complexity and making things easier. That's why customer insight is key. Truly meaningful innovation, however, requires more than understanding human needs in the context of the design challenge. Rather, it emerges as solutions to problems found at the intersection between the world's wicked problems, human needs, useful technology, and impact business models (ideally circular, and even regenerative), as shown in Figure 33.

Going forward, meaningful innovation should always start at the intersection between human needs and wicked problems and aim to identifying new potential ways to addressing these dilemmas. Then, useful and applicable technology should be developed and put into use in a sustainable way. And finally, impact business models (ideally circular or even regenerative) should be developed, tested, deployed and continuously challenged and improved. The business model should also safeguard the value creation for the company as well as for other relevant stakeholders.

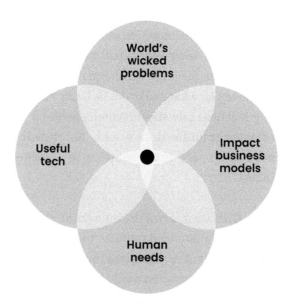

FIGURE 33

The sweet spot of meaningful innovation can be found in the intersection of human needs, the world's wicked problems, useful tech, and new business models.

Due to its complexity, the concept of meaningful innovation demands both knowledge and insight into all four dimensions: the world's wicked problems, human needs, useful technology and impact business models. This implies that a traditional innovation team will not be able to achieve this on its own. Instead, truly meaningful innovation can be most effectively pursued in cross-functional teams with diverse backgrounds and competencies spanning across the relevant areas, having an understanding of the SDGs and working in open innovation efforts with experts, or in different types of unconventional strategic partnerships and collaborations. To speed up the process, an alternative is to partner with, or even acquire, a promising new player in a relevant field. This should, however, be regarded as a complement to driving your own exploration and innovation agenda, rather than as a substitute.

A summary of good practices in this important step of exploration and innovation are:

- Strategically deciding to pursue meaningful innovation in the direction of Better Business.
- Understanding the concept of wicked problems and identifying relevant business opportunities connected to the SDGs.
- Being open, curious and continuously scouting emerging trends and opportunities.
- Reviewing your current portfolio and identifying how it could be systematically revitalized from a sustainability perspective and put to use in a more impactful and sustainable business model (e.g., circular).
- Designing sustainability and circularity into your products and adding maintenance services to support long life.
- Developing sustainability brands (i.e., brand innovation).

BETTER FUTURE

- Developing impact business models from scratch.
- Systematically exploring your value chain to identify potential innovation areas (e.g., process innovation).
- Start working as an ambidextrous organization that has the capacity to optimize the "old" core and explore the future in parallel, while redistributing resources to the strategically prioritized future growth areas.
- Collaborating with external partners to solve problems across your value chain.
- Learning fast through collaboration, testing and experimentation.

IKEA is a great example of living many of these practices. Let us now take a look at their recent focus on innovations for circularity.

GOOD PRACTICE EXAMPLE:
INNOVATIONS FOR CIRCULARITY AT IKEA

In line with their frugal mindset, IKEA has always been working on finding new innovative ways to reduce the use and cost of resources, albeit in a business model adapted to the traditional take-make-dispose logic of our consumer society.

Today, IKEA has realised that its linear business model and offering will not be sustainable going forward. To address the challenge, they have involved stakeholders across the company and beyond to innovate for a circular economy, with the goal of being fully circular by 2030. They have also entered a strategic partnership with the Ellen McArthur Foundation, a global thought leader on the circular economy. They have even created their own Circular Design Guide, which is openly available on their website.[186]

As a start in this important shift towards a circular business model, they assessed more than 9,500 articles to get a clearer picture of their status and their capabilities. One important insight turned out to be that all product types—from the big and bulky furniture to the many small, decorative products—had the potential to become circular. Material choice and how materials are combined turned out to be a key enabler, as well as designing for standardization and adaptability to enable maintenance and repair possibilities with standardized parts and remanufacturing by reusing parts in other products.

As part of their newfound focus on circular business model, they then defined four circular loops: reuse, refurbishment, remanufacturing and recycling, as shown in Figure 34.

"Reuse refers to how we describe the customer use of the product and includes all aspects of normal product use and care."

"Refurbishment is the process by which used, damaged or non-compliant IKEA products are restored to "like-new" condition with limited improvements."

"Remanufacturing of products is a process by which usable parts from dismantled products are utilized in the production of new products, increasing resource recovery and potentially lowering the cost for the IKEA business."

"Recycling is the process by which parts from products are transformed into new raw materials, which can then be utilized within the IKEA business or external supply chains. This is the last step for every product part." [188]

A few years into this journey, IKEA has already made important progress. Testing and experimentation with new concepts has been an im-

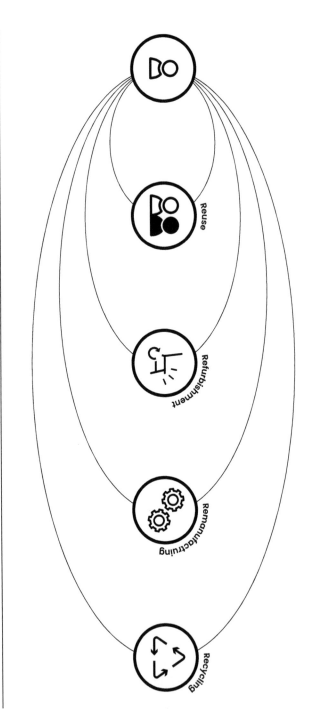

FIGURE 34

The four circular loops defined by IKEA. [187]

portant key. They have already decided to make more than 14 million spare parts easily available via convenient and easy-to-use online ordering solutions. This will make it easier for consumers to maintain and repair their products and increase their span of life. A few other concepts that they have tested and experimented with so far are refurbishments of sofas, furniture as a service and buy-back furniture.

Even though IKEA's approach to the circular economy may sound truly interesting, the company has even higher ambitions when it comes to its future exploration and innovation. Let me introduce you to Space10.

GOOD PRACTICE EXAMPLE: SPACE10

Any respectable company today seems to have an innovation hub for different types of breakthrough innovation that is not necessarily tightly connected to the current core of the company. So does IKEA. Space10 is their independent research and design lab, located in Copenhagen, Denmark, about one and a half hours' drive from their head office in Älmhult, Sweden, and a forty-five-minute drive from their international hub in Malmö, Sweden. They recently also opened a Space10 hub in India.

Space10 was founded to bring new perspectives and design new solutions that enable IKEA to live up to its promise of creating a better everyday life for people and the planet. In short, they research and design innovative solutions to some of the major societal changes expected to affect people and our planet in the years to come. Their projects include research and experiments into urban futures, the future of food, clean energy and technology at home, including digital safety and security. In one of their projects, called Everyday Experiments, they led a series of 18 experiments to answer the question, "How will tomorrow's technologies redefine the way we live at home?" In another project, they teamed up with a partner to create a book that gathered world-renowned experts to explore a better urban future for humanity. In yet another project, they concluded that the only way you can make sustainability win is if you make it more desirable than the alternative.

/ The only way you can make sustainability win is if you make it more desirable than the alternative /

With these short examples, I believe it is clear that IKEA aims to not only build circular offerings and business models, but also to explore new frontiers for both people and planet to survive and thrive far into the future. Exploration and meaningful innovation will be absolutely critical to getting there.

Let us now invite Too Good To Go to explore if businesses really can be designed to solving the worlds wicked problems through business model innovation. Because business model innovation does not only happen in the innovation labs of large corporations, but even more so in the startup world. Having been a pro bono mentor and guest lecturer for young entrepreneurs at the Master's degree program of Entrepreneurship and Innovation Lund University in Sweden over the past ten years, I can attest that this is very much a reality.

GOOD PRACTICE EXAMPLE: BUSINESS MODEL INNOVATION TO APPROACH WICKED PROBLEMS

A third of all food produced worldwide never reaches our plates – and this food waste provides an interesting problem to be solved by relevant business models. In the light of this Too Good To Go was founded in 2016 with a business model that addresses truly wicked problems. The company is today on a mission to inspire and empower everyone to take action against food waste. Currently, they have a presence in Europe and the US and are growing rapidly.

By reducing food waste, this company aims to tackle three of the greatest challenges faced today by humanity with the increasing emissions, growing populations, and natural degradation:

1. **CLIMATE CHANGE.** Emissions are on a continuous increase around the world, and the global food system has a major role to play in this. A vast majority of the emissions produced worldwide result from the food system – not merely in terms of food production and emissions from landfills, but all the energy used to produce and transport the food. The reduction of waste has a huge positive environmental impact, and global scientists have assessed that tackling food waste as the *best and number one* solution against climate change and stop warming at 2 degrees.[189]

2. **GROWING POPULATION.** With a growing population, there is a major threat on food security and the possibilities of feeding the world population and future generations. The amount of food waste produced today is enough to end world hunger four times over.

BETTER FUTURE

Solutions to tackle the unnecessary waste will make
sure that all food produced is consumed.

3. **DEPLETION OF NATURAL RESOURCES.** Degradation and
deforestation to make space for food production is
happening at a drastic scale, resulting in many animals going extinct. Reducing food waste avoids the
deforestation of unnecessary farmland and prevent
greenhouse gas emissions.

Founded on the insights above, Too Good To Go can most simply be described as a marketplace for food waste, connecting consumers with
local stores and restaurants that have unsold food. Everything made
possible through what has today become the #1 anti-food waste app
globally. The app uses a geo-targeted map to show users the restaurants closest to them with perfectly good leftover food available for
collection – at a special time and at a good price.

Since their business model is largely local, going into a new market
the company usually starts in large metropolitan areas. There Too
Good To Go connects restaurants, bakeries, cafés, and supermarkets
that have surplus food to consumers who can buy it at a reduced price.
The food is perfectly edible and would have otherwise gone to waste
at the end of the day – food that is just too good to be thrown away.

Their business model is a win for everybody involved, as restaurants,
cafés and food businesses that sell their surplus food can generate a
bit of revenue rather than throwing their surplus away – and customers can buy their surplus food at great prices, before it becomes
unsellable. It's also beneficial for Too Good To Go, as the company
takes a commission on each transaction. On top they are addressing
one of the world's wicked problems, and food waste gets reduced.

Convincing traditional restaurateurs to change their processes however showed to be harder than expected and was real barrier in the beginning. After some testing and experimentation – and moving from a website format to the app their concept however took off. So far, they have entered more than 15 countries, more than 41 million people have signed up for the service. Since their inception in 2015 the company has managed to save more than 80 million meals via their more than 65 000 partners. The service is today not only limited to food services, but multiple corporations and industry giants are now collaborating with Too Good To Go to reduce their food waste. Some examples include Starbucks, Unilever, 7-Eleven, and Netto.

With this said, I just wanted to demonstrate that solving wicked problems can indeed be an integrated part of your business model innovation agenda. Why not giving it a try? If a startup with extremely limited resources can, you can. For anyone interested in exploring new and exciting ideas within the field of Better Business innovation, I propose a quick scan of the Space10 website, but also of the impact startups supported by the Norrsken Foundation.[190]

This closes the second step—Explore and Innovate—of the StepUp Framework. In our third step, we will look closer at how to integrate sustainability into the core of a business.

 **NOTE TO SELF**

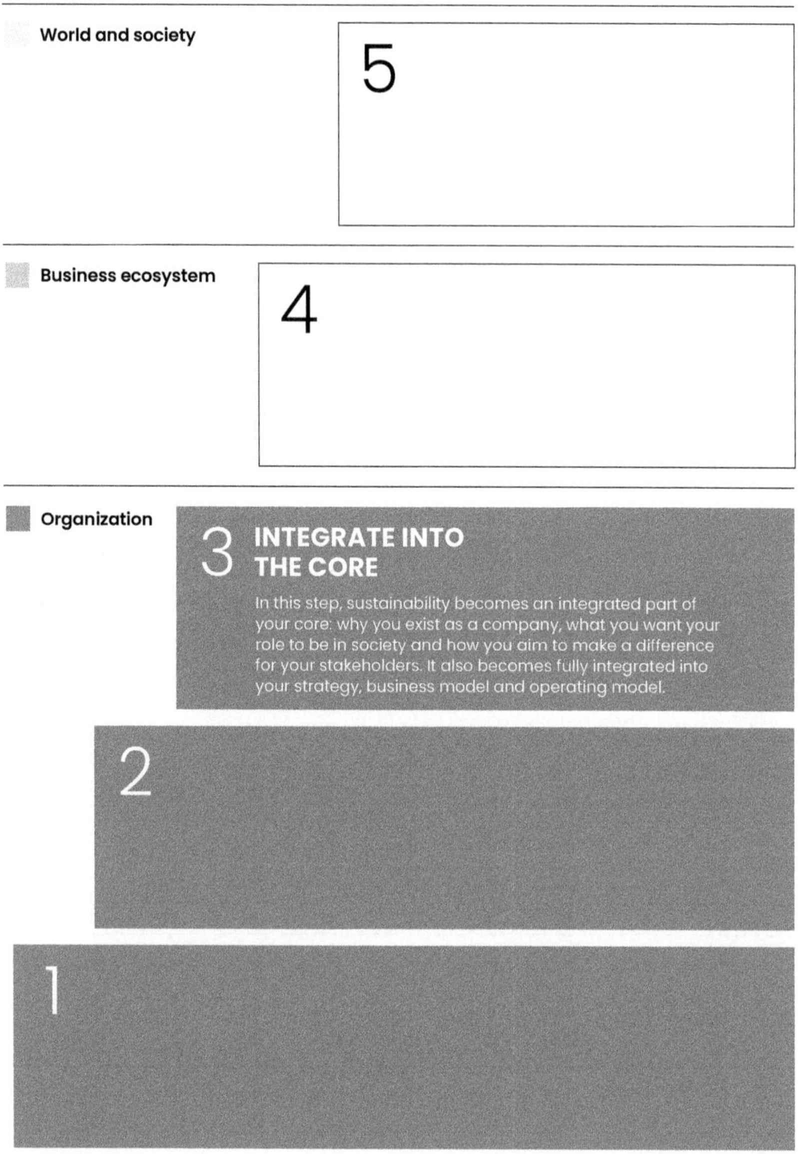

World and society

5

Business ecosystem

4

Organization

3 **INTEGRATE INTO THE CORE**

In this step, sustainability becomes an integrated part of your core: why you exist as a company, what you want your role to be in society and how you aim to make a difference for your stakeholders. It also becomes fully integrated into your strategy, business model and operating model.

2

1

FIGURE 35

The StepUp framework's third step of Better Business transformation: integrate into the core.

STEP 3
INTEGRATE INTO THE CORE

We have now come to the third step of the StepUp Framework: Integrating into the Core. This is a step tightly tied to why you exist as a company, what you want your role to be in society and how you aim to make a difference for your stakeholders. Sustainability here ultimately becomes an integrated part of your organization's overall purpose, values, culture, vision, strategy, business model and operating model. In short, it completely infuses who you are and what you do as an organization.

This step encompasses skills and experiences that are far from the competencies of an ordinary sustainability team. Rather, it is a transformational core-integration process in which the top team and the board of directors need to be highly involved. Why? Because this is a critical component to the success of any long-term transformational process of this magnitude. Also, the long-term development of the company is the ultimate responsibility of the board of directors.

Good examples on this level can, as we have already seen, be found with all of our six case companies, which have integrated sustainable practices and principles into their core. Some general examples of good practices observed in this step are, in summary:

- Living a higher purpose, which is embedded, aligned and integrated throughout the organization, its values, culture, business and operating model. It is not merely a strategy to create competitive advantage, it is a way of being.
- Having a long-term or even generational perspective (e.g., IKEA).
- Getting your people engaged and exited in shaping the future (e.g., Patagonia and Oatly).
- Actively building and managing a portfolio of sustainability products, brands, business models, and business units (e.g., Unilever).
- Strategically repositioning your business and brand to do good and create traction among customers and consumers (e.g., Patagonia and Oatly).
- Acquiring or investing in sustainability-focused companies or brands to speed up your transformation (e.g., Unilever).
- Becoming a Certified B-Corp (e.g., Patagonia).

What struck me when doing the research for this step is that only a few businesses are taking the opportunity that a higher purpose present. As late as 2017, most companies with a purpose had not related it to sustainable development, and only a few had truly embedded it in their strategy. A Deloitte report says: "While two-thirds of large businesses have a purpose of some description, only a quarter make an explicit link with a wider social, environmental or economic goal. Of those which link the purpose with sustainable development, half explicitly embed the purpose in strategy."[191] Research shows that companies linking sustainable development and commercial success have better long-term financial returns. A higher purpose simply provides a business with a platform for engagement with stakeholders, be they employees, consumers or investors. Also, it provides a North

Star for the organization to inform the highest levels of decision making, direction and strategy, as well as everyday operations.

Our six case companies all have higher purposes that point us in the direction of the greater good – for the future of our planet and humanity. The purpose statements of the top 10 global sustainability leaders in the SustainAbility survey by GlobeScan are equally powerful and can be found in Appendix 4.

- **PATAGONIA** – "To save our home planet"
- **IKEA GROUP** – "To create a better everyday life for the many people"
- **INTERFACE** – "Lead industry to love the world"
- **UNILEVER** – "Making sustainable living commonplace".
- **ØRSTED** – "Let's create a world that runs entirely on green energy."
- **OATLY** – "Oatly exists in order to create, and inspire others to create, global societal change that benefits the planet and all of us that live here."

A higher purpose that is not integrated in the organization is, however, powerless. The term *integration*, which is often used in the field of sustainability (e.g., "integrating sustainability into the core"), is actually very similar to *fit* or *alignment*, which are proven and powerful enablers of business success, as shown by Jonathan Trevor in the book *Align* (2019).[192] The best aligned companies are normally the best performing because their leaders approach alignment as part of their strategy. In his book Jonathan says: "This means that they arrange all elements of their enterprise... in such a way as to best support the fulfillment of its long-term purpose." He describes alignment as "a tightly managed enterprise value chain that connects to an enterprise's purpose (what we do and why we do it) to its business strategy (what we are trying to win at to fulfill our purpose), organizational capability (what we need to be good at to win), organizational architecture (what makes us good enough to win), and finally, management systems (what delivers the performance we need to win)."

Viewing the process of alignment from a business and operating model perspective rather than thru the lens of the value chain provides a slightly different set of questions, as we will see in the next section.

THE FIT FOR PURPOSE MODEL

The Fit for Purpose Model (see Figure 36) represents five building blocks of better business, all built around its higher purpose. Any building blocks that are literally not fit for purpose (or aligned with the higher purpose) simply need to be aligned for you to be trustworthy – as a leader and as a business. Otherwise, you risk being accused for 'purpose-washing' as you do not live as you preach.

The model was specifically designed to help you strategically align the higher purpose of your business with your business and operating model. It also helps you zoom out from the StepUp Framework and answer strategically critical questions in relation to your business.

The model was inspired by my own 25-plus-years of business experience and the research for this book, but also by several business thinkers who have already created powerful 'business mind maps', such as Simon Sinek (*Start with Why*); Roger Martin (*Playing to Win*); Alexander Osterwalder and Yves Pigneur (*Business Model Generation*) Oliver Gassman, Michaela Csik and Karolin Frankenberger (*The Business Model Navigator*); the above mentioned Jonathan Trevor (*Align*); the Better Business Blueprint, and others. The model has already been used as part of client strategy projects

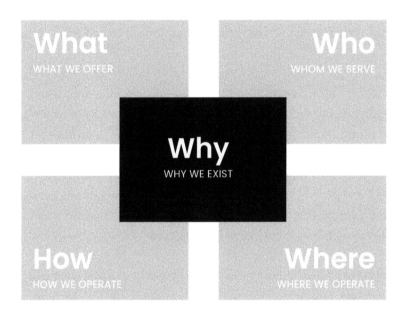

FIGURE 36
The Fit for Purpose Model.

and has been iterated through multiple rounds of client feedback.

The five building blocks of the Fit for Purpose Model are as follows:

1. Why the company exists (its purpose);
2. What it offers (e.g., value proposition, brand, products and services);
3. Whom it serves (e.g., target groups and key stakeholders);
4. Where it operates (e.g., geographic presence and channels);
5. How it operates (e.g., organization, culture, people and competencies, rewards, systems, processes and value chain).

As you have already observed in our case descriptions, an integration and alignment of the different building blocks have been necessary for our case companies to deliver on their purpose. They have for instance understood that you cannot have a sustainable value proposition if it is not supported by how you operate (that would simply be called 'greenwashing'). Further, they have understood that having a higher purpose that is not supported by your operating practices simply leaves employees cynical and disengaged.

Let us take a look at how to create the entry ticket to this level: a higher purpose. Following this, we will then apply the Fit for Purpose Model to Patagonia.

GOOD PRACTICE EXAMPLE:
CO-CREATING A HIGHER PURPOSE

There is no one way of constructing a higher purpose. One of the more relevant approaches comes from the University of Cambridge Institute for Sustainability Leadership (CISL). It was presented in their

2020 report *Leading With a Sustainable Purpose* and built through discussions and experience exchanges with five senior leaders from Unilever, Interface, IKEA Group, and DSM[193] The purpose statements of the books case companies are again as follows:

- **IKEA GROUP** – "To create a better everyday life for the many people."
- **INTERFACE** – "Lead industry to love the world."
- **UNILEVER** – "Making sustainable living commonplace."

These purpose statements may sound generical to the critical observer, but in the co-creation of a purpose statement, it is key that the purpose statement itself captures the 'sweet spot' for the business. According to the CISL report, this lies between:

- "The current or future potential for profitable long-term value propositions."
- "The domains where the trends point to opportunities to contribute to a sustainable economy."
- "Protecting and restoring the social and environmental dependencies the business relies upon across the value chain."
- "Optimising the company's distinctive capabilities, assets and offerings."

How would you then go about the co-creation of a higher purpose in more practical terms?

The report recommends that you start with an exploration of your external environment to identify relevant external trends and drivers for the business. Next, consult relevant external stakeholders on strategic issues and expectations of the business. It is then recommended to involve your employees and ask about their views as to what is already working well, such as what they value about the company and what their aspirations are for the company. It is also critical to engage the board to ensure a shared understanding, involvement and ownership of the purpose. That can be done through briefing sessions, workshops and regular meetings with a focus on understanding the external context and trends – and their potential implications for the business and its value chain, as well as general risks and opportunities.

You would then want to play back to employees what they have told you throughout the process (not just at the end) and share with them how this has contributed to your understanding and progress. You would also encourage ongoing involvement. You can also include questions about purpose in your employee surveys.

When you finally develop your purpose statement, you should make sure that it captures the domain(s) where the company's core capabilities can profitably benefit society: "Avoid trying to draft the specific wording during a workshop. This can be carefully crafted afterwards and presented back to the Executive team. The purpose should not try to be all things to all people but rather focus on the distinctive contribution the company makes to society and the world. A good purpose statement is often formatted into a short phrase that uses everyday language that inspires stakeholders, is distinctive to the business and specific enough to guide decision making while being flexible enough for local adaptation. The purpose can be tested and refined with external stakeholders."

The CISL report also gives advice on how to integrate your higher purpose into strategy and objective-setting in the next step, including throughout business unit and functional sub-strategies and plans: "Doing so aligns individual, team, departmental and functional objectives with the organizational purpose and strategy. This principle also brings the purpose alive by linking it to the delivery of commercial solutions that also benefit other stakeholders, such as customers and investors."[194] I have personally come to prefer a more conceptual model to visualize this high-level integration as a first step: the Fit for Purpose Model presented above. In the example below, we will apply the model to Patagonia.

GOOD PRACTICE EXAMPLE:
PATAGONIA'S INTEGRATION OF PURPOSE

You remember the journey of Patagonia—it started in business as usual and over time evolved into a Better Business. Today their business and operating model is completely designed around its updated purpose, which is to save our home planet.

In Figure 37, I have outlined the five current building blocks of Patagonia in the Fit for Purpose Model to identify how the different building blocks build an integrated and attractive whole. In summary, the five building blocks of Patagonia can be described as follows:

Why we are in business:
- To save our home planet.

What we offer?
- High quality, long-lasting minimalist style outdoor clothing and gear under the Patagonia brand.
- Added services for consumers to repair, share and recycle used Patagonia gear.
- Environmentalism and anti-consumerism as part of the brand identity.

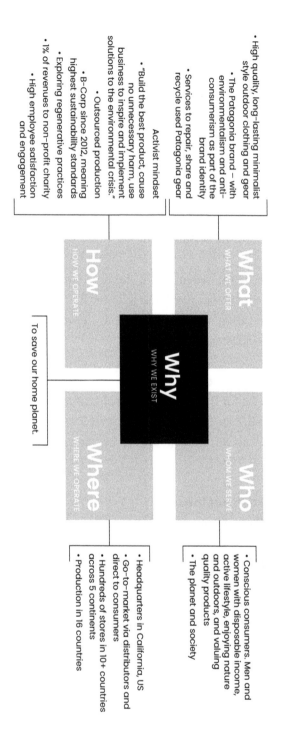

- High quality, long-lasting minimalist style outdoor clothing and gear
  - The Patagonia brand – with environmentalism and anti-consumerism as part of the brand identity
  - Services to repair, share and recycle used Patagonia gear

Activist mindset

- "Build the best product, cause no unnecessary harm, use business to inspire and implement solutions to the environmental crisis."
  - Outsourced production
  - B-Corp since 2012, meaning highest sustainability standards
- Exploring regenerative practices
- 1% of revenues to non-profit charity
  - High employee satisfaction and engagement

What
WHAT WE OFFER

How
HOW WE OPERATE

Why
WHY WE EXIST

Who
WHOM WE SERVE

Where
WHERE WE OPERATE

To save our home planet.

- Conscious consumers. Men and women with disposable income, active lifestyle, enjoying nature and outdoors, and valuing quality products
- The planet and society

- Headquarters in California, US
- Go-to-market via distributors and direct to consumers
- Hundreds of stores in 10+ countries across 5 continents
- Production in 16 countries

FIGURE 37

An overview of Patagonia through the lens of the Fit for Purpose Model.

Whom we serve?

- Primarily men and women with disposable income, valuing high-quality products, having an active lifestyle, enjoying nature and the outdoors, as well as the conscious consumer.
- The planet and society as a whole.

Where we operate?

- Head office in Ventura, California (US).
- Outsourced production in 16 countries.
- Go-to-market direct to consumers and via distributors, and reaching hundreds of stores in more than ten countries across five continents.

How we operate?

- An activist culture and mindset inspired by environmentalism and anti-consumerism.
- Operational focus on building the best product, causing no unnecessary harm, and in using business to inspire and implement solutions to the environmental crisis.
- Safeguarding the highest standards of sustainability (a Certified BCorporation since 2012).
- Experimentation with regenerative practices.
- Donating one percent of annual revenues to non-profit charities.
- High employee satisfaction and engagement, and 91 percent of employees saying that Patagonia is a great place to work.

As you can see, the Fit for Purpose model is straightforward and easy to apply. It helps to overview the whole and to identify potential misalignments. You can apply it to your business too. It will help you identify potential misalignments, and in building a more authentic, coherent and integrated business.

This puts an end to the third step of the StepUp Framework and leads us to the fourth step: Upgrade your business ecosystem.

NOTE TO SELF

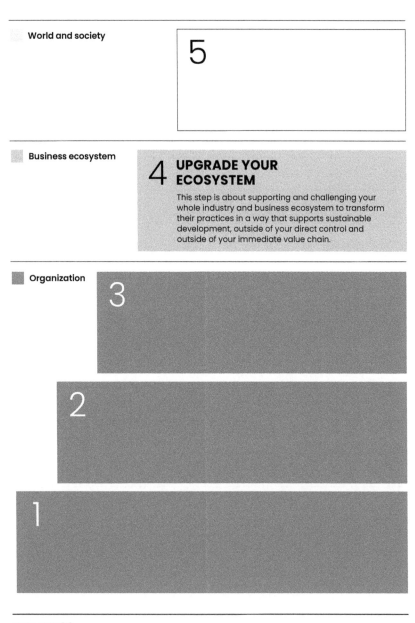

World and society

5

Business ecosystem

4 **UPGRADE YOUR ECOSYSTEM**

This step is about supporting and challenging your whole industry and business ecosystem to transform their practices in a way that supports sustainable development, outside of your direct control and outside of your immediate value chain.

Organization

3

2

1

FIGURE 38

The StepUp framework's fourth step of Better Business transformation: upgrade your ecosystem.

STEP 4
UPGRADE YOUR ECOSYSTEM

This fourth step is about challenging, supporting and ultimately upgrading your whole industry and business ecosystem in a way that supports sustainable and even regenerative development, both environmentally and socially.

As mentioned earlier, your organization is part of a larger human-made and natural system that I have here chosen to call your business ecosystem. For the purpose of this book, your business ecosystem is defined as a network of human-made organizations. It is made up of your extended value chain (e.g., suppliers and the suppliers of your suppliers as far out as to the producers and workers handling the raw materials you need; your customers and users; those responsible for the recycling of your goods at its end-of-life); competitors, substitutes, and new entrants; industry organizations; authorities, labor unions, investors, and other relevant stakeholders.

At this level, your first interest will most probably be to spark and accelerate the wheel of change in your business ecosystem, as suggested by Rebecca Henderson in her popular Harvard Business School course, *Sustainable Business*. This will be made possible by your work on the previous steps, where you have progressed enough to be trustworthy when sharing your experiences and learnings with your ecosystem peers to help them advance their practices, too. To enable your industry to become a force for good, you will also need to proactively cooperate with industry associations, authorities and even competitors to raise the bar for the whole industry. And as the factors of competition within your industry start to rise over time, you will need to continue to raise the bar even further to stay ahead of the curve.

Trailblazers on this step are companies such as Interface, Patagonia and Unilever. Why have they done it? Because this ultimately reduces the negative impact of the operations related to their business ecosystems and helps speed up the change that we all need. It has also made their work and brands even more credible, and safeguarded the parts of their value chain that are outside of their immediate control.

Good practices in this step for instance include:

- Mapping your enlarged value chain to understand its flow and key actors.
- Sharing good practices with peers across your industry and business ecosystem.
- Challenging your industry and ecosystem to step up and deal with its potential structural problems.
- Supporting your industry and the business ecosystem outside of your immediate control through knowledge, education and financial means.
- Cooperating within industry associations and other key stakeholder groups within your industry and business ecosystem to raise the ethics and practices of the industry, e.g., through self-regulation.
- Pursuing public affairs and building relationships with relevant authorities to speed up the development in

a direction that supports a better future, e.g., through stricter laws and further regulations.

- Becoming a thought leader and activist aiming to change your industry and business ecosystem.

In attempting to understand this step better, it often helps mapping or drawing out your enlarged value chain. Mapping the enlarged value chain and its stakeholders in more detail – including where problems arise – will help you understand where the real key issues of your complete value chain lie. For a tea or coffee brand that could very well be outside of their immediate control, e.g., in the farming and agricultural practices used for the production of tea leaves and coffee beans that they buy through distributors. When you are aware about the problems you can then work to find ways to address relevant issues more systematically.

In general, the food sector seems to have come comparably far on this step. A well-known and highly relevant Harvard Business Review (HBR) case on this step is Unilever's Lipton tea farmer initiative from 2011, where Unilever aimed to build a more sustainable supply chain.[195] A more recent HBR case (2020) is that of Danone, a Certified BCorporation and global dairy company striving to change the food system in the direction of regenerative agricultural practices.[196]

Rather than looking to these well-known food industry giants, we will this time, look to Paulig Group who was also early on the ball as they set out to support the business ecosystem outside of their immediate control in their coffee business.

BETTER FUTURE

GOOD PRACTICE EXAMPLE:
PAULIG GROUP SUPPORTS THEIR LOCAL COFFEE FARMERS

Paulig Group is a family-owned Finnish-based food and beverage company providing coffee, world foods, spices and plant-based options. The company has more than 2,000 employees in 13 different countries, with sales amounting to 920 million EUR in 2020.

Paulig Group is most well known for their coffee, especially in Finland. Coffee farming is, however, facing many great challenges, such as climate change and an insufficient income level for coffee farmers.

So, what can a company like Paulig do about that? They buy about 50 million kilograms of green coffee annually, which is equivalent to only 0.7% of the total world production. This nonetheless corresponds to the annual production of more than 75,000 average-sized coffee farms. Most of these coffee farms are run by families and ensuring a future for coffee starts with the realization that coffee farmers must be able to make a fair living from their work to be able to support themselves and their families.

Here, a win-win solution is sourcing certified coffee, or coffee from partnership programs where the coffee is verified sustainable by a third party. As to Paulig's experiences, this is actually the best way to ensure a sustainable and profitable coffee farming and support farmers.

Today, Paulig is an industry forerunner in terms of sustainable sourcing. In depth coffee knowledge, long-term relationships and continuous development have been key parameters here. Paulig's coffee sourcing experts have in fact spent a lot of time in coffee farming countries learning about the conditions in the farming communities: "We launched our first sustainably certified coffee product range in 2006. During that time, we started to consider the meaning of sustainability more broadly in our operations. In my job, I have visited many coffee farms and worked during Brazil in 2007-2008. I learned that sustainability in practice is about dialogue, cooperation and respect; all parties in the value chain must be doing well and receive sufficient financial compensation for their work so that the environment also does well", Katariina Aho, Director of Sourcing and Hedging at Paulig Group told Anita Laxén, who helped me document this case for the book.

For Paulig Group, these partnerships have been essential in driving progress towards more sustainable supply chains. The company has established several coffee partnership programs in cooperation with International Coffee Partners (ICP) – a leading promotor of impact-oriented support to coffee farmer families and youth in producing regions – as well as Coffee & Climate, Fairtrade and coffee export companies. To date, these initiatives have helped more than 100,000 coffee farmers improve their crops by implementing new farming methods while protecting natural resources.

Some of the key learnings from Paulig Group in working on upgrading their industry and business ecosystem are:

- Think long-term; change is not created overnight.
- Commitment from owners, the board, and leaders is a prerequisite to success.
- An engaged, committed and skilled team is key in making change happen.
- Build an ethical culture through values, ethical principles and code of conduct.
- Don't try to solve everything alone—build strong relationships with partners and through partnership programmes.

BETTER FUTURE

- Sustainable development increases pride and engagement among employees.
- Communicate, communicate, communicate.

Going forward, another huge topic for the future of coffee is climate change. Unexpected weather conditions have become more common and had an effect on both the quality and the quantity of the coffee crops. Extreme weather phenomena, drought and heat brought on by climate change have also introduced many factors of uncertainty to the sources of livelihoods of coffee farmers. If nothing is done, the question really is: Will there be any coffee in 2080? This brings the whole coffee industry's challenge up another level and makes the challenge even more pertinent.

In our next case, we will leave the coffee industry and instead move into waste and recycling. This will provide you some insights into how you can go about challenging a whole industry to change for the better (albeit in this case from a very basic level).

GOOD PRACTICE EXAMPLE:
A CEO DECIDES TO CHALLENGE HIS INDUSTRY

This good practice example originally comes from a Harvard Business School case about a new CEOs deciding to spark the wheel of change and to challenge his whole industry in becoming more sustainable.[197] I am talking about the waste management industry, which plays a critical role in the build-up of a circular economy and in addressing the increasing shortage of raw materials globally. It also has an important role when it comes to climate change.

This story starts in 2012, when Erik Osmundsen, who came from outside of the industry, was brough in as the new CEO of Norsk Gjenvinning (a Norwegian market leader) by their new owners. When accepting the position, he personally saw a huge potential in the future of waste management: – "I realized that our industry holds the key to achieving the circular economy—solving two global issues at the same time: the rapidly increasing global waste problem and the squeeze on the future supply of natural resources..."[198]

As he started to ride along with the waste trucks and spent some time at the depots, he however soon realized that the realities of the industry were far from rosy. It was clear that several rogue agents in the whole industry, including Norsk Gjenvinning, were disposing of waste illegally and entangled in other illegal practices. One study even suggested that 85 percent or more of all waste transported in the country was in violation of the regulations. A lot of waste was for instance exported to Asia (where we have seen plastic waste swamp rivers, oceans and beaches over the past decade) under unknown circumstances. In this competitive landscape, the price was the main lever as waste streams and associated services became increasingly commoditized. Hence, companies that attempted to abide to regulations were economically disadvantaged compared to those that were non-compliant.

When Erik asked about the behaviors observed, the explanations were always the same: "this is how it has always been done" and "everyone else is doing it". In a dialogue with his board of directors about the situation, he decided to act. Not only to clean up their own business, but the whole industry.

He started on the inside recognizing that willingness to change is strongest if it comes from a positive angle, employee yearning to reach a joint desired outcome and make a positive difference. First out was a new vision for the company: *"Our vision is that waste will be the solution to the resource problems of the future."* He also established a new

BETTER FUTURE

compliance policy that every employee had to sign. He then moved to zero-tolerance, where a violation of the policy would result in instant termination. Obviously not entirely popular move as almost half of the line managers and senior staff left the company in the first year – many taking their customers with them. When things did not move in the right direction, Erik concluded that he had to go public with the situation to change their internal culture. To his surprise no other company in the industry followed suit. Instead, Erik received a letter from one of the trade associations who threatened with expulsion if they continued informing the media about industry practices.

Erik then started to work on several fronts in parallel: industry peers, key customers, banks and investors, industry regulators and politicians, and the police.

1. **INDUSTRY PEERS:**
   Determined to make a difference, Erik reached out to leaders of three other waste management companies that had earlier shown an interest in changing the industry. Two agreed to publicly support Norsk Gjenvinning in their efforts.

2. **KEY CUSTOMERS:**
   Erik and his team also began to work on some of their key customers, where they made the case that corruption free operations would reduce their costs and risk.

3. **BANKS AND INVESTORS:**
   They engaged banks and investors across the country arguing that once legitimate business practices were in place – across the industry – investors would reduce risk and avoid the potential liability of hazardous investments.

4. INDUSTRY REGULATORS AND POLITICIANS:

Erik and his team also decided to educate industry regulators and politicians, as most were not aware of the problems and believed that organized crime did not play any significant role in the country. They simply launched an educational campaign to help explain the state of the industry. They also shared what the government needed to do to protect public interests.

5. THE POLICE:

Finally, Erik and his team started working actively in supporting and educating the police, as they had learned to identify signals of corrupt business practices that the police could benefit from.

These were probably not perceived as very popular moves by the majority of industry peers, who were now pushed to change and improve their practices from all sides, but as Erik said: -"We are not talking this industry down. We are talking about the truth. At the end of the day, this will bring the industry up."[199]

So, what happened next? Despite being threatened along the way, Erik stayed in the position as CEO for nine years and managed to transform Norsk Gjenvinning into one of Norway's more reputable companies. He also led a Nordic expansion of the company's sustainable recycling and waste treatment solutions. Erik has today moved on to a position as Partner at Verdane, a specialist growth equity investor. He is also a member of the Norwegian Ministry of Climate and Environment's Climate Council. From Verdane's website we get a brief insight into his journey: "Erik joined Verdane's Oslo office as a partner in 2021. He has more than two decades of experience as a chief executive, investment professional, board member, and sustainability expert with a proven ability to turn sustainability into competitive advantage and financial results... Driven by the firm belief that sustainable business practices can create competitive advantage for companies, Erik is widely acknowledged for his strong execution ability based on aligning interest in operations with solid overall strategic direction setting, both through line management and team work, and his solid track record in building company reputation and corporate culture."[200]

Despite the turmoil that Erik's initiatives must have created across the Norwegian waste management and recycling industry at the time, I am convinced that it ten years later (2012 vs. 2021) is in much better shape. More CEOs with the ethics, insights, guts and persistence of Erik would most certainly be able to make a meaningful difference and help their industries step up across the globe.

And what about Norsk Gjenvinning? It remains a reputable market leader of its industry and is today owned by Summa Equity, who on their website describe themselves as an investment firm defined by a purpose to address the global challenges: "We focus on companies in industries supported by megatrends within three themes: Resource Efficiency, Changing Demographics and Tech-Enabled Business. Our investments across the three themes have the potential for long term sustainable outperformance because they address some of the social, environmental, and business challenges we need to solve as a society."[201]

This now leads us to the fifth and final step of the StepUp framework: Collaborate to change the world.

NOTE TO SELF

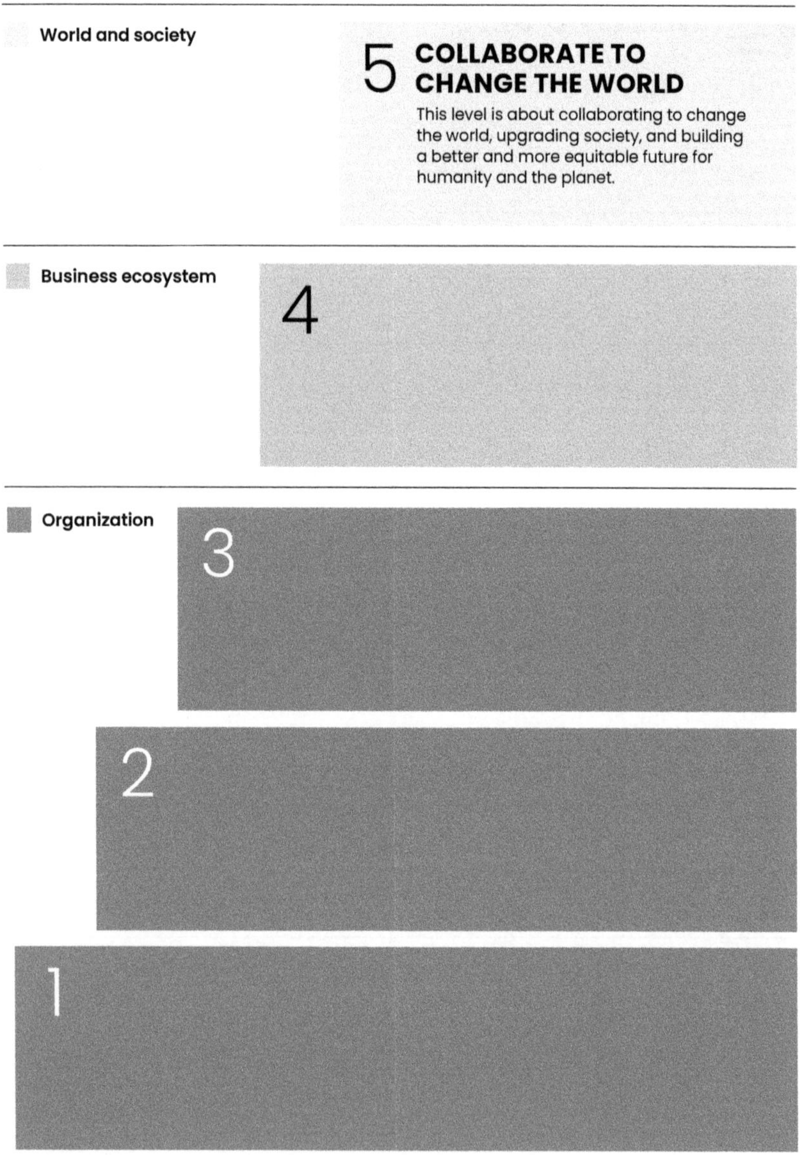

World and society

5 COLLABORATE TO CHANGE THE WORLD

This level is about collaborating to change the world, upgrading society, and building a better and more equitable future for humanity and the planet.

Business ecosystem

4

Organization

3

2

1

FIGURE 39

The StepUp framework's fifth step of Better Business transformation: aspire to change the world.

STEP 5
COLLABORATE TO CHANGE THE WORLD

This level is about aspiring to change the world, upgrading society, and building a better and more equitable future for humanity and the planet. As such it is probably far from your current comfort zone and stronghold as a business leader.

Playing on this level requires an understanding of – and interest in – unfolding megatrends, wicked problems, and complex adaptive systems. Understanding the 17 SDGs and their background is a good start, but far from enough.

This level relates to everything on this planet that is outside of what we have earlier defined as your industry and business ecosystem: the biosphere and humanity, including human-made systems, infrastructures and organizations, such as institutions for global collaboration and development (e.g., UN Global Compact), international associations (e.g., WBCSD and the World Economic Forum), iNGOs (e.g., the World Wide Fund For Nature, and Greenpeace), and philanthropic foundations (e.g., 1% for the Planet Foundation, and the Bill and Melinda Gates Foundation).

BETTER FUTURE

This playing field also requires more of you as a leader, your team, and your organization. To truly contribute to changing the world, you will for instance be helped by a flair for systems thinking, a solid Theory of Change, and a series of unconventional partnerships to get things moving. Tools that successful iNGOs, NGOs and charitable foundations have been using for decades to identify the most efficient and effective use of their limited funding in relation to the impact that they want to create. You could of course also just follow your inherent values and inner ethical compass, as I believe is what happened when Patagonia started to support different grass-root movements supporting the conservation of the environment in the US. You may also be inspired to create a social movement as for instance Too Good To Go, the young company that we learned about before with the ambition to create the world's biggest movement against food waste. Possibly inspired by Greta Thunberg and her Fridays for the Future.

Some of the good practices observed in this step are:

- Becoming a member of UN Global Compact (as for instance IKEA, Unilever, Interface and Ørsted) – "the world's largest corporate sustainability initiative... to align strategies and operations with universal principles of human rights, labour, environment and anti-corruption, and to take action that advances societal goals"[202]

- Becoming a member of the World Business Council of Sustainable Development (WBCSD) as IKEA and Unilever for collaboration across multinational companies and industry sectors globally "to accelerate the transition to a sustainable world and to help make more sustainable businesses more successful." [203]

- Applying a systems perspective to understand the complex adaptive systems that you aim to change.

- Building your Theory of Change – and systematically working to create the systemic change that you want to see.

- Collaborating with iNGOs, NGOs, other foundations and academia – and across disciplines and industries – to address systemically complex challenges through unconventional and unexpected partnerships.

- Starting a foundation with a focus on the high-level systems change you want to co-create.

- Starting a think tank to impact policymakers and other relevant stakeholders through research, articles, books and reports.

- Investing in multiple impact startups and scale-ups, as they have already developed and tested solutions and business models that will help build a better future for the planet and society.

- Engaging in corporate activism to support grass-root movements (as for instance Patagonia).

- Utilizing your position as a business leader or CEO to build coalitions and collaborations on the global stage (e.g., Paul Polman during his time as Unilever CEO).

- Building a movement and nudging consumer behaviour into more sustainable ones (e.g., Too Good To Go and Oatly).

In our first good practice example on this level, we will look into how to potentially map and understand a complex adaptive system.[204] Because, as a systems thinker, you will need to understand complex problems holistically, from different angles and multiple perspectives.

GOOD PRACTICE EXAMPLE:
MAPPING THE FOOD SYSTEM

Creating a systems map will help you and your team to understand and navigate the complex adaptive system that you have set out to change (after having identified its boundaries). Understanding the system is of course also a prerequisite to intentionally changing it.

Now, we are all part of the food systems in our roles as consumers. Any company active in the food sector is also a part of the larger food system – and most probably "belong" to one or a few of the many smaller subsystems that they are active within. The food system is indeed extremely complex. It is in fact a complex adaptive system that is hard to predict. It accounts for roughly one third of all greenhouse gas emissions[205], and the vast majority of biodiversity loss on this planet[206]. Hence, understanding and addressing issues within the food system could potentially deliver substantial impact on a global level. Something that for instance Oatly has understood.

Systems mapping is an interesting way to starting this journey. To go about this, your team will most probably need the help of system thinking experts, as well as a diverse group of systems experts (in this case from different parts of the food sector).

A systems map can be done in detail, or in a highly simplified way to help visualize the complex and its interconnectedness – which in turn creates a common ground for identifying challenges and opportunities for intervention among identified stakeholders and collaborators.

A great example – which could be very useful in a business context – is the mapping of the global food system through a trend and foresight perspective that was performed by the RAND Corporation (a US think tank) as input to the UK Food Standard Agency (FSA). See Figure 40. As a background, the FSA is responsible for ensuring food safety in the UK and "to provide consumers with access to an affordable, healthy diet while being able to make informed choices about what they eat, now and in the future". In order to do this, the FSA wants to have a good overview and a long-term perspective on the global food system.

In short, the Rand Corporation used a horizon-scanning and prioritization approach, involving a review of available literature, as well as a series of interviews, and an expert workshop to identify the different system parts, as well as the overarching themes and subthemes. What emerged was *a foresight driven global food systems map* identifying many interdependent and interconnected features and trends, that in different ways could impact the future of the global food system and FSA: from new technologies, and alternative food production methods, to alternative proteins and synthetic biology, changing consumer behaviors and demand, contaminants, and packaging and food-waste.

The next step of this project was to map *systemic interdependencies*. Why would RAND choose to do that? Any system is complex in nature and has interdependencies both within and outside of the system that you want to try to understand. A map of systemic interdependencies tries to capture this in a simplified overview. See Figure 41.

BETTER FUTURE

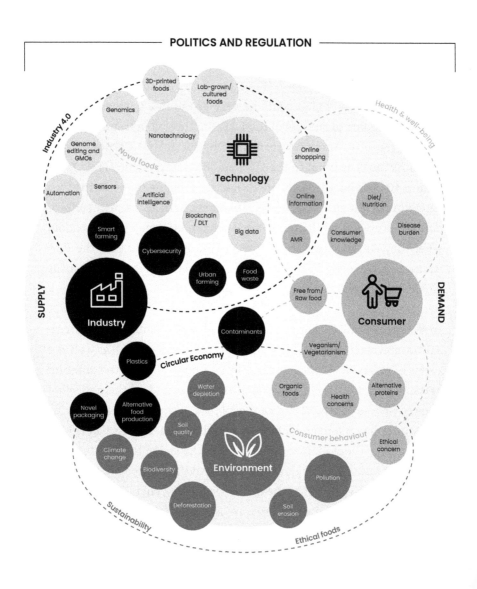

FIGURE 40

RAND's map of the global food system.[207]

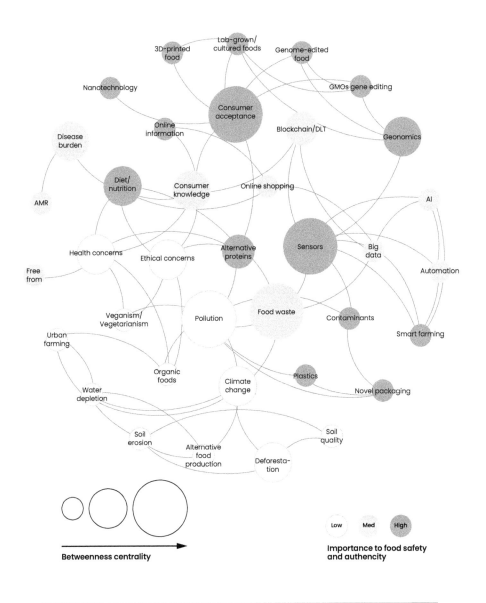

FIGURE 41

RAND's map of food system interdependencies.[208]

This map of the identified system interdependencies was then used by the FSA "as a tool to help place-specific issues in the context of a wider food systems network and to quickly identify pathways through which they could have an impact on food safety and authenticity. The map could help the FSA explore potential 'flash points' or cascading impacts, where a shock or solution to one issue may have wider repercussions to neighbouring and even distantly related issues."[209]

A company like Unilever could for sure use the same type of maps to identify potential risks and opportunities related to their relevant parts of the food system, including evolving trends, potential intervention points and future business.

In our next good practice example, we will stay within the food system and learn from a recently (2019) started a coalition of corporations that decided to join forces to change the broken food system and help heal the planet.

GOOD PRACTICE EXAMPLE:
FORMING A COALITION TO CHANGE THE FOOD SYSTEM

By now you may have already understood that the global food system is one of the pillars of human life on this planet. Scientists, and even large parts of the industry, today seem to agree that the industrialization of agriculture practices and the resulting monoculture have been taken too far in the race for increased crops and lower consumer prices.

An initiative addressing the regenerative health of the food system is *One Planet Business for Biodiversity (OP2B)*.[210] This is a cross-sectoral and action-oriented coalition between a number of forward-thinking agriculture-oriented companies that was launched at the UN Climate Action Summit 2019 in corporation with the World Business Council for Sustainable Development (WBSCD). The companies involved are multinationals such as Unilever, Danone, Mars, Nestlé, Kellogg Company, Arla, and Mondeléz. As this is written in mid 2021, 27 companies have joined the initiative.

Interestingly many of the companies involved in the initiative have been involved in forging the unsustainable agricultural practices that they now aim to address. When Emmanuel Faber, then Chairman and Chief Executive Officer at Danone, formally launched the project at the Climate Action Summit, he was clear on what was (and still is) at stake: - "The food system that we've built over the last century is a dead end for the future. In essence, we thought that our science could change the cycle of life and its rules. We thought that we could engineer the life that we needed and kill the rest of the fields. The resulting monocropping consequences are standing right in front of us now. We depend for two thirds of our food, on this planet, on only nine plants today. And 40 percent of our lands are already degraded. In a nutshell, we have broken the cycle of life."[211]

The idea behind the *One Planet Business for Biodiversity* initiative is in short to join forces to promote biodiversity and catalyze systemic change. All engaged businesses have committed to take tangible actions to develop innovative solutions to protect and enhance biodiversity in agricultural systems. This for instance means working with farmers and other stakeholders across their value chain and product portfolios, to drive systemic change for the benefit of the people and the planet. They will approach this through three focus areas:[212]

1. "Scaling up regenerative agriculture practices to protect soil health."

2. "Developing product portfolios to boost cultivated biodiversity and increase the resilience of the food and agriculture models.

3. "Eliminating deforestation, enhancing the management, restoration and protection of high value natural ecosystems."

This coalition is not expected to come up with any quick answers to these wicked problems. Peter Bakker, President and CEO, World Business Council for Sustainable Development (WBCSD), however truly believes in the value of this long-term collaboration: "This coalition has specific and ambitious goals that will drive real change in preserving biodiversity. We know that the path forward will be challenging. However, I am confident that, over time, the OP2B platform will transform existing food and agricultural models and achieve a significant, positive impact for both healthy people and a healthy planet."[213]

Even though I personally truly admire this initiative, my business experience tells me that 27 multinationals in a coalition will not move at the speed of light, or even the speed that we as a humanity need to transform the food system. On the other hand, this type of collaborations can potentially create a healthy peer pressure where everyone involved wants to perform and to be seen as 'the good guy'. If nothing else, this will help them safeguard their own value chains and make them fit for the future while doing good for humanity and the planet in the process.

This leads us to the end of this good practice example and the beginning of the next. This time we are going to explore the work of an innovative non-profit 'think and do tank' and how they approach the wicked problems and systemic challenges with a hands-on methodology in a more agile fashion than that of a global coalition of multinationals.

GOOD PRACTICE EXAMPLE:
AXFOUNDATION

Starting out in 1993 as a foundation supporting scientific research on sustainable development in Sweden, Axfoundation has today grown into something of a "think-and-do-tank" that works hands-on towards a sustainable society. [214] They see themselves as collaborators and bridges between different areas of society, where their role is to bring people together. On their website, they write, "We are confident that broad collaborations between relevant actors in society can solve complex problems. Our position as an independent and non-profit player with strong networks in several sectors enables us to form a bridge between parties who would likely not otherwise cooperate. Axfoundation's work is always knowledge based and we work together with over 40 researchers to find solutions to complex business problems and ensure our ventures and results are research based."[215] When talking to their Secretary General, Maria Smith, about their focus areas and approach, I came to realise that this 'think-and-do-tank' applies many of the good practices that I had already then identified on this step of the StepUp Framework. Especially:

- Applying a systems perspective to understand the complex adaptive systems that you aim to change.
- Collaborating with stakeholders across disciplines and industries – to address systemic change through unconventional and unexpected partnerships.

- Aiming to impact policymakers and other relevant stakeholders through research, articles, books and reports.

On top – based on their close business connection with the Axel Johnson Group and other parts of the business world – they also develop and test impact solutions and business models with a potential to alleviate or remove the systemic issues they have set out to change.

Their three strategic focus areas of today are:

- **FUTURE FOOD,** which works in three areas to address the problem: the protein shift, efficient use of resources and sustainable farming, and aquaculture methods. Central to the program is Axfoundation's operation at Torsåker farm together with academia and actors within the whole-food chain.

- **CIRCULAR ECONOMY,** where Axfoundation and its partners identify, pilot and scale circular business models, including future resource and material flows. To facilitate a mindset shift and speed up the shift towards a circular economy, Axfoundation is also bridging researchers and practitioners, and providing opportunities for collaboration across sectors and industries.

- **SUSTAINABLE PRODUCTION AND CONSUMPTION,** where Axfoundation collaborates with public and international bodies, as well as Swedish and international companies, on improving the working and living conditions of employees, migrant workers and smallholder farmers in global production chains. Axfoundation also tests and develops new methods, including possibilities with blockchain technology, for increased transparency and traceability along value chains to make it possible to detect and address problems, place responsibility where it belongs, and provide accurate product information to customers. Finally, Axfoundation also aims to contribute to changing consumer behaviour by assisting customers in making sustainable choices, both in the store and online.

What may be particularly interesting about Axfoundation for a for-profit business leader like yourself is the easily accessible, high-level overview of their hands-on approach (see Figure 42) to rather wicked problems. If you have worked in the innovation field, you will be happy to see that it is very similar to the ways of working of an advanced innovation team. Compared to the approach of IKEA's innovation hub Space10, the most important difference seems to be that Space10 focuses fully on fuelling the future pipeline of IKEA, while Axfoundation has a higher purpose than only fuelling its corporate relatives. The companies of the Axel Johnson sphere, however, participate in many of the projects and get to share their insights and opportunities.

Axfoundation has had very positive experiences from its approach to exploring new solutions to different types of systemic challenges through smart collaborations. For those who are interested, the outcomes of the Axfoundation programmes are presented in their yearly progress report, which is available on their website (www.axfoundation.se/en). There they also provide examples of when things did not go as planned. Because, as Axfoundation writes, "to innovate sustainable solutions and achieve transformative change, we need to have courage to fail." I could not have said it any better myself.

BETTER FUTURE

AXFOUNDATION'S APPROACH

Axfoundation's ambition is to contribute to transformative and positive development in society by exploring new solutions through smart collaborations. They work concretely and practically to bring about long-term change.

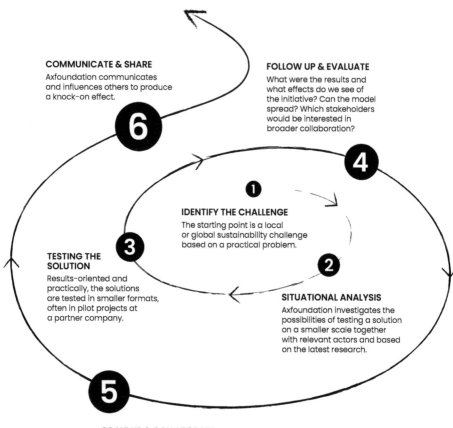

COMMUNICATE & SHARE
Axfoundation communicates and influences others to produce a knock-on effect.

6

FOLLOW UP & EVALUATE
What were the results and what effects do we see of the initiative? Can the model spread? Which stakeholders would be interested in broader collaboration?

4

1

IDENTIFY THE CHALLENGE
The starting point is a local or global sustainability challenge based on a practical problem.

3

TESTING THE SOLUTION
Results-oriented and practically, the solutions are tested in smaller formats, often in pilot projects at a partner company.

2

SITUATIONAL ANALYSIS
Axfoundation investigates the possibilities of testing a solution on a smaller scale together with relevant actors and based on the latest research.

5

SCALE UP & COLLABORATE
A small-scale solution can now be transformed into an industry collaboration, international collaboration or other types of collaboration with companies, researches, practitioners and public bodies. Axfoundation scales up with the goal of achieving transformative change.

FIGURE 42

The hands-on approach of Axfoundation in solving some of the local or global sustainability challenges they identify

Coalitions and collaborations are as we have seen instrumental in aspiring to change the world. You as a corporate business leader is however more influential than you may think. In our next and final good practice example of this book, we will briefly look into how a CEO of a large multinational built his own activist platform on the global scene.

GOOD PRACTICE EXAMPLE:
PAUL POLMAN AS AN ACTIVIST CEO

You as a corporate business leader can have an influence on this playing field if you have the interest and know-how to approach it – especially if you are a business leader in a large corporation.

Just consider how Paul Polman wisely utilized his position as the CEO of Unilever as a force for good. Under his leadership this multinational – as we have seen – set out the ambitious vision to decouple its growth from overall environmental footprint (doubling its sales while keeping its footprint flat), and to increase its positive social impact through touching one billion people and improving the lives of suppliers around the world. They also created a new framework for decision-making in the organization. A framework that brought in a multiple stakeholder perspective and long-term value creation.

During this time with Unilever (2009-2019) Paul actively also sought cooperation with other companies and different global bodies to drive systemic change. He was for instance involved in the development of the UN Sustainable Development Goals, and actions to tackle climate change; he was a member of the SDG Advocacy Group and promoting its cause and actions; he was the chair of the World Business Council for Sustainable Development (WBCSD); and he was a board member of the UN Global Compact; and much more.[216] He just seemed to be as comfortable on the big scenes as in his day-to-day job. How he had time for all this while being the CEO for one of the world's largest FMCG companies? I do not know.

Paul Polman is today the co-founder and Chair of IMAGINE, a foundation with the purpose to help combat poverty and climate change and mobilizing businesses around the UN Global Goals. He is also the co-author of the book *Net Positive* (2021), in which he and his co-author present how businesses can profit by fixing the world's problems rather than in creating them.

Looking at his career from the outside, it can only be described as a quite unexpected journey by this former Nestlé Chief Financial Officer and Head of Americas (2006-2008) who started his career as a cost analyst at Proctor & Gamble (P&G) in 1979 and stayed within that corporation in many different roles till 2006, for 27 years. An amazing journey, which can indeed help inspire corporate leaders from any background into doing good.

But you do not have to be Paul Polman or the CEO of a corporate giant to make a difference, even on this level. Business leaders in smaller – yet iconic – corporations like Interface (Ray Anderson) and Patagonia (Yvon Chouinard) may have inspired many more to change the world, especially in setting aspirational visions, challenging the status quo, and generously sharing their insights and experiences along the way. Yvon Chouinard has even co-founded several charitable foundations for the conservation of nature, whereof the most well-known is the 1% for the Planet Foundation. Also remember the many founders and entrepreneurs that now aspire to change the world through their impact startups, leveraging meaningful innovation, new technology and impact business models.

What is considered good practice will of course evolve over time and it is up to you to stay up to stay informed going forward. The world is indeed moving beyond business as usual.

We have now reached the end of the StepUp framework and are only a few pages away from the closing of this book with a few important words about you as a business leader. In our final chapter, let us also remind ourselves of what we have learned so far.

 **NOTE TO SELF**

CHAPTER 5

SUMMARY AND WAY FORWARD

This book was written for business leaders with a genuine interest in building Better Business. It is based on a rigorous search for a holistic, yet strategically and practically applicable perspective, and intended to inspire you to step up to the challenge of our lifetime, integrate sustainability into the core of your business, capture what may be the biggest business opportunity in our history, and co-create a better future for your children and the generations to come. I hope I have managed to do so by helping you understand the big picture that is unfolding and in sharing good practice examples from the frontline.

In the start of this book, you were introduced to the concepts of business as usual, Better Business and Regenerative Business. I suggested that Regenerative Business is where we will need to go over the coming decades, but that Better Business will help us bridge the gap from business as usual into the emerging future, and as such, help reduce risks and increase the likelihood of successful corporate transformations. I also helped you define some of the lingo often used in relation to sustainability.

You were then guided through some of the key drivers of the sustainability revolution. From the unintended consequences of the industrial revolutions and the age of the Anthropocene to the planetary boundaries, the Doughnut model, the biodiversity crisis and the steadily increasing amount of CO_2 in the atmosphere. We explored the concepts of wicked problems, social tipping points, inflection points and the role of technology. We also investigated whether we are currently stuck in a paradigm paralysis—between the old (business as usual) and that which is trying to emerge. Next, you were encouraged to rise to the challenge and move beyond business as usual. You were also asked to reimagine the future and consider how to capture this opportunity of a lifetime.

You also had the opportunity to learn from six companies already on the frontline of Better Business: Patagonia, Interface, Ørsted, Unilever, IKEA and Oatly. You were further introduced to models and good practices that will help you shape your own integrated Better Business strategy going forward – from the Three Playing Fields of Better Business to the StepUp Framework and the Fit for Purpose Model. You also learned that today's sustainability leaders seem to have a few things in common.

You were further introduced to 14 good practice examples presented along the StepUp Framework. A far more detailed and systematic checklist for those aspiring to uphold the highest standards in the field of sustainability and Better Business can be found with BLab. Their B Impact Assessment tool is open for all and can be used (for free and confidential) for an evaluation of your current practices and business – whether you qualify to become a Certified BCorporation or not. More information and instructions are available at: https://bimpactassessment.net.

WAY FORWARD

One of the most important conclusions that I arrived at in the research for this book is that only a few of the studied sustainability leaders (i.e., Tesla, IKEA and Microsoft) appear on the global rankings of innovative companies. The lists of top global innovators instead seem to be dominated by companies with a base in the digital revolution. Hence, there is still a tremendous opportunity for meaningful innovation in this field. A lot of wicked problems are simply waiting to be solved through exponential technologies, innovative business models and truly meaningful solutions. And as we have seen, even though a technology may look unattractive at first glance (due to high costs and small volumes) evidence from the past show us that what is a small experimental start can scale to become both efficient and effective with an innovative business model. Remember our example of solar photovoltaic, where prices dropped by 89 percent over the 10-year period 2009-2019. What started with extremely expensive solutions for satellites in the late 1950s has developed to a mass market product for regular households. Today even IKEA is developing home solar solutions to democratize clean energy. With this, IKEA wants to empower as many people as possible to produce and use clean energy and play a part in creating a better future for the planet. IKEA has of course not developed the original technology – they have simply applied it and found a viable and attractive way to package the value proposition with an interesting business model and an already existing market reach. This is of course good for IKEA, but also good for people and good for the planet. As such it is a case of '3W' – a Win-Win-Win. Something that we all will need to strive for going forward.[217] Here your existing market reach and customer base can for sure be used as a lever to explore and accelerate identified business opportunities.

As we have seen, not only large corporations are now exploring this field. There are also many venture capital backed impact startups driven by entrepreneurial spirit, personal values and conviction, purpose, cool technical solutions, innovation, impact business models, scaling to solve relevant wicked problems, and doing well by doing good in the process. This dynamic will most certainly lead to the creation of completely new markets, but also a number of low-end disruptions in market segments today underserved by incumbents—as has been the case throughout the digital revolution.

As the experienced corporate business leader that you are, I know that being disrupted would not feel like an attractive option. So, what are you waiting for? Not acting is most probably riskier than proactively exploring the potential. Even more so, the business opportunities available are in plentiful supply. Whether you decide to go for organic innovation and growth, a partnership, an acquisition of an interesting technology, brand or business model, or all in parallel.

To summarise the necessary strategic transformation for your corporation from a more general perspective, this is ultimately all about enabling the long-term relevance and attractiveness of your business in relation to its stakeholders. Companies that choose not to proactively surf the waves of the Sustainability Revolution simply risk becoming irrelevant and unattractive to their stakeholders over time. These laggards will be the losers in this game. The winners are instead both people and planet, as this process of creative destruction will wipe out the old while giving life to what needs to emerge. Managing this process wisely will also help investors steer 'old capital' into where it makes a true difference, as was the case in the example of Blackstone and Oatly.

Surfing the Sustainability Revolution takes an understanding of the world and society that is deep enough to identify relevant trends and wicked problems to address. You will also need to explore and understand how your business can best contribute to co-creating and shaping a desirable future. Not only for your organization, but for your ecosystem, as well as for the planet and humanity.

You will further need to co-create an authentic and meaningful higher purpose and supporting values, and a clear strategic ambition and direction. Further, you will need to pursue meaningful innovation to identify solutions for wicked problems, while in parallel transforming your old business with more sustainable practices, net zero carbon solutions, and circular business models. This takes engaging in fruitful collaborations inside and outside of your traditional industry as well as generously sharing your experiences and expertise to help others accelerate their Better Business transformations too.

Finally, becoming a Better Business will require that you connect your heart and mind, mobilize your people and culture and build a future-fit, creative, innovative and dynamic organization based on ongoing learning, experimentation and collaboration for continuous evolution. This will also help your organization to utilize its full human potential – your own included. You as a business leader are hence an important key to this purpose-led corporate transformation.

/ You as a business leader are an important key to this purpose-led corporate transformation /

12 GUIDING PRINCIPLES

Leading Better Business companies...

1 ... have a long-term view and see business as usual as riskier than exploring new ways forward.

2 ... show an interest in understanding the world around them and see the potential in contributing to the solutions of truly wicked problems.

3 ... take proactive measures to co-create the future.

4 ... proactively play on three systemic levels (their own organization, their business ecosystem, and the world and society).

5 ... have been through journeys of evolutionary change sparked by strategic insight, crisis, or even epiphanies – still, they continue to renew themselves over time.

6 … are guided by a higher purpose, which they have fully integrated into who they are and how they operate. Something that makes them highly attractive to talents.

7 … set high goals – or even Moonshots – and may even aspire to accomplish what others believe to be impossible.

8 … systematically work to improve their already solid foundations to further reduce their negative footprint.

9 … explore regenerative practices and meaningful innovation.

10 … apply transparent reporting practices and get rewarded by high ESG scores, which in turn attracts investor interest.

11 … work on challenging and supporting their industries and business eco-systems to elevate their practices.

12 … collaborate with others to change the world and society for the better.

YOUR ROLE AS A BUSINESS LEADER

"You can't stop the waves, but you can learn to surf."

JON KABAT-ZINN

This book has highlighted the importance of understanding your strategic playing fields in relation to Better Business:

- The organization itself
- Its business ecosystem
- The world and society

It has also suggested that you can expand your circle of influence as a corporate business leader to go beyond that of your organization, out into your business ecosystem, and beyond. With this expanded playing field you can share your experiences in a wider circle, truly contribute as a leader and leave a legacy worth remembering beyond your own organization. This most probably takes you far beyond your current comfort zone and out into the more challenging zones of learning and growth.

Therefore, we now add a fourth level to this playing field: *you*, as the potentially impactful business leader that you are with a responsibility to your stakeholders, and for bringing life to the higher purpose of

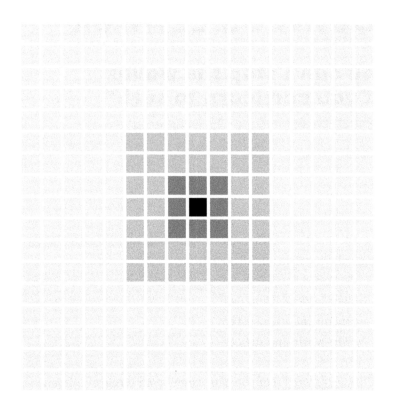

■ World and society

■ Business ecosystem

■ Organization

■ You

FIGURE 43

The four playing fields of a Better Business leader.

your organization - today and into the future. Even more so, with an ethical responsibility for the future of your children and the generations to come. And we are going to place you at the very center of this model (see Figure 43). That is how important you are!

Now, the question that remains with me is why not many more corporate business leaders have seriously moved on these opportunities so far—at least not very far beyond adapting some of their goals and corporate communication to suitable SDG goals or ESG metrics, and the soon to be mandatory NetZero ambitions for 2050. Could this even be an opportunity reserved for venture capital backed impact entrepreneurs with an idea that could transform the world as we know it? I do not think so. I think it is an opportunity that is open to us all. If we dare to step into it.

In my last book (Navigera in i Framtiden, 2018), I explored why companies have a hard time adapting to the accelerating change in their business environments. What I found is also relevant here. One of the largest traps seems to be success itself. Successful companies – and successful business leaders - simply have no apparent reason to change and no sense of urgency. Instead, a crisis is often necessary to propel an organization forward and catch it up with its ever-changing business environment. But even in those cases where a sense of urgency and motivation exists, the ability to change is still limited by the individual and collective beliefs and assumptions of an organization. This makes not only us as business leaders, but the whole organization, immune to change, as explained in the book *Immunity to Change*, by Lisa Lahey and Robert Kegan (2009). Identifying and dealing with those underlying beliefs and assumptions is hence critical to making change happen – on an individual level as well as on an organizational level. Let us take a brief chance to examine a common situation in relation to responsible and sustainable business.

BETTER FUTURE

In this case, you, as a corporate business leader, see what is going on in your business environment and have come to realise the need for change. You have even set out goals to move into that direction. The problem is that competing commitments and underlying assumptions hinder your progress and instead make you act in ways that do not support your overall goal. In business, such competing commitments are often the short-term focus of quarterly reports, reward packages and analyst recommendations. You might soon realise that your big assumption behind this struggle is very simple, e.g., that the underlying system is not rewarding your long-term ambitions and that your successful career may be damaged if you fail to deliver on these short-term expectations. It may also be a more complex realization of an underlying inner fear that you are not the right person to accomplish this transformation. That you do not know how to go about it but still believe that you as the big boss should have all the answers (which is, of course, not true). All in all, this pretty much means that you have a foot on the gas and a foot on the break at the same time and ultimately do not make progress towards the desired goals.

This is important. Because, as corporate business leaders, we certainly do not have to be passive bystanders or the victims of circumstance. We have the capability to change and even the capability to co-create and shape the future we want. Here, the potential of corporate business and corporate business leaders as drivers of change, mobilizing to reach sustainability goals and solve wicked problems, is significant and pertinent.

As always, there are leaders and laggards also in this race. Some business leaders, companies and industries will, as in history, fail to take action, become disrupted and fall into oblivion as they become irrelevant and unattractive to their stakeholders over time. Some, those that manage to capture the opportunity, however, will learn to successfully navigate the challenge to ride the waves of change and use the extra wind in their sails to positively contribute to shaping the future of our planet and society.

To a large extent this will depend on our willingness as a business leader to work on expanding our own consciousness to access our own full potential, including our ability to deal with an increasingly complex and uncertain world. This calls for us as business leaders to elevate our perspective, see the big picture and look beyond the horizon to imagine the future that we want—and collaborate to co-create it. Hence, the sustainability revolution will demand an equally transformative leadership revolution. Why do I say that? Simply because leadership research has shown that mature leaders at later levels of vertical development are more successful in orchestrating organization-wide and ecosystemic transformations, not only navigating but leveraging a VUCA world.[218]

Vertical leadership development is about an expansion of who you are as an adult and as a leader to utilize more of your full potential as a human being.[219] It can be described as an evolution from a conventional to a mature post-conventional mindset. Leaders with a conventional mindset may, for instance, struggle with limiting beliefs about what is right and wrong, get triggered by issues of the ego, singlehandedly focus on reaching their own goals without really caring about how they get there or how that could impact others or the environment, and in general have a hard time seeing the benefit of different perspectives. They also have a hard time sensing, changing and even navigating the system(s) that they are part of. Leaders with a mature post-conventional mindset have worked on their self-awareness and personal shadows to relieve much of the unconscious triggers of their egos; they are open to alternative perspectives; able to hold many points of view; can anticipate change and operate in conditions of ambiguity; easily navigate the systems that they are part of, and even co-create completely new systems.[220] And much more. Get the picture?

BETTER FUTURE

Disturbingly, research shows that only a small portion of the leadership community has reached this mature post-conventional mindset. As stated by the authors to the article *Elevating leadership development practices to meet emerging needs* in the Journal of Leadership Education: "Currently, less than 10% of leaders have the qualities of mind to optimally lead in volatile, uncertain, complex and ambiguous (VUCA) environments... This shortage of prepared leaders is often referred to as 'The Leadership Gap', a concept that emphasizes the growing difference between the leadership skills currently possessed by leaders in today's organizations, and the skills that are needed to solve the complex problems of the future..."[221]

/ Currently, less than 10% of leaders have the qualities of mind to optimally lead in volatile, uncertain, complex and ambiguous (VUCA) environments /

This is nothing that we can cure through the traditional leadership development programmes that dominate the current scene and narrative. Instead, we need leaders who dare to go on a personal evolutionary journey connecting mind and heart, resolving shadows and triggers, growing mindset agility, and growing the capacity to lead in a dynamic, complex and uncertain world. Accelerating Vertical Leadership Development is simply an important key to helping business leaders elevate their perspective, increase their positive impact, and move beyond business as usual. Ultimately to build a Better Business and a better future.

This is vital because vertically evolved leaders are seriously needed in solving the world's wicked and systemic problems. And you are crucial in this transformation. By growing vertically in conscious awareness, providing purpose, direction and resources, you can contribute to meaningful, purpose-led transformation, evolutionary growth, the creation of healthier systems—and help enhance the wellbeing of both people and planet, while future-proofing your own business and organization in the process.

Starting by asking yourself five key questions, inspired by Harvard Business School professor Cynthia Montgomery and her book *The Strategist*, will help you take a few first steps on the way:[222]

1. What does our company bring to the world?
2. Do we make a difference?
3. Are we relevant?
4. How do we add value?
5. How can we be relevant and add value in the future?

Then look yourself in the mirror and ask the next five questions:

1. What do I bring to the world?
2. Do I make a difference?
3. Am I relevant?
4. How do I add value?
5. How can I be relevant and add value in the future?

I would also add:

- Are you leading a purposeful and meaningful life?
- Will you look back from your deathbed and realize your life made a significant difference to the world your grandchildren will inherit?

Food for thought.

As you have understood by now, this journey ultimately starts with you. You are critical to any change and transformational process of the magnitude needed going forward. The more vertically developed and mature you are as a leader, the likelier it is that you will succeed in transforming your organization and in creating meaningful change for the benefit of all.

Here, what we are particularly looking for are business leaders with the willingness and openness to mindfully develop into what is often called the Strategist or Synergist level. A Synergist leader is distinguished by a mature post-conventional mindset with an expanded capacity to integrate the broader organizational and ecosystem context that they are surrounded by and an integral part of.[223]

After having read this book, you will have already expanded your perspectives and started to surf the waves of the sustainability revolution. Remember the words of Christina Figueres and Tom Rivett-Carnac from the very beginning of the book, "The future is unwritten. It will be shaped by who we choose to be now."[225]

ELEMENTS OF A SYNERGIST LEVEL BUSINESS LEADER[224]

When led by a *Synergist*, the organization shifts from being customer-centric to community-centric, or eco-centric. It succeeds in achieving medium- to long-term sustainable outcomes that make a real, significant, and beneficial impact on the people they serve and affect now and in future generations.

NEEDS/VALUES

The *Synergist* is defined by their capacity to engage more collaboratively, think more systemically, demonstrate more curiosity in relation to other people's viewpoints, actively step in to resolve conflict more readily, and look into situations with greater insight and discernment. They show a genuine interest in developing others and capitalizing on the interconnections across situations, regions, and cultures.

Causation is recognized as circular, relational, and systemic. The realization is that people share a common humanity, the same breadth and depth of emotions, dreams, hopes, and fears within, that make us a single human community.

STRENGTHS

At this point in their journey of increasing expanding consciousness, *Synergists* have become self-aware and other-aware and have the ability to be discerning and self-validating. They do not seek approval or permission from others. They have developed strength of character and their integrity is evident. *Synergists* have the vision, conviction, and presence to generate and sustain transformative change by standing up for what they believe in and articulating their perspective graciously and wisely.

TABLE 6
Elements of a Synergist level business leader.

NOTE TO SELF

> "Be the change
> you want to see
> in the world."
>
> MAHATMA GANDHI

SELF-ASSESSMENT

As we now close this book, I invite you to assess your own business in relation to some of the good practices of the Better Business trailblazers studied for this book.

INSTRUCTIONS	
a	Start by reading each question and mark the current status of your company. Are you a beginner? Have you made some progress? Have you made significant progress? Or are you even worldclass in the field?
b	Next, mark where you aspire to be five years from now.
c	Review you answers and write a final note to self about your current situation and potential next steps.

Visit www.elisabetlagerstedt.com or www.future-navigators.com for more inspiration and support.

1. LAY A SOLID FOUNDATION

	Beginner	Some progress made	Significant progress made	Worldclass
We understand our stakeholders, and their needs, concerns and priorities in relation to our business.	☐	☐	☐	☐
We have identified the key sustainability challenges along our value chain.	☐	☐	☐	☐
We conduct a materiality analysis on a yearly basis.	☐	☐	☐	☐
We set aspirational goals and science based targets in relation to identified issuess, connected to the SDGs.	☐	☐	☐	☐
We have a well working governance structure in place.	☐	☐	☐	☐
We work systematically to reach our sustainability goals.	☐	☐	☐	☐
We transparently communicate the outcome of our work in the field.	☐	☐	☐	☐
We explore regenerative practices along our value chain.	☐	☐	☐	☐

BETTER FUTURE

2. EXPLORE AND INNOVATE

	Beginner	Some progress made	Significant progress made	Worldclass
We work from an outside-in perspective, well anchored in trends and customer insight.	☐	☐	☐	☐
We have identified the business opportunities connected to the SDGs and global wicked problems.	☐	☐	☐	☐
We understand the life cycle impact of our current products and services.	☐	☐	☐	☐
We work systematically to make our range of products and services sustainable and circular.	☐	☐	☐	☐
We work on transforming the core and exploring sustainable future bets in parallel.	☐	☐	☐	☐
We explore new technologies and business models to approach wicked problems and new potential.	☐	☐	☐	☐
We learn fast through collaboration, testing and experimentation.	☐	☐	☐	☐

3. INTEGRATE INTO THE CORE

	Beginner	Some progress made	Significant progress made	Worldclass
We have a long term and stakeholder oriented perspective.	☐	☐	☐	☐
Our organization is guided by a meaningful higher purpose (i.e., why we exist).	☐	☐	☐	☐
We have an aspirational vision for 2030.	☐	☐	☐	☐
We have strategically repositioned our core business and brands to do good.	☐	☐	☐	☐
Sustainabilty is fully integrated in our company strategy, offering, business model, operating model and culture.	☐	☐	☐	☐
We are aquiring sustainability companies and brands to speed up our transformation	☐	☐	☐	☐
Our people are engaged and exited in the meaningful co-creation of a sustainable future.	☐	☐	☐	☐

BETTER FUTURE

4. UPGRADE YOUR ECOSYSTEM

	Beginner	Some progress made	Significant progress made	Worldclass
We challenge our whole industry and ecosystem to step up to the global challenges.	☐	☐	☐	☐
We share good practices with peers across our industry and eco-system.	☐	☐	☐	☐
We back change across our business ecosystem through financial means and support.	☐	☐	☐	☐
We cooperate with key stakeholder groups to raise the ethical practices of our business ecosystem, e.g., through self-regulation.	☐	☐	☐	☐
We work together with national authorities to help raise the minimum level of practices across our business ecosystem, e.g., through regulation.	☐	☐	☐	☐
We are considered a sustainability thought leader in our industry.	☐	☐	☐	☐

5. COLLABORATE TO CHANGE THE WORLD

	Beginner	Some progress made	Significant progress made	Worldclass
We apply a systems perspective to better understand the complex adaptive systems that we aim to change.	☐	☐	☐	☐
We collaborate with iNGOs, NGOs, foundations and academia – and across diciplines and industries – to address systemically complex challenges.	☐	☐	☐	☐
We have started a foundation with a focus on the societal and/or environmental changes that we want to create.	☐	☐	☐	☐
We engage in corporate activism to support grass-root movements.	☐	☐	☐	☐
We are part of co-creating a movement to help nudge consumer behaviours into more sustainable ones.	☐	☐	☐	☐
I am personally engaged in building coalitions and collaborations promoting change on the global stage.	☐	☐	☐	☐

BETTER FUTURE

NOTE TO SELF

_____

_____

_____

_____

_____

_____

_____

_____

_____

_____

_____

_____

_____

_____

_____

_____

METHODOLOGY

As stated in the preface, this book finally came to life through the discussions and contributions of an amazing network of business leaders and sustainability experts in the frontline of Better Business transformation and I have indeed learned a lot from our dialogues.

The first parts of the book are largely the result of my never-ending attempt to understand the world. A journey that started decades ago. Over the past decade it includes a broad literature and article review deep diving into the fields of global mega-trends, scenarios, strategy, innovation, transformation, sustainability and personal development. Even so, every article, every report, and every book still remind me of how much more there is still to learn.

The second part of the book is largely the result of my own business experience, combined with an empirical study of 40 organizations that have in different ways come far in integrating sustainability into their core and/or is proactively working to build a better future. This empirical study started early 2020 with a review of a wide range of articles, literature, reports and surveys to identify good and evolving practices in the field. This produced a first short report called the Better Business Playbook that was published in June 2020.

Being especially interested in strategy, innovation and transformation, I then decided to deepen this study and make the identification of good and evolving practices more systematic. After an evaluation of different ranking frameworks within the field of sustainability and ESG, I finally chose to use the corporate ranking of the *GlobeScan SustainAbility Survey 2020*, where 700 global and local experts were interviewed and specifically asked, "What specific companies do you think are leaders in integrating sustainability into their business strategy?"[226]

The other source I decided to use was the *CSRHub*, an easy-to-use online sustainability management platform that has rated and ranked more than 46,800 companies in 153 countries globally based on more than 700 sources relevant for corporate ESG practices and performance. They cover more than 99 percent of listed (publically traded) companies worldwide, and also provide high-level comparisons between industries. Here I mainly double checked the respective company ratings in relation to GlobeScan's SustainAbility survey to safeguard that they all had ESG ratings that were generally better than their industry peers. And indeed, most proved to top the sustainability rankings of their respective industries. Cynthia Figge, CEO at the CS-RHub, also helped provide a more general understanding of the overall ESG development of industries over the past ten years (as it has not moved substantially across industries).

This resulted in a selection of the top 10 performers on the GlobeScan SustainAbility Survey's list: *Unilever, Patagonia, IKEA, Interface, Natura & Co., Danone, Tesla, Nestlé, Microsoft* and *Ørsted*. Tesla and Interface did however not reach the high ESG ratings of the rest of the group (see Appendix 2). The others all have a long history and reputation of being good corporate citizens. Most have also gradually transformed their business models over the past decades in different ways. Five of these companies were apart from being part of the study, also selected for the book's case descriptions. This selection was based on my personal contact network and ability to access relevant in depth information about each company. Those companies were: Unilever, Patagonia, IKEA, Interface and Ørsted.

As a next step, I decided to add a strategic selection of differently sized companies that have in some way been recognized for their good practices in the field. Rather than focusing on any global company ranking, I here decided to focus on Scandinavia, as the region is globally renowned for its responsible companies and good practices within the fields of sustainability and innovation.

In this phase, I reached out to my own network for recommendations of companies that, for different reasons, have stood out for their particularly good, interesting and innovative practices, for their integration of sustainability into their strategy, and/ or for their high ESG ratings. I then decided to focus in on companies where I could potentially get a personal connection at the top management team level to enable a deeper dialogue for a better understanding of their strategic choices and operational practices. This resulted in a strategic selection of 20 companies from across industries, lifecycles, ownership structures and sizes to identify the widest possible spectrum of good practices among the studied companies. Information was retrieved from their websites, press releases, yearly reports and articles in media, as well as from the CSRHub (ESG ratings). I also had exploratory interviews with 16 company representatives (mostly executives) around their practices and learnings. These organizations were initially *Oatly, Max Burgers, TooGoodToGo, Nudie Jeans,*

Bona Group, Fristads, H&M Group, Paulig Group, Fiskars Group, Volvo Group, SKF, Thule Group, Södra (Building System). I later added *Scania, Electrolux, Danfoss, Essity, Vattenfall, Stora Enso* and *Norsk Gjenvinning*. I finally selected Oatly to be added to the case presentation based on their exponential growth and unique transformational journey in the field, and my own insight into the company from my work as a consultant.

Finally, the study also came to include a scanning of good practices of a selection of ten (10) forward-thinking non-profits in relevant fields. Why? Because some of their good and evolving practices can be an inspiration to us all, especially when it comes to the aspiration to change the world and build a better future. These were, *the B Lab* (providing the B Corporation Certification for businesses that meet the highest standards of verified social and environmental performance); *the Better Business Blueprint* (an independent foundation whose purpose is to create a better society through better business, and help business to be inspired and guided by a purpose that benefits society and respects people and planet); *1% for the Planet* (co-created by the founder of Patagonia, Yvon Chouinard); *IKEA Foundation* (IKEAs independent charitable organization); *Axfoundation* (a 'do and think tank' exploring local and global sustainability challenges connected to the Axel Johnson Group); *Ellen McArthur Foundation* (a foundation leading the exploration and development of the circular economy); *Norrsken Foundation* (with a focus on helping entrepreneurs to solve the world's greatest problems, founded by one of the co-founders of Klarna); *Ekskäret Foundation* (aiming to facilitate a more conscious and sustainable society, founded by the entrepreneur and Club of Rome member Tomas Björkman); *Cloudera Foundation* (part of the Patrick J. McGovern Foundation's focus on data and AI for impact as of March 2021); and *Animals Australia* (Australia's leading animal protection organization). Also here, information was initially mainly retrieved from their websites, press releases and yearly reports. I also reached out to some of their senior leaders and have had a rewarding dialogue with seven (7) representatives and leaders.

Note that I throughout this research aimed to qualitatively identify and cluster good and evolving practice and not to quantify any frequency of occurrence. This led to the design, testing and evolution of the frameworks and models that has been presented in this book. From this research I also selected 14 examples of good practices that I in the book present along the five steps of the StepUp Framework. These examples were selected based their potential usefulness to other companies, and to help the reader discover and understand some of good practices practically applied on each step.

Inspired by Thomas Kalling, Professor in Strategy and Innovation at Lund University School of Economics and Management, I made an effort to use a structured approach in developing the frameworks and models for the book. Namely a design thinking and research approach commonly used in Design Science Research[227] under the guidance of Camilla van den Boom at Eindhoven University of Technology, who is also a strategy consultant and a lecturer in Strategic Management at TIAS School for Business and Society in the Netherlands.

This approach can be visualized in *The three cycle view of design science research* by Alan R. Hevner, which starts with three blocks: the Knowledge base (i.e., what we already know), the Design Science Research, and the Environment. See Figure 44. The method suggests an iterative approach that circles back and forth within and between the three fields (the Rigor Cycle, The Design Cycle and The Relevance Cycle). As Alan R. Hevner explains it in his own words: "The Relevance Cycle inputs requirements from the contextual environment into the research and introduces the research artifacts into environmental field testing. The Rigor Cycle provides grounding theories and methods along with domain experience and expertise from the foundation's knowledge base into the research and adds the new knowledge generated by the research to the growing knowledge base. The central Design Cycle supports a tighter loop of research activity for the construction and evaluation of design artifacts and processes. The recognition of these three cycles in a research project clearly positions and differentiates design science from other research paradigms."[228]

This process was indeed iterative and involved a solid initial knowledge base coming from both own business experience, observations for the studied companies and literature; then sketching out (i.e., designing) the first ideas for the models; then testing their relevance and application with cases in the real world (i.e., the studied organizations); going back to the drawing board to improve on the models; check-ins with the knowledge base and already existing visualizations in related fields; back to the drawing board and literature for further iterations; and then back out into the real world and trying to apply it again. I followed this process, over and over again, till I felt that the models well mirrored a simplified reality of what I could observe, and till the models were easy to understand and apply, for myself as well as for those they were introduced to.

BETTER FUTURE

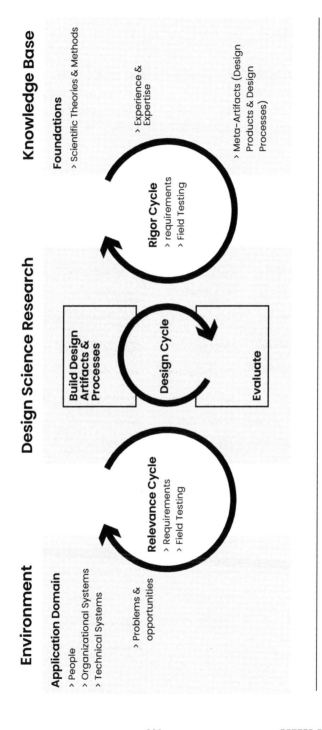

FIGURE 44

The three cycle view of design research.[229]

BETTER FUTURE

APPENDIX 1.

An overview of the 60 biggest (high-level) market opportunities within food and agriculture, cities, energy and materials, and health and well-being, related to the 17 Global Goals (SDGs) as to the UN Business and Sustainable Development Commission in their Better Business Better World Report 2017. [230]

SDG	Food & Agriculture	Cities	Energy & Materials	Health & Well-being
1	Reducing food waste in value chain	Affordable housing	Circular models – automotive	Risk pooling
2	Forest ecosystem services	Energy effeciency – buildings	Expansion of renewables	Remote patient monitoring
3	Low-income food markets	Electric and hybrid vehicles	Circular models – appliances	Telehealth
4	Reducing consumer food waste	Public transport in urban areas	Circular models – electronics	Advanced geonomics
5	Product reformulation	Car sharing	Energy effeciency – non-energy intensive industries	Activity services
6	Technology in large-scale farms	Road safety equipment	Energy storage systems	Detection of counterfeit drugs
7	Dietary switch	Autonomous vehicles	Resource recovery	Tobacco control
8	Sustainable aquaculture	ICE vehicle fuel efficiency	End-use steel efficiency	Weight management programs
9	Technology in smallholder farms	Building resilient cities	Energy effeciency – energy intensive industries	Better disease management
10	Micro-irrigation	Municipal water leakage	Carbon capture and storage	Electronic medical records
11	Restoring degraded land	Cultural tourism	Energy access	Better maternal and child health
12	Reducing packaging waste	Smart metering	Green chemicals	Healthcare training
13	Cattle intensification	Water and sanitation infrastructure	Additive manufacturing	Low-cost surgery
14	Urban agriculture	Office sharing	Local content in extractives	
15		Timber buildings	Shared infrastructure	
16		Durable and modular buildings	Mine rehabilitation	
17			Grid interconnection	

APPENDIX 2.

Overview of sustainability related good practice indicators among top 10 sustainability leaders*.

RANKING AS TO GLOBESCAN SUSTAINABILITY SURVEY 2020**	Communicated, transparent and ambitious sustainability program on website	Science Based Targets (SBT)	UN Global Compact member	World Business Council for Sustainable Development member	BCorporation Certification *****	MSCI ESG rating *****
Unilever	Yes	Targets set	Yes	Yes	Partly (8 out of 400+ brands certified)	AA
Patagonia	Yes	No	No	No	Yes	N/A
IKEA	Yes	Targets set	Yes	Yes	No	N/A
Interface	Yes	Committed	Yes	No	No	N/A
Natura & Co	Yes	Committed	Yes	Yes	Yes	AA
Danone	Yes	Targets set	Yes	Yes	Halfway***	AAA
Tesla	No****	No	No	No	No	A
Nestlé	Yes	Targets set	Yes	Yes	No	AA
Microsoft	Yes	Targets set	Yes	Yes	No	AAA
Ørsted	Yes	Targets set	Yes	Yes	No	AAA

*   Overview of sustainability and ESG related metrics summarized as to information available on the respective company websites on August 24, 2021

**   Highest ranking companies based on the answers of 701 qualified sustainability experts on the question: "What specific companies do you think are leaders in integrating sustainability into their business strategy?" (GlobeScan SustainAbility Survey 2020).

***   Danone's BCorporation certifications represented approximately 50% of sales 2020. Danone aims to be the first fully BCorporation certified multinational.

****   Tesla's sustainability report ('impact report') was somewhat difficult to find on their website (even though it was presented at the top of their first page). Their first materiality assessment was according to their report done last year, which indicates that their systematic focus on foundational practices is lagging. Hence, they are a sustainability leader in terms of their purpose, in their application of sustainable technology to their offering (electrical vehicles), and in challenging their ecosystem, but not in relation to their foundational practices.

*****   An observation is that ESG and B Corp scoring criteria point in the same direction. If a company has a strong rating on the B Impact Assessment, they are hence likely to be a strong ESG performer.

BETTER FUTURE

APPENDIX 3.

Overview of the 20 Scandinavian companies that were selected for the enlarged study.

RANKING AS TO EST NET SALES 2020**	Stock listed	Est net sales 2020**	ESG score (max 100)*	ESG score relative to all companies (max 100)*	Why selected for the enlarged study of good sustainability practices?
Volvo Group	Yes	35 bill Euro	62	92	Early global sustainability leader (1990ies). The health, safety and wellbeing of people a main priority since decades.
H&M Group	Yes	18 bill Euro	64	95	CEO with sustainability background and exploring innovative business models. Included in the Dow Jones World Sustainability Index for the eighth year running.
Electrolux	Yes	15 bill Euro	63	92	Included in Dow Jones Sustainability World Index; named one of the top 5 % corporate global leaders acting against climate change (CDP Climate A Lis); and more. Studied already for my previous book.
Scania	Yes	12.5 bill Euro	65	96	Sustainability well integrated into purpose and strategy. Their former CEO in 2021 published the book Sustainability Leadership, where he shares his learnings.
Vattenfall	Yes	12 bill Euro	61	90	Sustainability well integrated into purpose, business model and strategy.
Essity	Yes	11.6 bill Euro	61	89	Recognized as one of the world's 100 most sustainable companies in 2021 by Corporate Knights; top rated (platinum) by EcoVadis 2020.
Stora Enso	Yes	8.6 bill Euro	59	84	Focus on renewable materials. Highest score in the 2019 'Walking the talk' study on sustainability communications by the Mistra Center for Sustainable Markets (Misum) at the Stockholm School of Economics.
SKF	Yes	7.5 bill Euro	64	94	Innovative business model (servitization) promoting long-life and remanufacturing. One of the world's most sustainable companies as to the Dow Jones Sustainability World Index.

RANKING AS TO EST NET SALES 2020**	Stock listed	Est net sales 2020**	ESG score (max 100)*	ESG score relative to all companies (max 100)*	Why selected for the enlarged study of good sustainability practices?
Danfoss	Yes	6 bill Euro	62	92	Sustainability well integrated into purpose and strategy. Work to drive the sustainable transformation of tomorrow through smart solutions for climate, urbanization and food.
Södra	Yes	2 bill Euro	N/A	N/A	Innovative building solutions from renewable materials (wood) replacing CO_2 intensive concrete and metal constructions
Fiskars Group	Yes	1.1 bill Euro	56	75	Innovation hub exploring circularity with digital solutions.
Paulig Group	No	920 mill Euro	N/A	N/A	Systematic sustainability and ecosystem practices.
Thule Group	Yes	800 mill Euro	64	94	Excellent ESG practices.
Norsk Gjenvinning	No	500 mill Euro	N/A	N/A	Challenged their industry to improve standards, as earlier highlighted in a Harvard Business School case
Oatly	Yes	400 mill Euro	N/A	N/A	Leading the 'plant-based-revolution' and challenging the dairy industry
Max Burgers	No	350 mill Euro	N/A	N/A	Innovative sustainability work
Bona Group	No	234 mill Euro	N/A	N/A	Systematic sustainability practices and conscious leadership
Nudie Jeans	No	40 mill Euro	N/A	N/A	Innovative and transparent ecosystem practices
Fristad Kansas (part of Hultafors Group)	No	N/A	N/A	N/A	Lifecycle Assessments of garments finding organic cotton to be an inferior solution to regular cotton
TooGoodToGo	No	N/A	N/A	N/A	Innovative business model to tackle a wicked problem (food waste)

*   ESG rating by www.CSRHub.com Aug 31, 2021. "All companies" equals the 46,800 ESG relevant companies in 153 countries covered by the database. Max ESG score relative to all companies is 100.

**   Est revenue 2020 as to relevant online sources.

APPENDIX 4.

Overview of top 10 global sustainability leaders and their purpose statements.

TOP 10 AS TO GLOBESCAN SUSTAINABILITY SURVEY 2020*	Purpose statement** (as of their websites, Aug 21, 2021)
Unilever	'To make sustainable living commonplace'
Patagonia	'To save our home planet'
IKEA	'To create a better everyday life for the many people'
Interface	'To lead the industry, to love the world'
Natura & Co	'To create and sell products and services that promote the harmonious relationship of the individual with oneself, with others and with nature'
Danone	"Bringing health through food to as many people as possible."
Tesla	'To accelerate the world's transition to sustainable energy'
Nestlé	'Unlocking the power of food to enhance quality of life for everyone, today and for generations to come'
Microsoft	'To empower every person and every organization on the planet to achieve more'
Ørsted	To 'create a world that runs entirely on green energy'

*   Highest ranking companies based on the answers of 701 qualified sustainability experts on the question: "What specific companies do you think are leaders in integrating sustainability into their business strategy?" (GlobeScan SustainAbility Survey 2020).

**   NB. What has here been interpreted as a purpose statement is on the respective company websites called purpose, reason to exist, mission and vision.

ENDNOTES

PREFACE

1   *The Future We Choose: Surviving the Climate Crisis*, by Christiana Figueres and Tom Rivett-Carnac, 2020, https://www.amazon.com/Future-We-Choose-Surviving-Climate-ebook/dp/ B07Y7HZLX8

2   As to the latest reports by the UN Intergovernmental Panel on Climate Change (IPCC), https://www.ipcc.ch/reports/ (retrieved 2021-08-09)

3   *Vision 2050: Time to Transform*, by The World Business Council for Sustainable Development https://www.wbcsd.org/Overview/About-us/Vision-2050-Refresh/News/Time-to-Transform-Leading-multinational-companies-set-urgent-action-agenda-for-all-people-to-live-well-within-planetary-boundaries (retrieved 2021-06-01)

INTRODUCTION

4   *A climate-change fix is the 'biggest investment opportunity in history'*: Al Gore to millennials, by Rachel Koning Beals at MarketWatch, Nov22, 2019, https://www.marketwatch.com/story/a-climate-change-fix-is-the-biggest-investment-opportunity-in-history-algore- to-millennials-2019-11-22 (retrieved 2021-02-07)

5   *The Future We Choose: Surviving the Climate Crisis*, by Christiana Figueres and Tom Rivett-Carnac, 2020, https://www.amazon.com/Future-We-Choose-Surviving-Climate-ebook/dp/ B07Y7HZLX8

6   *Why Sustainability is the new Digital*, by Orit Gadiesh and Jenny Davis-Peccoud, World Economic Forum, Jan13 2021, https://www.weforum.org/agenda/2021/01/davos-agenda-sustainability-digital-revolution/ (retrieved 2021-02-06)

7   *The Limits of Growth*, by Donatella H. Meadows et al, 1972, Can be downloaded for free as PDF via donatellamedows.org: https://donellameadows.org/wp-content/userfiles/ Limits-to-Growth-digital-scan-version.pdf

8   *Report of the United Nations Conference on the Human Environment*, Stockholm 5-16 June 1972, https://documents-dds-ny.un.org/doc/UNDOC/GEN/NL7/300/05/IMG/ NL730005.pdf?OpenElement

9   *Net Zero: a fiduciary approach*, from a client letter by BlackRock's Global Executive Committee, https://www.blackrock.com/corporate/investor-relations/blackrock-client-letter (retrieved 2020-12-16)

10 *Credit Suisse CEO says sustainable investing no longer means lower returns*, by Anmar Frangoul at CNBC, Jul1 2021, https://www-cnbc-com.cdn.ampproject.org/c/s/ www.cnbc.com/amp/2021/07/01/credit-suisse-ceo-sustainable-investing-no-longer-means-lower-returns-.html (retrieved 2021-07-05)

11 As to CSRHub data 2010-2020, pulled together by Cynthia Figge, CEO and Co-founder of CSRHub and https://www.csrhub.com/CSR_industry_ratings/ (retrieved 2021-05-11)

12 Inspired by *Digital Vortex*, by Michal R. Wade et al, 2016, https://www.imd.org/research-knowledge/books/digital-vortex/

13 *A Friedman doctrine – The Social Responsibility of Business Is to Increase Its Profits*, by Milton Friedman, Sep13, 1970, published in the New York Times https://www.nytimes.com/1970/09/13/archives/a-friedman-doctrine-the-social-responsibility-of-business-is-to.html (retrieved 2021-02-01)

14   See for instance:
      Business Roundtable redefines the purpose of a corporation to promote an economy that
      serves all Americans, by Business Roundtable Aug19, 2019,
      https://www.businessroundtable.org/business-roundtable-redefines-the-purpose-of-a-
      corporation-to-promote-an-economy-that-serves-all-americans (retrieved 2021-02-01)
      Beyond Sustainability: the Regenerative Business, by Navi Radjou in Forbes, Oct22, 2020,
      https://www.forbes.com/sites/naviradjou/2020/10/24/beyond-sustainability-the-
      regenerative-business/?sh=3f93f921ab35 (retrieved 2020-12-03)

15   *Regeneration Report 2021*, by Sustainable Brands https://sustainablebrands.com
      (retrieved 2021-08-03)

16   *What is net positive?* by Forum for the Future https://www.forumforthefuture.org/
      net-positive (retrieved 2021-09-12), *Net Positive: How Courageous Companies Thrive by*
      Giving More Than They Take, by Paul Polman and Andrew S. Winston, 2021

17   *What is Regenerative Business? And why do we need it?* by Jenny Andersson at Medium,
      Oct22 2018, https://medium.com/activate-the-future/what-is-regenerative-busi-
      ness-3e562f909707 (retrieved 2021-02-08)
      Beyond Sustainability: The Regenerative Business, by Navi Radjou in Forbes, Oct22 2020,
      https://www.forbes.com/sites/naviradjou/2020/10/24/beyond-sustainability-the-
      regenerative-business/?sh=3f93f921ab35 (retrieved 2020-12-03)
      The rising frugal economy, by Navi Radjou in MIT Sloan Management Review, Aug6 2020,
      https://sloanreview.mit.edu/article/the-rising-frugal-economy/ (retrieved 2020-12-03)
      Introducing Handprints – a net positive approach to sustainability, by Gregory A. Norris,
      Harvard Extension School, Nov30 2017, https://extension.harvard.edu/blog/introducing-
      handprints-a-net-positive-approach-to-sustainability/ (retrieved 2020-12-03)

18   *Regeneration Report 2021*, Sustainable Brands https://sustainablebrands.com
      (retrieved 2021-08-03)

19   https://guayaki.com (retrieved 2021-08-03)

20   *Stefan Kozak announced as new CEO of Guayaki Yerba Mate Beverage Company*, press
      release by Guayaki published at CISION Apr28 2021, https://www.prnewswire.com/
      news-releases/stefan-kozak-announced-as-new-ceo-of-guayaki-yerba-mate-
      beverage-company-301279434.html (retrieved 2021-08-06)

21   Stefan Kozak's LinkedIn profile: https://www.linkedin.com/in/stefan-kozak-44b8495a/
      (retrieved 2021-08-06)

22   *Stefan Kozak announced as new CEO of Guayaki Yerba Mate Beverage Company*, press
      release by Guayaki published at CISION Apr28 2021, https://www.prnewswire.com/
      news-releases/stefan-kozak-announced-as-new-ceo-of-guayaki-yerba-mate-beverage-
      company-301279434.html (retrieved 2021-08-06)

23   Inspired by:
      Better Business Better World, a report by The UN Business and Sustainable Development
      Commission, Jan 2017, https://sustainabledevelopment.un.org/content/documents/
      2399BetterBusinessBetterWorld.pdf
      The Third Wave of Change described in Organizational Change for Corporate
      Sustainability, by Susanne Benn, Melissa Edwards and Tim Williams (2018), and
      Also, inspired by The B Corp movement (https://bcorporation.net), the Better Business
      Blueprint Foundation (https://www.blueprintforbusiness.org) and TrendWatching.com
      (https://www.trendwatching.com) (retrieved 2021-02-27)

24   Inspired by several books and articles, including:
      Green Swans: The Coming Boom in Regenerative Capitalism, by John Elkington (2020);
      The Regenerative Business, by Carol Sanford (2017);
      Designing Regenerative Cultures, by Daniel Christian Wahl (2016);

Regenerative Enterprise, by Ethan Roland (2013);

The Future We Choose: Surviving the Climate Crisis, by Christiana Figueres and Tom Rivett-Carnac (2020);

What is Regenerative Business? by Jenny Andersson at Medium, Oct22, 2018 https://medium.com/activate-the-future/what-is-regenerative-business-3e562f909707 (retrieved 2021-02-08);

Beyond Sustainability: The Regenerative Business, by Navi Radjou in Forbes, Oct22, 2020 https://www.forbes.com/sites/naviradjou/2020/10/24/beyond-sustainability-the-regenerative-business/?sh=3f93f921ab35 (retrieved 2020-12-03);

The rising frugal economy, by Navi Radjou in MIT Sloan Management Review, Aug6, 2020 https://sloanreview.mit.edu/article/the-rising-frugal-economy/ (retrieved 2020-12-03);

Introducing Handprints – a net positive approach to sustainability, by Gregory A. Norris, Harvard Extention School, Nov30, 2017 https://extension.harvard.edu/blog/introducing-handprints-a-net-positive-approach-to-sustainability/ (retrieved 2020-12-03)

25   This is the most common definition of sustainability and sustainable development, developed by the Brundtland Commission in 1987: "The aim of the Brundtland Commission was to help direct the nations of the world towards the goal of sustainable development. The commission is also known as the World Commission on Environment and Development (WCED). It operated from 1984 to 1987. The commission published its results in the Brundtland report in 1987. Thereafter, sustainable development became an important concept in the vocabulary of politicians, practitioners, and planners... The report by the Brundtland Commission developed the most widely used definition of sustainable development as "development which meets the needs of current generations without compromising the ability of future generations to meet their own needs" (WCED, 1987)." https://link.springer.com/referenceworkentry/10.1007%2F978-94-007-0753-5_441 (retrieved 2020-12-03) and https://en.wikipedia.org/wiki/Brundtland_Commission (retrieved 2020-12-03)

26   Read more about the sustainable development goals at https://www.un.org/sustainabledevelopment/ (retrieved 2020-12-01)

27   https://www.un.org/sustainabledevelopment/ (retrieved 2020-12-01)

28   Read more about UN Global Compact at: https://www.unglobalcompact.org/about and https://www.unglobalcompact.org/what-is-gc/mission/principles (retrieved 2021-08-25)

29   *Corporate social responsibility & Responsible business conduct*, definitions by the EU Commission, https://ec.europa.eu/growth/industry/sustainability/corporate-social-responsibility_en (retrieved 2020-12-01)

30   *Six steps to improve your ESG performance*, by Lizzy Walsh at Simply Sustainable, https://simply-sustainable.co.uk/insights/six-steps-to-improve-your-esg-performance (retrieved 2021-08-28)

31   Read more about B Corporations on their website: https://bcorporation.net/about-b-corps (retrieved 2021-02-13)

32   Top ESG rating providers, by Gabriella L. Jun2021, BrokerChooser, https://brokerchooser.com/how-to-invest/top-esg--rating-providers
For insights into different ESG rating methodologies, see for instance:
What a Difference an ESG Ratings Provider Makes, Feifei Li, Jan2020, Research Affiliates https://www.researchaffiliates.com/en_us/publications/articles/what-a-difference-an-esg- ratings-provider-makes.html (retrieved 2021-08-28)

33   https://en.wikipedia.org/wiki/Benefit_corporation and https://benefitcorp.net (retrieved 2021-02-13)

34   https://simple.wikipedia.org/wiki/Non-governmental_organization
     (retrieved 2020-12-10) and
     https://en.wikipedia.org/wiki/International_non-governmental_organization
     (retrieved 2020-12-10)

35   https://simple.wikipedia.org/wiki/Non-governmental_organization
     (retrieved 2020-12-10) and
     https://en.wikipedia.org/wiki/International_non-governmental_organization
     (retrieved 2020-12-10)

36   https://en.wikipedia.org/wiki/Foundation_(nonprofit) (retrieved 2020-12-10) and
     https://www.axfoundation.se (retrieved 2021-09-15)

37   *What is a social business?* by Management Study Guide, see https://www.management-
     studyguide.com/what-is-social-business.htm (retrieved 2020-12-08)

38   *22 awesome social enterprise business ideas*, at thesedge.org, Jan2018,
     https://www.thesedge.org/socent-spotlights/22-awesome-social-enterprise-
     business-ideas (retrieved 2020-12-10)

39   *22 awesome social enterprise business ideas*, at thesedge.org, Jan2018,
     https://www.thesedge.org/socent-spotlights/22-awesome-social-enterprise-
     business-ideas (retrieved 2020-12-10)

40   *Conscious Business: How to build value through values*, by Fred Kofman, 2013,
     https://www.amazon.com/Conscious-Business-Build-through-Values/dp/1622032020
     Conscious Business, by The Arthur W. Page Center, Public Relations Ethics,
     https://www.pagecentertraining.psu.edu/public-relations-ethics/corporate-social-
     responsibility/lesson-2-introduction-to-conscious-capitalism/conscious-businesses/

41   *What is a circular economy?* by Ellen McArthur Foundation,
     https://www.ellenmacarthurfoundation.org/circular-economy/concept
     (retrieved 2021-02-08)

42   *What is biodiversity?* by World Wildlife Fund, https://www.worldwildlife.org/pages/
     what-is-biodiversity
     You can find more information about the state of biodiversity on the website of the Inter-
     governmental Science-Policy Platform on Biodiversity and Ecosystem Services (ipbes),
     https://ipbes.net (retrieved 2021-08-27)

43   *What is biodiversity?* by World Wildlife Fund, https://www.worldwildlife.org/pages/
     what-is- biodiversity (retrieved 2021-08-27)

44   *Overview: Weather, Global Warming and Climate Change*, NASA Global Climate Change
     site, https://climate.nasa.gov/resources/global-warming-vs-climate-change/
     (retrieved 2021-08-24)

45   *Overview: Weather, Global Warming and Climate Change*, NASA Global Climate Change
     site, https://climate.nasa.gov/resources/global-warming-vs-climate-change/
     (retrieved 2021-08-24)

46   The Intergovernmental Panel on Climate Change (IPCC) is the United Nations body
     for assessing the science related to climate change. More information on their website:
     https://www.ipcc.ch (retrieved 2021-08-24)

47   *How does the IPCC review process work?* IPCC factsheet available at: https://www.ipcc.ch/
     site/assets/uploads/2021/07/AR6_FS_review_process.pdf (retrieved 2021-08-24)

48   More information about the Paris Agreement on: https://unfccc.int/process-and-
     meetings/the-paris-agreement/the-paris-agreement (retrieved 2021-08-24)

49   *What is the difference between carbon neutral, net zero and climate positive?* by PlanA
     Academy, more information at: https://plana.earth/academy/what-is-difference-
     between-carbon-neutral-net-zero- climate-positive/ (retrieved 2021-07-27)

50 More information about the GreenHouse Gas Protocol available at: https://ghgprotocol.org/ about-us (retrieved 2021-08-24)

51 *Briefing: What are Scope 3 emissions?* by CarbonTrust.com. More resources and information on their website: https://www.carbontrust.com/resources/briefing-what-are-scope-3-emissions (retrieved 2021-08-17)

52 Learn more about the Science Based Target initiative on their website: https://sciencebasedtargets.org (retrieved 2021-07-27)

CHAPTER 1

53 *The Lab That Discovered Global Warming Has Good News and Bad News*, by Lamont Doherty, New York Times, Apr2020, https://www.nytimes.com/2020/04/24/nyregion/lamont-doherty-earth-observatory-global-warming.html (retrieved 2021-07-27)

54 http://www.connerpartners.com/frameworks-and-processes/the-real-story-of-the-burning-platform (retrieved 2020-11-15)

55 *The New Nature Report II: The Future of Nature and Business*, by World Economic Forum (2020), http://www3.weforum.org/docs/WEF_The_Future_Of_Nature_And_Business_2020.pdf (retrieved 2020-11-10)

56 *Economic Growth*, by Max Roser, Our World in Data, updated daily https://ourworldindata.org/economic-growth (retrieved 2020-11-15)

57 *The 100 year March of Technology in One Graph*, by Derek Thomson, The Atlantic (2012) https://www.theatlantic.com/technology/archive/2012/04/the-100-year-march-of-technology-in-1-graph/255573/ (retrieved 2021-02-05)

58 *World Population Growth* by Max Roser, Hannah Ritchie and Esteban Ortiz-Ospina, Our World in Data, article updated in May2019, https://ourworldindata.org/world-population-growth (retrieved 2021-02-05)

59 *The trajectory of the Anthropocene: The Great Acceleration*, W. Steffen et al, The Anthropocene Review, 2015, https://scinapse.io/papers/2139274755 (retrieved 2020-12-03)

60 *The trajectory of the Anthropocene: The Great Acceleration*, W. Steffen et al, The Anthropocene Review, 2015, https://scinapse.io/papers/2139274755 (retrieved 2020-12-03)

61 *2050 Scenarios – Four Plausible Futures*, by Aarup, 2019, https://www.arup.com/perspectives/publications/research/section/2050-scenarios-four-plausible-futures (retrieved 2020-11-30)

62 Read more about *The Planetary Boundaries* on the Stockholm Resilience Center website: https://www.stockholmresilience.org/research/planetary-boundaries.html (retrieved 2020-11-13)

63 *How food connects all SDGs*, by Johan Rockström and Pavan Sukhdev (video), Stockholm Resilience Center, Jun2016, https://www.stockholmresilience.org/research/research-news/2016-06-14-how-food-connects-all-the-sdgs.html

64 *How food connects all SDGs*, by Johan Rockström and Pavan Sukhdev (video), Stockholm Resilience Center, Jun2016, https://www.stockholmresilience.org/research/research-news/2016-06-14-how-food-connects-all-the-sdgs.html

65 https://www.oxfordlearnersdictionaries.com/definition/english/ecosystem (retrieved 2021-09-09)

66 IPBES Global Assessment, https://www.un.org/sustainabledevelopment/blog/2019/05/nature-decline-unprecedented-report/ https://ipbes.net/global-assessment (retrieved 2021-09-09)

67 IPBES Global Assessment, https://ipbes.net/sites/default/files/2020-02/ipbes_global_assessment_report_summary_for_policymakers_en.pdf (retrieved 2021-09-09)

68   *About Doughnut Economics*, from the Doughnut Economics Action Lab website: https://doughnuteconomics.org/about-doughnut-economics (retrieved 2020-11-13)

69   *About Doughnut Economics*, from the Doughnut Economics Action Lab website: https://doughnuteconomics.org/about-doughnut-economics (retrieved 2020-11-13)

70   Read more about Earth Overshoot day and Country Overshoot days at: https://www.overshootday.org/newsroom/country-overshoot-days/ (retrieved 2021-07-27)

71   *Climate Change Report 2021*, summary for policymakers, by IPCC, 2021, https://www.ipcc.ch/report/ar6/wg1/downloads/report/IPCC_AR6_WGI_SPM.pdf (retrieved 2021-08-24)

72   *You Asked: If CO2 Is Only 0.04% of the Atmosphere, How Does it Drive Global Warming?* by Renee Cho, Jul2019, Columbia Climate School, https://news.climate.columbia.edu/2019/07/30/co2-drives-global-warming/ (retrieved 2021-07-30)

73   *Carbon dioxide peaks near 420 parts per million at Mauna Loa observatory*, by Theo Stein, NOAA Research News, Jun2021, https://research.noaa.gov/article/ArtMID/587/ ArticleID/2764/Coronavirus-response-barely-slows-rising-carbon-dioxide (retrieved 2021-07-30)

74   *Climate Change: Atmospheric Carbon Dioxide*, by Rebecca Lindsey, NOAA, Climate.Gov, Aug2020, https://www.climate.gov/news-features/understanding-climate/ climate-change-atmospheric-carbon-dioxide (retrieved 2021-09-13)

75   Graph by NOAA Climate.gov based on data from Lüthi et al., 2008, via the NOAA NCEI Paleoclimatology Program: https://www.climate.gov/news-features/understanding-climate/climate-change-atmospheric-carbon-dioxide (retrieved 2021-09-13)

76   *A critical assessment of the wicked problem concept: relevance and usefulness for policy science and practice*, by Catrien J.A.M Termeer, Art Dewulf and Robbert Biesbroek, in Policy & Society, Vol38, 2019, issues 2, https://www.tandfonline.com/doi/full/10.1080/ 14494035.2019.1617971, and https://en.wikipedia.org/wiki/Wicked_problem (retrieved 2020-12-22)

77   *The Global Risk Report 2020*, World Economic Forum, Jan2020, https://www.weforum.org/reports/the-global-risks-report-2020 (retrieved 2020-12-22)

78   *The 25 Percent Tipping Point for Social Change*, by Damon Centola, Psychology Today, 2019, https://www.psychologytoday.com/intl/blog/how-behavior-spreads/201905/ the-25-percent-tipping-point-social-change
New analysis show social norms can cross tipping points faster if new behavior is difficult for others to ignore, by Stockholm Resilience Center, in Phys.org, Oct2016, https://phys.org/news/2016-10-analysis-social-norms-faster-behavior.html
Stay committed, and change will come! by Cecilia Larrosa, Oxford University Martin School, Jul2018, https://www.oxfordmartin.ox.ac.uk/blog/stay-committed-and-change-will-come/

79   For more information about LOHAS, please visit: https://www.lohas.se/about-lohas/ (retrieved 2020-12-21) and https://www.ekocentrum.se/ar-du-en-lohas/ (in Swedish, retrieved 2020-12-21)

80   See for instance: https://www.fashionrevolution.org (retrieved 2020-12-21)

81   According to several studies and reports available with a corporate account at Statista: https://www.statista.com

82   *Healthy & Sustainable Living Report 2020*, by GlobeScan 2020, https://globescan.com/ healthy-sustainable-living/ (retrieved 2021-07-29), GlobeScan Healthy & Sustainable Living Study 2021 (a global survey of 30,000 people in the general public, 2021 vs 2019)

83 *The European Green Deal sets out how to make Europe the first climate-neutral continent by 2050, boosting the economy, improving people's health and quality of life, caring for nature, and leaving no one behind,* a pressrelease from the European Union Dec 2019, https://ec.europa.eu/commission/presscorner/detail/e%20n/ip_19_6691 and, *A European Green Deal, as part of the strategic priorities 2019-2024,* by the European Commission, https://ec.europa.eu/info/strategy/priorities-2019-2024/european-green-deal_en (retrieved 2020-11-25)

84 *If we want more companies like Patagonia, we need laws to enforce it,* by Kristin Toussaint, Fast Company, 2020, https://www.fastcompany.com/90560496/patagonia-ben-jerry-bcorp-woke-capitalism (retrieved 2020-11-30)

85 *8 Sustainably Trends to Watch For in 2020,* by Natalia Olynec, IMD, https://www.imd.org/research-knowledge/articles/sustainability-trends-to-watch-out-for-in-new-decade/ (retrieved 2020-12-22)

86 *Revolutionary Change Theories: A Multilevel Exploration of the Punctuated Equilibrium Paradigm,* by Connie Gersick, The Academy of Management Review, Vol. 16, No. 1 (Jan., 1991), pp. 10-36

87 *Organizations, environmental management and innovation,* from an online course by Open University, https://www.open.edu/openlearn/nature-environment/organisations-environmental-management-and-innovation/content-section-1.7 (retrieved 2020-11-15)

88 *Organizations, environmental management and innovation,* from an online course by Open University, https://www.open.edu/openlearn/nature-environment/organisations-environmental-management-and-innovation/content-section-1.7 (retrieved 2020-11-13)

89 https://www.merriam-webster.com/dictionary/paradigm%20shift (retrieved 2020-11-13)

90 More inspiration about the edges of the evolving paradigms of leadership and the process of a paradigm being replaced by another can be found at Berkana Institute: https://berkana.org/wp-content/uploads/2020/04/Emergence-Booklet-English.pdf

CHAPTER 2

91 *Business as usual will not save the planet,* by Mark R. Kramer, Rishi Agarwal, Aditi Srinivas, Harvard Business Review, Jun2019, https://hbr.org/2019/06/business-as-usual-will-not-save-the-planet (retrieved 2021-08-06)

92 Read more about the 17 Global Goals on the UN website: https://sdgs.un.org/goals (retrieved 2020-12-22)

93 *Business as usual will not save the planet,* by Mark R. Kramer, Rishi Agarwal, Aditi Srinivas, Harvard Business Review, Jun2019, https://hbr.org/2019/06/business-as-usual-will-not-save-the-planet (retrieved 2020-12-22)

94 *2019 Research Report: An analysis of the sustainability reports of 1000 companies pursuant to the EU non-financial directive,* by Alliance for Corporate Transparency, 2020 https://www.allianceforcorporatetransparency.org/assets/2019_Research_Report%20_Alliance_for_Corporate_Transparency.pdf (retrieved 2021-09-14)

95 *Corporate Greenwashing is all the Rage, how can we stop it?* by Paul Polman, Fortune, Apr2021, https://fortune.com/2021/04/11/greenwashing-esg-businesses-corporations-climate-change/ (retrieved 2021-07-17)

96 *State of Green Business 2021,* report by GreenBiz 2021, https://www.greenbiz.com/report/2021-state-green-business-report (retrieved 2021-07-13)

97 *Seeing Around Corners,* by Rita McGrath, 2020, https://www.ritamcgrath.com/books/seeing-around-corners/ (retrieved 2020-12-22)

98   *The S Curve of Business: The Key Levers to Sustaining Momentum for Your Brand*,
      by Buckley Barlow at Rocketsource, https://www.rocketsource.co/blog/s-curve-of-
      business/ (retrieved 2021-08-26)

99   *Why Sustainability is the new Digital*, by Orit Gadiesh and Jenny Davies-Peccoud,
      World Economic Forum, Jan2021, https://www.weforum.org/agenda/2021/01/
      davos-agenda-sustainability-digital-revolution/ (retrieved 2021-02-07)

100 *Why Sustainability is the new Digital*, by Orit Gadiesh and Jenny Davies-Peccoud,
      World Economic Forum, Jan2021, https://www.weforum.org/agenda/2021/01/
      davos-agenda-sustainability-digital-revolution/ (retrieved 2021-02-07)

101 *The Future of Purpose report*, by TrendWatching, 2020, https://trendwatching.com/
      quarterly/2020-02/the-future-of-purpose/ (retrieved 2021-09-14) and,
      The Trend Radar Study 2020 by TrendOne, https://www.trendone.com/en/ and
      https://www.trendone.com/en/trend-radar-study-2020#c3388 (retrieved 2021-09-14)

102 *Klarnamiljardären lifter 100 bolag som ska rädda världen*, by Jonas Leijonhufvud,
      Dagens Industri, Jun2020, https://www.di.se/digital/klarnamiljardaren-lyfter-100-
      bolag-som-ska-radda-varlden/

103 *Do you manage an explore/exploit portfolio?* by Michael Tushman at the ChangeLogic
      blog, updated Dec2020, https://www.changelogic.com/single-post/do-you-manage-
      an-explore-exploit-portfolio (originally retrieved 2020-11-23) and,
      Lead & Disrupt–How to solve the innovators dilemma, by Michael Tushman and Charles
      O'Reilly, 2016 https://www.gsb.stanford.edu/faculty-research/books/lead-disrupt-
      how-solve-innovators-dilemma (retrieved 2021-09-14)

104 *Global Direct Primary Energy Source 1800-2019*, chart by Our World In Data,
      https://ourworldindata.org/grapher/global-primary-energy?country=~OWID_WRL
      (retrieved 2021-09-17)

105 *Why did renewables become so cheap so fast?* by Max Roser at Our World in Data, Dec2020,
      https://ourworldindata.org/cheap-renewables-growth (retrieved 2021-01-24), and
      Energy (facts and figures) by Hannah Ritchie and Max Roser at Our World in Data, 2020
      https://ourworldindata.org/energy-mix (retrieved 2021-01-24)

106 *Why did renewables become so cheap so fast?* by Max Roser at Our World in Data, Dec2020,
      https://ourworldindata.org/cheap-renewables-growth (retrieved 2021-01-24)

107 *Why did renewables become so cheap so fast?* by Max Roser at Our World in Data, Dec2020,
      https://ourworldindata.org/cheap-renewables-growth (retrieved 2021-01-24)

108 *Why did renewables become so cheap so fast?* by Max Roser at Our World in Data, Dec2020,
      https://ourworldindata.org/cheap-renewables-growth (retrieved 2021-01-24)

109 The story of the boiling frog is cited from my own memory and from Wikipedia:
      https://en.wikipedia.org/wiki/Boiling_frog (retrieved 2020-11-15)

110 *2050 Scenarios: Four plausible futures*, by Arup, 2020, https://www.arup.com/
      perspectives/publications/research/section/2050-scenarios-four-plausible-futures
      (retrieved 2020-11-30)

111 *2050 Scenarios: Four plausible futures*, by Arup, 2020, https://www.arup.com/
      perspectives/publications/research/section/2050-scenarios-four-plausible-futures
      (retrieved 2020-11-30)

112 *Sustainarama–How sustainability will change the world in 2050*, by Roland Berger, 2020
      https://www.rolandberger.com/en/Insights/Publications/Sustainarama-How-
      sustainability-will-change-the-world-in-2050.html (retrieved 2021-01-31)

113 *Sustainarama–How sustainability will change the world in 2050*, by Roland Berger, 2020
      https://www.rolandberger.com/en/Insights/Publications/Sustainarama-How-
      sustainability-will-change-the-world-in-2050.html (retrieved 2021-01-31)

114 *New Nature Economy Report: The future of nature and business 2020*, by World Economic Forum, 2020, http://www3.weforum.org/docs/WEF_The_Future_Of_Nature_And_Business_2020.pdf (retrieved 2020-11-10)

115 *More than philanthropy: SDGs represent an estimated US12 trillion in market opportunities for private sector through inclusive business*, by UN BusinessCallToAction, 2017 https://www.businesscalltoaction.org/news/more-than-philanthropy-sdgs-present-an-estimated-us12-trillion-in-market-opportunities-for-private-sector-through-inclusive-business (Originally retrieved 2020-11-07 via the UNDP.org blog)

116 *Circular economy, sustainability and business opportunities*, by By Rashmi Anoop Patil, Sudiptal Seal, and Seeram Ramakrishna, in European Business Review, Jan2020, https://www.europeanbusinessreview.com/circular-economy-sustainability-and-business-opportunities/ (retrieved 2020-11-23)

117 *Circular economy, sustainability and business opportunities*, by Rashmi Anoop Patil, Sudiptal Seal, and Seeram Ramakrishna, in European Business Review, Jan2020, https://www.europeanbusinessreview.com/circular-economy-sustainability-and-business-opportunities/ (retrieved 2020-11-23)

118 *The New Climate Economy Report 2018*, by the Global Commission on the Economy and Climate, https://newclimateeconomy.report/2018/executive-summary/ (retrieved 2020-12-03), https://newclimateeconomy.report//2018 (retrieved 2021-08-27), and http://newclimateeconomy.net/content/about (retrieved 2021-08-27)

119 A note to this meta-analysis wisely mentions that Corporate Responsibility programs may contribute to the overall success, but that they – as always - are highly dependent on the overall business context. Clever Corporate Responsibility practices simply cannot replace poor product quality, or make up for major deficiencies in other areas, such as strategy, finance, marketing, HR, supply chain, manufacturing and R&D. Corporate Responsibility can however drive benefits in marketing and sales, as well as in Human Resources for the firm. As to the meta-analysis, this is mainly achieved by reflecting the customer's own values and creating a pathway from guilt to pride; through building awareness and engagement; and through differentiation from competition. It can furthermore enhance employees' commitment and engagement; enhance how attractive an employer looks; improve job satisfaction and sense of pride; and increase the employees' confidence in and affinity towards the company's leaders.
See *Project ROI: Defining the Competitive and Financial Advantages of Corporate Responsibility and Sustainability*, by Steve Rochlin, Richard Bliss, Stephen Jordan, Cheryl Yaffe Kiser, Babson College, 2015: http://www.impactroiglobal.com/wp-content/uploads/2019/05/Project-ROI-Report-Impact-ROI.pdf (retrieved 2020-11-25)

120 *The power of hidden teams*, by Marcus Buckingham and Ashley Goodall, Harvard Business Review, May2019, https://hbr.org/2019/05/the-power-of-hidden-teams?autocomplete=true (retrieved 2020-11-25)

121 *The power of hidden teams*, by Marcus Buckingham and Ashley Goodall, Harvard Business Review, May2019, https://hbr.org/2019/05/the-power-of-hidden-teams?autocomplete=true (retrieved 2020-11-25)

122 *How much are your disengaged employees costing you?* by Karlyn Borysenko, Forbes, Apr2019, https://www.forbes.com/sites/karlynborysenko/2019/05/02/how-much-are-your-disengaged-employees-costing-you/?sh=6e1294e03437 (retrieved 2021-02-08)

123 *Bridging The Gap: How to Unlock Untapped Potential in the Workplace*, by Emily Grace Peck, Medium, May2019, https://medium.com/jalapeno-app/bridging-the-gap-how-to-unlock-untapped-potential-in-the-workplace-1bae644c1c56 (retrieved 2021-02-08)

124 *Put purpose at the core of your strategy*, by Thomas W. Malnight, Ivy Buche, and Charles Dhanaraj, Harvard Business Review, Sep2019, https://hbr.org/2019/09/put-purpose-at-the-core-of-your-strategy (retrieved 2021-02-05)

125 As to the Task Force on Climate Related Financial Disclosures, https://www.fsb-tcfd.org (retrieved 2021-09-01)

126 *Rate the Raters Report 2020*, by The SustainAbilty Institute, https://www.sustainability.com/thinking/rate-the-raters-2020/ (retrieved 2021-08-31)

127 See for instance MSCI's Industry Materiality Map on https://www.msci.com/our-solutions/esg-investing/esg-ratings/materiality-map (retrieved 2021-09-09

128 A company's Market Capitalization is used as a measurement of company size based on a calculation of the company's share price times the number of outstanding shares. In general, large market cap companies are considered good long-term investments with less risk than small cap companies. The latter are in general considered to potentially produce faster growth and bigger returns (but at higher risk) by investors. Read more about ESG risks in large vs small cap companies on MSCI.com: https://www.msci.com/research/global-investing-trends/esg-credentials-how-have-small-caps-stacked-up (retrieved 2021-09-10)

129 From an interview presented on the website of Nordsip, an association for Nordic sustainable investment, https://nordsip.com/2020/03/20/the-esg-challenges-of-small-caps/ (retrieved 2021-09-12)

130 I have utilized the CSRHub's aggregated ESG ratings as of Aug 31st, 2021. Please visit www.csrhub.com for more information on their methodology. Also note that ESG ratings are normally only available for stock-listed companies, even though there are exceptions (e.g., IKEA and Patagonia which are both privately held).

131 *What is sustainability communication? Is it different than ESG communication?* by Mack Bhatia on The Sustainability.io website, https://www.thesustainability.io/what-is-sustainability-communication-esg (retrieved 2021-09-12)

CHAPTER 3

132 *The state of Fashion 2020,* a report by The Business of Fashion and McKinsey and Company, https://www.mckinsey.com/~/media/mckinsey/industries/retail/our%20insights/the%20state%20of%20fashion%202020%20navigating%20uncertainty/the-state-of-fashion-2020-final.pdf (retrieved 2021-03-04)

133 *Five 'Ridiculous' Ways Patagonia Has Built a Culture That Does Well and Does Good,* by Bruce M. Anderson, LinkedIn Talent Blog, Sep2019, https://business.linkedin.com/talent-solutions/blog/talent-connect/2019/5-ways-patagonia-built-ridiculous-culture (retrieved 2021-03-09)

134 *Let My People Go Surfing,* by Yvon Chouinard, 2005 and 2016. https://www.patagonia.com/product/let-my-people-go-surfing-revised-paperback-book/BK067.html (retrieved 2021-09-14)

135 About the Conservation Alliance: http://www.conservationalliance.com/who-we-are/ (retrieved 2021-02-28)

136 *How we fund,* by Patagonia: https://eu.patagonia.com/se/en/how-we-fund/ (retrieved 2021-02-28)

137 Quote from https://www.onepercentfortheplanet.org/about (retrieved 2021-02-28)

138 The annual Benefit Corporation reports of Patagonia from 2013, 2015 and 2016: https://eu.patagonia.com/se/en/b-lab.html (retrieved 2021-03-09)

BETTER FUTURE

139 *Benefit Corporation update: Patagonia passes B-impact assessment, improves score to 116*, on Patagonia's website: https://www.patagonia.com/stories/benefit-corporation-update-patagonia-passes-b-impact-assessment-improves-score-to-116/story-17871.html (retrieved 2021-02-28)

140 *Benefit Corporation update: Patagonia passes B-impact assessement, improves score to 116*, on Patagonia's website: https://www.patagonia.com/stories/benefit-corporation-update-patagonia-passes-b-impact-assessment-improves-score-to-116/story-17871.html (retrieved 2021-02-28)

141 *Changing the fabrics of our lives*, by Lindsay Morris, Feb2020, published on Patagonia's website: https://eu.patagonia.com/se/en/stories/changing-the-fabric-of-our-lives/story-79355.html (retrieved 2021-02-28)

142 "The questions in the B Impact Assessment are organized into five Impact Areas: Governance, Workers, Community, Environment, and Customers. Click into an Impact Area to see topics covered in each. Topics in blue are Impact Business Models associated with that Impact Area where the company has earned additional credit. Due to rounding, displayed totals may not add up exactly. The B Impact Assessment is customized to a company's size, sector, and geographic market." See the 2019 Patagonia assessment here: https://bcorporation.net/directory/patagonia-inc (retrieved 2021-02-28)

143 *How Patagonia and Allbirds set the pace on their journeys as sustainability leaders*, BCorp website article, Feb2021, https://bcorporation.net/zbtcz02z09/how-patagonia-and-allbirds-set-pace-their-journey-sustainable-leaders (retrieved 2021-02-28)

144 See the Great Place to Work ranking of 2019, https://www.greatplacetowork.com/certified-company/1000745 (retrieved 2021-07-28)

145 *Spotlight on Patagonia: core values key to employee engagement*, by Andrew Heath, WeThrive, Feb2019, https://wethrive.net/employee-engagement/spotlight-patagonia-core-values-key-employee-engagement/ (retrieved 2021-07-28)

146 *How Patagonia and Allbirds set the pace on their journeys as sustainability leaders*, BCorp website article, Feb2021, https://bcorporation.net/zbtcz02z09/how-patagonia-and-allbirds-set-pace-their-journey-sustainable-leaders (retrieved 2021-02-28)

147 *Executive on a Mission: Saving the Planet*, by Cornelia Dean, New York Times, May2007, https://www.dailygood.org/more.php?n=2981 (retrieved 2021-07-30)

148 Read more about Interface and their Climate Takeback initiative on their website, https://www.interface.com/US/en-US/sustainability/climate-take-back-en_US (retrieved 2021-06-15)

149 The company changed names from Dong Energy – Danish Oil and Gas - to Ørsted in 2018. These interviews were done as part of the research for my previous book, *Navigera in i framtiden* (2018).

150 See video with transcript: *Ørsted's move to offshore wind: an interview with Thomas Brostrøm*, by Innosight (date not available), https://www.innosight.com/insight/transformation-20-orsteds-move-to-offshore-wind/ (retrieved 2021-07-31)

151 *Ørsted's renewable energy transformation*, by Christer Tryggestad, McKinsey.com, 2020, https://www.mckinsey.com/~/media/mckinsey/business%20functions/sustainability/our%20insights/orsteds%20renewable%20energy%20transformation/orsteds-renewable-energy-transformation-final.pdf?shouldIndex=false (retrieved 2021-07-31)

152 *Has quarterly capitalism made us overhasty?*, by Dan Matthews in ThinkAct Magazine, Jul2019, Roland Berger, https://www.rolandberger.com/en/Insights/Publications/Has-quarterly-capitalism-made-us-overhasty.html (retrieved 2021-02-18)

153 See more information about the Sustainable Living Plan on the Unilever website, https://www.unilever.com/sustainable-living/ (retrieved 2021-02-27)

154 Quote from *Does B-Corp Work for Multinationals and Publicly Traded Companies*, in the LiftEconomy blog, May2019, https://www.lifteconomy.com/blog/2019/5/21/ does-b-corp-work-for-multinationals-and-publicly-traded-companies (retrieved 2021-02-18)

155 I end the Unilever case with a big thank you to Karen Hamilton, Global Vice President Sustainability at Unilever, and Richard Aldwinckle, Sustainability and Purpose consultant, who has supported Unilever over the past decades. I would also like to extend a special thanks to Soulla Kyriacou, Chief Operating Officer at Better Business Blueprint, for bringing us all together.

156 Based on the IKEA document *The IKEA direction NOW-2025. Three Roads Forward: Our to-do-list.* and a face-to-face interview with the Inter IKEA Group CEO Torbjörn Lööf in Stockholm, February 2019.

157 https://gbl-sc9u2-prd-cdn.azureedge.net/-/media/aboutikea/pdfs/people-and-planet-sustainability-strategy/people-and-planet-positive-ikea-sustainability-strategy-august-2020.pdf?rev=3a3e9a12744b4705b9d1aa8be3b36197&hash= 099EADD58A6B850BD522866B8E01F518 (retrieved 2021-06-15)

158 More information about the progress of their sustainability strategy and initiatives can be found on the IKEA website, https://www.ikea.com/ms/en_AU/pdf/reports-downloads/ sustainability-strategy-people-and-planet-positive.pdf (retrieved 2020-12-02)

159 More information about their sales performance can be found on the INGKA website, https://www.ingka.com/news/solid-sales-performance-when-life-at-home-has-never-been-more-important/ (retrieved 2020-11-24)

160 From the IKEA sustainability strategy 2020... "IKEA: one brand – many companies. The IKEA business is operated through a franchise system. That means many companies with different owners work under the IKEA trademark. All work towards the shared IKEA vision – to create a better everyday life for the many people – that guides every decision. The IKEA business idea is to offer a wide range of well-designed, functional home furnishing products at prices so low that as many people as possible will be able to afford them. The IKEA retail business is operated by independent franchisees under franchise agreement with Inter IKEA Systems B.V. The whole value chain means from supplier to customer."

161 More information in the IKEA Sustainability Report 2012, https://www.ikea.com/ms/ ar_KW/pdf/sustainability_report/sustainability_summary_2012.pdf (retrieved 2021-08-15)

162 Oatly has certainly chosen their own path, which has not always been perceived as politically correct by outside observers, or the traditional dairy industry. Before their IPO they for instance had their underlying purpose and motives questioned due to their ownership structure, which was a mix of investment companies such as China Resources and Blackstone, with far from sustainable pasts. Oatly has however working hard to live up to their own standards and promises of being a transparent and sustainable company, while admitting that everything is not perfect and still in development.

163 Quote from Oatly's Sustainability Report 2020, https://www.oatly.com/uploads/ attachments/ckqv4y5xd001f9xgil61zhso2-oatly-sustainability-report-2021-web.pdf (retrieved 2021-07-10)

164 Quote from The Challenger Project, https://thechallengerproject.com/blog/2016/oatly (retrieved 2021-07-12)

165 *Livsstilsvarumärke i livsmedelsindustrin*, Hanna Meinl et al (2018), Lunds Universitet https://lup.lub.lu.se/luur/download?func=downloadFile&recordOId=8951722& fileOId=8951734 (retrieved 2021-07-10)

166 *Activists sour on Oatly vegan milk after stake sold to Trump-linked Blackstone,* by Edward Helmore, The Guardian, Sep2020, https://www.theguardian.com/food/2020/sep/01/oatly-vegan-milk-sale-blackstone (retrieved 2021-07-07)

167 Oatly shares soar 18% in company's public market debut on Nasdaq, by Amelia Lucas, CNBC.com, May2021, https://www.cnbc.com/2021/05/20/oatly-ipo-otly-starts-trading-on-nasdaq.html (retrieved 2021-07-10)

168 Quote from *Oatly's Sustainability Report 2020,* https://www.oatly.com/uploads/attachments/ckqv4y5xd001f9xgil61zhso2-oatly-sustainability-report-2021-web.pdf (retrieved 2021-07-10)

169 See for instance Dunphy and Griffiths (2007), and Mirvis and Googins (2006)

170 Suzanne Benn, Melissa Edwards and Tim Williams, *Organizational change for corporate sustainability* (2020), building on the work of Dexter Dunphy and Andrew Griffiths.

171 Suzanne Benn, Melissa Edwards and Tim Williams, *Organizational change for corporate sustainability* (2020), building on the work of Dexter Dunphy and Andrew Griffiths.

172 Model from the transformation toolbox of StrategyTools, https://www.strategytools.io

CHAPTER 4

173 *The next corporate sustainability goal: Capturing all of the CO2 a company has ever emitted,* by Adele Peters, FastCompany.com, Sep2020, https://www.fastcompany.com/90545475/the-next-corporate-sustainability-goal-capturing-all-of-the-co2-the-company-has-ever-emitted (retrieved 2021-08-25)
Velux partners with WWF to capture lifetime carbon emissions, by Sarah George, Edie.net, Sep2020, https://www.edie.net/news/6/Velux-partners-with-WWF-to-capture-lifetime-carbon-emissions/ (retrieved 2021-08-25)

174 *SDG Ambition Guide,* by UN Global Compact, learn more at: https://www.globalcompact.de/migrated_files/wAssets/docs/Reporting/SDG_Ambition_AmbitionGuide_200922.pdf (retrieved 2021-08-26)

175 *2019 Research Report: An analysis of the sustainability reports of 1000 companies pursuant to the EU Non-Financial Reporting Directive,* The Alliance for Corporate Transparency, 2019, https://www.allianceforcorporatetransparency.org (retrieved 2021-01-25)

176 Even though a large amount of impact startups is on the go, small companies in general (at least in Scandinavia) still do not prioritize sustainability. In particularly as to ESG-performance, where a large share of smaller companies has not yet identified and understood potential risks related to their operations and value chain. A reviewed study (Nordea Business Insight Report 2019) of Scandinavian companies found that large companies to a higher extent incorporate ESG and sustainability into their strategy as well as into their operations, mainly as means of risk reduction. Large companies perceive sustainability as more important than smaller companies and have higher competencies in the field. Interestingly only 20 percent of the companies in that same study – big and small - referred to their mission or purpose as the main reason for focusing on sustainability, and only 19 percent claimed that they focused on sustainability because of the business opportunity and potential future profits. Instead, the top three reasons to focus on sustainability were: the need to meet customer demands, potential improvements in brand value and reputation, and the need to meet legal demands. Something that also seem to shine through in the studied population, even though purpose seem to have a more prominent position.
The Nordea Business Insight Report 2019 can be retrieved via their website: https://insights.nordea.com/wp-content/uploads/2020/06/Nordea-Business-Insight-Report-2019-ESG.pdf (retrieved 2021-01-19)

177 Set strategic, ambitious, achievable sustainability goals, by UN GlobalCompact, https://www.unglobalcompact.org/take-action/leadership/integrate-sustainability/set-goals (retrieved 2021-08-02)

178 *Ørsted Sustainability Report* 2020, https://orstedcdn.azureedge.net/-/media/annual2020/sustainability-report-2020.ashx?la=en&rev=552cd4dd7bc3499c8bf2311549d-36b94&hash=53664FE832CA1812F310DE35856DA3F4 (retrieved 2021-07-14)

179 *Ørsted Sustainability Report* 2020, https://orstedcdn.azureedge.net/-/media/annual2020/sustainability-report-2020.ashx?la=en&rev=552cd4dd7bc3499c8bf2311549d-36b94&hash=53664FE832CA1812F310DE35856DA3F4 (retrieved 2021-07-14)

180 *Ørsted Sustainability Report 2020*, https://orstedcdn.azureedge.net/-/media/annual2020/sustainability-report-2020.ashx?la=en&rev=552cd4dd7bc3499c8bf2311549d-36b94&hash=53664FE832CA1812F310DE35856DA3F4 (retrieved 2021-07-14)

181 Ørsted Sustainability Report 2020, https://orstedcdn.azureedge.net/-/media/annual2020/sustainability-report-2020.ashx?la=en&rev=552cd4dd7bc3499c8bf2311549d-36b94&hash=53664FE832CA1812F310DE35856DA3F4 (retrieved 2021-07-14)

182 More information on the Unilever website, https://www.unilever.com/planet-and-society/ (retrieved 2021-09-01)

183 More information on the Unilever website, https://www.unilever.com/planet-and-society/sustainability-reporting-centre/sustainability-performance-data/ (retrieved 2021-09-01)

184 *Ranked: The Most Innovative Companies in 2021*, by Carmen Ang, Visual Capitalist, https://www.visualcapitalist.com/ranked-the-most-innovative-companies-in-2021/ (retrieved 2021-08-03)
Most innovative companies 2021, Overcoming the Innovation Readiness Gap, BCG, Apr2021, https://web-assets.bcg.com/93/a7/7d03fff34baa993929c81f220e72/bcg-most-innovative-companies-2021-apr-2021-r.pdf (retrieved 2021-09-17)

185 *Business Models for Sustainability: Origins, Present Research, and Future Avenues*, by Stefan Schaltegger, Erik G. Hansen, and Florian Lüdeke-Freund, Organization & Environment 2016, Vol. 29(1) 3–10, https://journals.sagepub.com/doi/pdf/10.1177/1086026615599806 (retrieved 2021-09-09)

186 *IKEA Circular Design Guide*, https://about.ikea.com/en/about-us/our-view-on/designing-for-circularity-and-our-future (retrieved 2021-07-14)

187 *IKEA Sustainability Report 2020*, https://gbl-sc9u2-prd-cdn.azureedge.net/-/media/aboutikea/pdfs/ikea-sustainability-reports/ikea_sustainability-report_fy20_.pdf?rev=51556c50bb594d1391e8a56f5ca05bed&hash=DFE0FADC2F7827888B-421CACD310BB44 (retrieved 2021-07-14)

188 *IKEA Sustainability Report 2020*, https://gbl-sc9u2-prd-cdn.azureedge.net/-/media/aboutikea/pdfs/ikea-sustainability-reports/ikea_sustainability-report_fy20_.pdf?rev=51556c50bb594d1391e8a56f5ca05bed&hash=DFE0FADC2F7827888B-421CACD310BB44 (retrieved 2021-07-14)

189 *The Drawdown Review, Climate solutions for a new decade*, 2020 https://drawdown.org/sites/default/files/pdfs/TheDrawdownReview–2020–Download.pdf (retrieved 2021-08-04)

190 https://www.norrsken.org (retrieved 2021-08-06)

191 *Purpose 2030: Good business and a better future*, Deloitte, 2016. The report can be downloaded on their website: https://www2.deloitte.com/global/en/pages/about-deloitte/articles/purpose-2030-good-business-better-future.html (retrieved 2021-08-04)

192   *Align: a Leadership Blueprint for Aligning Enterprise Purpose, Strategy and Organisation,* Jonathan Trevor (2020), https://www.amazon.com/Align-Leadership-Blueprint-Enterprise-Organization/dp/1472959396 (retrieved 2021-07-29)

193   *Leading with a sustainable purpose,* a report published by Cambridge Institute of Sustainability Leadership (CISL), Nov2020, https://www.cisl.cam.ac.uk/resources/ sustainability-leadership/leading-with-a-sustainable-purpose (retrieved 2021-08-04)

194   *Leading with a sustainable purpose,* a report published by Cambridge Institute of Sustainability Leadership (CISL), Nov2020, https://www.cisl.cam.ac.uk/resources/ sustainability-leadership/leading-with-a-sustainable-purpose (retrieved 2021-08-04)

195   *Sustainable Tea at Unilever,* a Harvard Business School case by Rebecca Henderson and Fredric Nelleman, 2011, https://www.hbsp.harvard.edu/product/712438-PDF-ENG (retrieved 2021-08-04)

196   *Danone: Changing the Food System,* a Harvard Business School case by David E. Bell et al, 2019, https://store.hbr.org/product/danone-changing-the-food-system/520053 (retrieved 2021-08-04)

197   The story is the authors interpretation of the development, based on a Harvard Business School Case: *Turnaround at Norsk Gjenvinning (A),* by George Serafeim and Shannon Gombos (2015) and the copyright of Harvard Business School; and *Reimagining capitalism in a world on fire,* by Rebecca Henderson, 2020
I have also been in contact with the CEO in the case, Erik Osmundsen, to hear him describe the journey in his own words.

198   *Turnaround at Norsk Gjenvinning (A),* a Harvard Business School case by George Serafeim and Shannon Gombos, 2015, https://www.hbsp.harvard.edu/ product/116012-PDF-ENG?Ntt=turnaround%20at%20norsk%20gjenvinning (retrieved 2021-08-04)

199   *Turnaround at Norsk Gjenvinning (A),* a Harvard Business School case by George Serafeim and Shannon Gombos, 2015, https://www.hbsp.harvard.edu/ product/116012-PDF-ENG?Ntt=turnaround%20at%20norsk%20gjenvinning (retrieved 2021-08-04)

200   From the presentation of Erik Osmundsen on the Verdane website, https://verdane.com/team/erik-osmundsen/ (retrieved 2021-08-14)

201   From the presentation of Summa Equity on their website, https://summaequity.com/story/about-summa/ (retrieved 2021-08-14)

202   Read more about UN Global Compact on their website, https://www.unglobalcompact.org/what-is-gc (retrieved 2021-08-17)

203   Read more about the wbscd members from their website, https://www.wbcsd.org/Overview/Our-members (retrieved 2021-08-17)

204   To learn more about complex adaptive systems and systems thinking, please explore: Video: *Systems Thinking: Fundamental Concepts,* by Joel Hartter, Associate Professor and Faculty Director MENV, at Coursera.com, https://www.coursera.org/lecture/effective-engagement/systems-thinking-fundamental-concepts-A6rnJ (retrieved 2021-08-17)
Embracing Complexity, by Tim Sullivan, Harvard Business Review, Sep2011, https://hbr.org/2011/09/embracing-complexity
Academy for Systems Change, the Donatella Meadows Project, https://donellameadows.org
Tools for Systems Thinkers: The 6 Fundamental Concepts of Systems Thinking, by Leya Acaroglu, Medium, Sep2017, https://medium.com/disruptive-design/tools-for-systems-thinkers-the-6-fundamental-concepts-of-systems-thinking-379cdac3dc6a

205 *Greenhouse gas emissions from food systems: building the evidence base*, by Francesco N Tubiello et al, Environmental Research Letters, Vol16, no6, Jun2021, https://iopscience.iop.org/article/10.1088/1748-9326/ac018e

206 *Food System Impacts on Biodiversity Loss*, by Tim G. Benton et al, Chatham House, Feb2021, https://www.chathamhouse.org/sites/default/files/2021-02/2021-02-03-food-system-biodiversity-loss-benton-et-al_0.pdf

207 *Using foresight to explore the global food system*, RAND Corporation. More information on their website: https://www.rand.org/randeurope/research/projects/global-food-system-foresight.html (retrieved 2021-08-02)

208 *Using foresight to explore the global food system*, RAND Corporation. More information on their website: https://www.rand.org/randeurope/research/projects/global-food-system-foresight.html (retrieved 2021-08-02)

209 *Using foresight to explore the global food system*, RAND Corporation. More information on their website: https://www.rand.org/randeurope/research/projects/global-food-system-foresight.html (retrieved 2021-08-02)

210 More information on the One Planet Business for Biodiversity (op2b) website, https://op2b.org (retrieved 2021-08-14)

211 *Danone: Changing the Food System*, by David E. Bell, Frederica Gabrieli, and Daniela Beyersdorfer, Harvard Business School case, 2020, https://store.hbr.org/product/danone-changing-the-food-system/520053 (retrieved 2021-08-04)

212 More information on the One Planet Business for Biodiversity (op2b) website, https://op2b.org (retrieved 2021-08-14)

213 More information on the One Planet Business for Biodiversity (op2b) website, https://op2b.org/testimonials/wbcsd-peter-bakker/ (retrieved 2021-08-14)

214 Axfoundation is a non-profit organization founded by Antonia Axel Johnsson, a respected member of the owner family of Axel Jonson Group in Sweden—a group of companies originally founded in 1873 through which the owners aim to be a positive force for change in the communities of which they are a part. The group builds and develops profitable trade and service businesses in the European market, with a focus on the Nordic countries. In 2019, the partly and fully owned companies within the group had a total annual turnover of approximately €8 billion and employed 25,000 people.

215 More information about Axfoundation on their website: https://www.axfoundation.se (retrieved 2021-03-01)

216 More information about Paul Polman on Wikipedia, https://en.wikipedia.org/wiki/Paul_Polman (retrieved 2021-08-10), and on the CommonPurpose website, https://commonpurpose.org/biographies/paul-polman/ (retrieved 2021-09-17). You can also follow Paul Polman on Twitter @PaulPolman.

CHAPTER 5

217 Considering the urgency or the situation the analogy of '3W' is especially interesting. '3W' is also used in the emergency handbook of UNHCR, the UN Refugee Agency. It represents *'Who's doing what, where' in situations of distress and disasters. If we as a business community do not act, it will indeed end up there – in global climate and biodiversity distress and disasters. We are already seeing signs of this unfolding. A situation neither of us wants. For more information about the use of 3W in emergency situation, please visit:* https://emergency.unhcr.org/entry/42801/who-does-what-where-3w

218 *Organizational Transformation as a Function of CEOs' Developmental Stage*, D. Rooke and W.R. Torbert (1998), Organization Development Journal, 16 (1): 11-29.

219 A brief introduction to Vertical Leadership Development can be found in Harvard Business Review, *Seven Transformations of Leadership*, by David Rooke and William R. Torbert, Apr2005, https://hbr.org/2005/04/seven-transformations-of-leadership (retrieved 2021-09-17)

220 *Elevating leadership development practices to meet emerging needs*, by Julie A. Chesley, PhD, Terri Egan, PhD and Hannah E. Jones, Journal of Leadership Education, vol. 19, issue 4, 2020 https://journalofleadershiped.org/jole_articles/elevating-leadership-development-practices-to-meet-emerging-needs/ (retrieved 2021-07-15)

221 *Elevating leadership development practices to meet emerging needs*, by Julie A. Chesley, PhD, Terri Egan, PhD and Hannah E. Jones, Journal of Leadership Education, vol. 19, issue 4, 2020 https://journalofleadershiped.org/jole_articles/elevating-leadership-development-practices-to-meet-emerging-needs/ (retrieved 2021-07-15)

222 From *The Strategist*, by Cynthia Montgomery, 2012, https://www.amazon.com/Strategist-Leader-Your-Business-Needs/dp/0062071017 (retrieved 2021-09-17)

223 *Executive Coaching in Strategic Holistic Leadership: The Drivers and Dynamics of Vertical Development*, by Antoniette Braks, 2020, https://www.amazon.com/Executive-Coaching-In-Strategic-Holisti/dp/0335249116 (retrieved 2021-04-01)

224 The fact box is an edited extract from the StageSHIFT Vertical Holistic Leadership Profile, developed by Dr. Antoniette Braks, the founder of the StageSHIFT approach and the author of *Executive Coaching in Strategic Holistic Leadership: The Drivers and Dynamics of Vertical Development* (2020).

225 *The Future We Choose: Surviving the Climate Crisis, Christiana Figueres and Tom Rivett-Carnac*, 2020, https://www.amazon.com/Future-We-Choose-Surviving-Climate-ebook/dp/B07Y7HZLX8

METHODOLOGY

226 This rating is done by 700 sustainable development experts across sectors in 71 countries, answering the question "What specific companies do you think are leaders in integrating sustainability into their business strategy" in the GlobeScan SustainAbilty Survey 2020. The top ten corporations 2020 were:
1. Unilever
2. Patagonia
3. IKEA
4. Interface
5. Natura & Co
6. Danone
7. Tesla
8. Nestlé
9. Microsoft
10. Ørsted
https://globescan.com/2020-sustainability-leaders-report/ (retrieved 2020-12-09)

227 See for instance *A Design Science Approach to Evidence-Based Management*, by Joan Ernst van Aken and George L Romme, in The Oxford Handbook of Evidence-Based Management, pp 43-57, Oxford University Press, 2012, https://www.researchgate.net/publication/235945854_A_Design_Science_Approach_to_Evidence-Based_Management (retrieved 2021-09-17)

228 *The three cycle view of design science research*, by Alan R. Hevner, Scandinavian Journal of Information Systems, Volume 19, issue 2, 2007, https://aisel.aisnet.org/cgi/viewcontent. cgi?article=1017&context=sjis (retrieved 2021-02-01)

229 *The three cycle view of design science research*, by Alan R. Hevner, Scandinavian Journal of Information Systems, Volume 19, issue 2, 2007, https://aisel.aisnet.org/cgi/viewcontent. cgi?article=1017&context=sjis (retrieved 2021-02-01)

APPENDIX 1

230 *Better Business Better World Report*, UN Business and Sustainability Commission, 2017, https://sustainabledevelopment.un.org/content/documents/2399BetterBusinessBetter-World.pdf

ABOUT THE AUTHOR

Elisabet Lagerstedt is a Senior Executive Consultant, Advisor and Coach, and an experienced facilitator of strategy, innovation, and transformation. She is also the Founder and Principal of Future Navigators.

Her clients are CEOs, C-level executives, and Board of Directors aiming for strategic and transformational change - more and more often with a desire to explore purpose-led and sustainable business opportunities, impact business models, and how to integrate sustainability into the very core of the company. Elisabet is personally deeply engaged in the amazing potential for business as a force for good, and her mission is simple: to inspire business leaders in building Better Business and a Better Future.

You can contact Elisabet at **elisabet.lagerstedt@future-navigators.com** or visit her website at **www.elisabetlagerstedt.com** or **www.future-navigators.com** for more information.